Praise for
MONEY MACHINE

"Gary Smith's *Money Machine* should be on the shelf of any investor right next to *Security Analysis* by Graham and Dodd."
—Andrew D. Sloves, Former Managing Director, JP Morgan

"Filled with common sense and an uncommon level of insight, Smith delivers a book that should be required reading for all investors."
—Chris Nelson, Chief Financial Officer,
Universal Studios Hollywood

"Smith combines key concepts from finance, statistics, and psychology into a must read book for any investor."
—Karl J. Meyer, Business Development,
Kleiner Perkins Caufield & Byers

"*Money Machine* is an essential read for any investor looking to improve their understanding of how to make money in financial markets today."
—Mike Schimmel, Managing Director/Portfolio Manager,
Kayne Anderson Capital Advisors

"This is the most comprehensive book I've read regarding faults in logic and math that plague investors, amateur and professional. This is an outstanding book! "
—Bob McClure, McClure Investment Management, LLC

"A joyful crusade through the world of economics, behavioral science, value investing, market dynamics and their intersection with common sense. Gary Smith's *Money Machine* is a must read."
—Simeon Nestorov, Managing Director, Berkeley Square Inc.

"Smith has again done a masterful job of simplifying the complicated and provides an insightful fact-based, common sense tool for investing."

—Joe Berchtold, Chief Operating Officer,
Live Nation Entertainment

"Smith is a brilliant writer who uses statistical analysis and common-sense storytelling to articulate his important message . . . Cash is King. I highly recommend this book to any serious long-time investor."

—Scott Green, Venture Capitalist, 270 Capital

"Psst! I got a tip for ya! Gary Smith's *Money Machine* is a rare pleasure—a book about investing that makes you laugh out loud. Smith uses a series of telling stories about investors, students, friends, and so-called experts to drive home his point that investing is about creating value, year after year, and not about yelling "Buy! Sell!" all day in response to the latest blips on the ticker board."

—Charles Euchner, Center for an Urban Future

"A modest investment of time with Smith's book will yield outsized returns to those looking to build personal wealth in a reliable and steady manner."

—Bryan White, Founder, Sahsen Ventures

"In *Money Machine*, Gary Smith does what he does best: he provides a clear, readable, accessible overview on the fundamentals of investing, its opportunities, and the pitfalls."

—Sebastian Thomas, CFA, MBA, Portfolio Manager,
Head of US Technology Research, Allianz Global Investors

"Shocking—An economist who can be clear and funny while actually conveying great insights into rational and irrational approaches to stock market valuation! This book will be a great gift to give to my friends and clients who definitely need to read it."

—Davis D. Thompson, Corporate Attorney

"Both engaging and insightful, *Money Machine* appeals to anyone who wants to understand the forces that drive the stock market. Using simple and entertaining examples, Smith provides a practical guide to making smart investments."

—Anita Arora, MD, MBA,
RWJF Clinical Scholar at Yale University

"In *Money Machine*, Smith dispels many common myths of technical data, data mining, and market bubbles through entertaining and engaging examples. A thoroughly enjoyable read. "

—Andrew Voth, CPA/CFF, CVA, CIRA/CDBV, CFE,
Senior Director, Alvarez & Marsal

"Over his more than 40 years of observing markets and teaching at some of America's top academic institutions, Dr. Smith has accumulated a wealth of insights that he shares with you in *Money Machine*. If you want to increase your investing IQ, I'd highly recommend this book."

—Jeffrey H. Ellis, CFA, MBA, Managing Member,
L Street Capital Management, LLC

MONEY MACHINE

MACHINE

The Surprisingly Simple
Power of Value Investing

GARY SMITH

AMACOM
AMERICAN MANAGEMENT ASSOCIATION
New York • Atlanta • Brussels • Chicago • Mexico City • San Francisco
Shanghai • Tokyo • Toronto • Washington, D.C.

American Management Association: www.amanet.org
This publication is designed to provide accurate and authoritative information in regard to the subject matter covered. It is sold with the understanding
that the publisher is not engaged in rendering legal, accounting, or other professional service. If legal advice or other expert assistance is required, the services of a competent professional person should be sought.

Library of Congress data is available upon request.

ISBN: 978-08144-3856-5
EISBN: 978-08144-3857-2

About AMA
American Management Association (www.amanet.org) is a world leader in
talent development, advancing the skills of individuals to drive business
success. Our mission is to support the goals of individuals and organizations
through a complete range of products and services, including classroom and
virtual seminars, webcasts, webinars, podcasts, conferences, corporate and
government solutions, business books, and research. AMA's approach to
improving performance combines experiential learning—learning through
doing—with opportunities for ongoing professional growth at every step of
one's career journey.

10 9 8 7 6 5 4 3 2 1

To James Tobin
For those who knew him, no explanation is necessary.
For those who didn't, no explanation could be sufficient.

CONTENTS

FOREWORD

Most people who buy and sell stocks have heard the story of the two finance professors who see a shiny $100 bill on the sidewalk. One professor is tempted, but the other cautions that if it were real, someone would have picked it up already. The lesson is supposed to be that, in the stock market, anything that looks like free money is an illusion. Some people actually believe this—I do not. *Money Machine: The Surprisingly Simple Power of Value Investing* makes clear why others should not believe it either.

Professor Smith reminds us of the South Sea Bubble, when even Isaac Newton bought stock in companies that lacked a compelling story but touted a whimsical expectation of reselling the stock at a higher price to an even bigger fool. More recently, investors bought into the same ill-founded illusions with Beanie Babies, gold, and dot-coms. At the other end of the spectrum—from greed to fear—the 2002 and 2009 stock market crashes left suitcases full of $100 bills on the sidewalks.

So, how does an investor distinguish a bubble from a bargain? Both Professor Smith and I believe the answer is through value investing: thinking about the intrinsic value of a stock and not about the stock's old price or a guess of its future price.

Professor Smith clearly explains the two keys to being a successful value investor.

First, no one is able to predict how prices will wiggle and jiggle as fear and greed batter the markets. But you can think of stocks as money machines. Think of the cash you will receive if you own the machine (and leave yourself a margin of error).

Second, do not let lust or panic sway your investment decisions. Many investors had a hard time sitting on the sidelines when Yahoo, AOL, and other internet companies soared during the dot-com boom in the late 1990s, but value investors did exactly that, they sat. Many investors could not think about buying stocks when prices fell more than 40 percent between 2000 and 2002 and, again, between 2007 and 2009. Value investors did exactly that; they bought because those were buying opportunities of a lifetime.

Professor Smith also explains how you could find bargains even in ordinary times—for example, in companies that are out of fashion and in closed-end funds selling at a discount. Some may think it counterintuitive that companies with analysts who are pessimistic usually do better than companies with analysts who are optimistic, or that stocks that are booted out of the Dow usually do better than the stocks that replace them . . . but not a value investor.

Let others make decisions driven by fear and greed, and thank them silently for the opportunities they give you—for the $100 bills they leave on the sidewalk. If you want to be a great investor, look for these $100 bills and do not be afraid to pick them up off the ground!

This is another great, well-thought-out book by Professor Smith that I enjoyed reading, and you will too.

MICHAEL LARSON
Chief Investment Officer of BMGI,
the Investment Office of Bill Gates

INTRODUCTION

*The stock market is filled with individuals who know the price of
everything, but the value of nothing.*
—PHILIP FISHER

I made it through Yale graduate school on a $200 monthly sti-
pend—$100 for rent in a nasty part of New Haven and $100 for
food, secondhand clothes, and not much else. My shoes were held
together with duct tape, and dinners at the end of the month were
often bread and orange juice, sometimes bread and water. I started
teaching economics at Yale in 1971, a newly minted PhD with a
three-month-old son, $12,000 annual income, and less than $100 in
the bank.

The Yale economics department asked students what courses
they would like added to the curriculum and the runaway winners
were Marx and the stock market. I wasn't interested in Marx, but
the chair of my thesis committee was James Tobin, who would be
awarded the Nobel Prize in Economics, in part for his analysis of financial markets. So, I volunteered to create a stock market course
and asked Jim to recommend a textbook. His immediate answer was
The Theory of Investment Value, by John Burr Williams, which had
been published more than thirty years earlier, in 1938, and was not
really a textbook. It was Williams's PhD thesis and had been rejected by several publishers for being overly academic (it had alge-
braic symbols!). Harvard University Press published it, but Williams
had to pay part of the printing cost himself.

Tobin's recommendation was inspired. John Burr Williams and
Benjamin Graham laid the foundation for value investing—assessing
stocks based on the cash they generate rather than trying to predict

zigs and zags in stock prices. Their way of thinking is central to the success of many legendary value investors, including Warren Buffett, Laurence Tisch, and Michael Larson.

I didn't use Williams's treatise as a textbook but, over and over, I have relied on the insights I learned from Tobin, Williams, Graham, and Buffett. I've been investing and teaching investing for more than forty years now, and I've learned that some lessons are well worth learning, others are not. Their lessons are worth learning.

Financial markets are always changing, but underneath these innovations are some core concepts like present value, leverage, hedging, efficient markets, and the conservation of value. These enduring principles are more important than temporary details. Investing is not a multiple-choice test that can be passed by memorizing soon-obsolete facts like the name of the largest brokerage firm or the number of stocks traded on the New York Stock Exchange.

The great British economist John Maynard Keynes wrote:

> The master-economist must possess a rare combination of gifts. He must be mathematician, historian, statesman, philosopher—in some degree. He must understand symbols and speak in words. He must contemplate the particular in terms of the general, and touch abstract and concrete in the same flight of thought. He must study the present in the light of the past for the purposes of the future. No part of man's nature or his institutions must lie entirely outside his regard.

The same could be said of the master investor. How can we calculate present values without mathematics? How can we gauge uncertainty without statistics? However, a deep understanding of investments requires recognition of the limitations of mathematical and statistical models, no matter how scientific they appear, no matter if they were developed by Nobel laureates.

Tobin came to Yale in 1950 when the economics department decided that it needed a mathematical economist. Yes, one mathematical economist among a faculty of perhaps sixty. When Tobin retired, every Yale economist was more mathematical than Tobin had been in 1950, some frighteningly so. Mathematicians had become the gods of economics, and knowing nothing about the real world was almost a badge of honor. When Gérard Debreu was awarded the Nobel Prize in Economics in 1983, reporters tried to get him to say something about Ronald Reagan's economic policies. Debreu firmly refused to say anything, some suspected because he didn't know or care—and was proud of it.

Mathematical models are too often revered more for their elegance than their realism. Too many economists assume whatever is needed—no matter how preposterous—in order to make their models mathematically tractable. I listened to a finance lecture at Yale where a future Nobel laureate began his talk with a brutally candid statement: "Making whatever assumptions are needed, here is my proof."

This cavalier attitude may work great for publishing academic papers that no one reads, but it is a recipe for disaster on Wall Street where real people risk real money and may literally be betting the bank based on a model concocted out of convenience.

At about the same time I heard this lecture, the *New Statesman* gave an award for this definition of an economist:

> An inhabitant of cloud-cuckoo land; one knowledgeable in an obsolete art; a harmless academic drudge whose theories and laws are but mere puffs of air in face of the anarchy of banditry, greed, and corruption which holds sway in the pecuniary affairs of the real world.

In recent years, the inhabitants of cloud-cuckoo land have been joined on the economics pedestal by new gods: number crunchers.

When I first started teaching investments, computers were just becoming popular, and my wife's grandfather ("Popsie") knew that my PhD thesis used Yale's big computer to estimate an extremely complicated economic model. Popsie had bought and sold stocks for decades. He even had his own desk at his broker's office where he could trade gossip and stocks.

Nonetheless, he wanted advice from a twenty-one-year-old kid who had no money and had never bought a single share of stock in his life—me—because I worked with computers. "Ask the computer what it thinks of Schlumberger," he'd say. "Ask the computer what it thinks of GE."

Things haven't changed much. Too many people still think that computers are infallible. No matter what kind of garbage we put in, computers will spit out gospel. Nope. Garbage in, garbage out. As with theoretical models based on convenient assumptions, statistical patterns uncovered by torturing data are worse than worthless. They have bankrupted investors large and small.

Mathematics is not enough. Statistics is not enough. Master investors need common sense; they need to understand human nature, and they need to control their emotions.

FEAR AND GREED

I have a friend, Blake, who netted a million dollars in cash when he downsized by selling a McMansion and buying a smaller home. About a year after the sale, I asked him what he had done with the money and I was flabbergasted when he told me that he had been holding it in his checking account. He didn't know what the interest rate was, so I checked. It was 0.01 percent. That's right, one one-hundredths of a percent.

I asked why and Blake said he didn't want to lose any money. True enough, his money wasn't going to go below $1 million, but it wasn't going to go much above $1 million, either. He was losing a lot of money compared to how much money he might have if he invested in stocks. A return of 0.01 percent on $1 million is $100 in a year's time. A portfolio of blue-chip stocks with 2 percent dividend yields would generate $20,000 in dividends in a year's time. There is a pretty big difference between $100 and $20,000.

It gets worse. With normal 5 percent dividend growth, the anticipated long-return from the blue-chip stock portfolio is 7 percent. If dividends and prices go up by 5 percent the first year, the first-year return is $70,000, compared to $100. That's a heavy price to pay for safety.

It is true, as Blake said adamantly, there is no guarantee what stock prices will be day to day, week to week, or year to year. Stock prices could drop 5, 10, even 20 percent in a single day, even more in a year.

I tried to convince Blake of the wisdom of a value-investor perspective. Invest in ten, twenty, or thirty great companies with 2 percent dividend yields and then forget about it. Don't check stock prices every day. He could think about something else—his family, his job, his hobbies. While he is minding his own business, his stock portfolio will pay $20,000 dividends the first year, somewhat more the next year, and even more the year after that, with all dividends automatically reinvested.

Ten years from now, he can check his portfolio. He will have accumulated ten years of healthy dividends reinvested to earn even more dividends. The market prices of his stocks will almost surely be higher ten years from now than they are today, probably much higher. The economy will be much larger, corporate earnings will be much higher, and dividends will be much higher—so will stock prices. If the dividends and earnings on his stocks grow by an average of 5 percent a year and price-earnings ratios are about the same then as they are today, his portfolio will be worth about $2 million, as opposed to $1,001,000 if he leaves his money in a checking account paying 0.01 percent interest for ten years

Blake reluctantly agreed to invest $500,000 in stocks. Wouldn't you know it, he called me the next day to complain that the value of his portfolio had dropped by $195. (No, I am not making this up.) He wanted to sell his stocks before he lost any more money.

Other people are the exact opposite. I have another friend, Emma, who gets the same thrills from buying and selling stocks that other people get from winning and losing money in Las Vegas. Every weekday morning, Emma bolts out of bed, excited to start a new day filled with buying and selling stocks. News tidbits, stock price blips, and chat-room rumors provide jolts of excitement as Emma moves quickly to buy or sell before others do. By the end of the day, she has sold everything she bought during the day because she doesn't want to be blindsided by overnight news. Emma wants to be in control, to begin every day with cash that she can deploy during the day as she does battle with other investors.

On weekends, Emma is bored and restless. For some people, Monday is Blue Monday—the day they have to go back to work. For Emma, Monday is Merry Monday—the day she gets to start living again.

Emma is a gambling addict. Some people love to watch slot-machine wheels spin; Emma loves to watch stock prices dance. Profits are exhilarating. Losses are an incentive to keep betting, hoping to recoup those losses and believing that she is due for a win. Day-trading stocks is entertainment, but it is not cheap.

I hope this book will convince you that Blake and Emma are bad role models. Sensible investors can make a lot more money than Blake's checking account without taking as many risks as Emma's dice rolls. The secret is value investing—buying solid stocks at attractive prices, and leaving them alone.

Value investing is admittedly more adventurous than checking accounts and more boring than day-trading, but it is more rewarding than both.

Part I of this book will argue that a value-investing strategy can help intelligent investors select profitable investments without unbearable financial stress. Part II will describe several detailed examples of value investing.

VALUE INVESTING

SEEING THROUGH THE HYPE

*If you don't know who you are, the stock
market is an expensive place to find out.*
—GEORGE GOODMAN

On March 11, 2000, I participated in a conference on the
booming stock market and the widely publicized "36K" prediction that the Dow Jones Industrial Average would soon more
than triple, from below 12,000 to 36,000. James Glassman and
Kevin Hassett, two scholars at the American Enterprise Institute,
had written a cover story for the *Atlantic Monthly* and a book published by Random House arguing that "stock prices could double,
triple, or even quadruple tomorrow and still not be too high." Their
"conservative" estimate of "the right price" was 36,000. It was a provocative assertion and it was taken seriously by serious people.

The first speaker at the conference talked about Moore's Law
(transistor density on integrated circuits doubles every two years). I
listened intently and agreed that technology is wonderful. But I
didn't hear a single word about whether stock prices were too high,
too low, or just right.

The next speaker talked about how smart dot-com whizzes were.
When you bought a dot-com stock, you were giving your money to
clever people who would figure out something profitable to do with
it. I again listened intently and I agreed that many dot-com companies were started by smart, likable people. Heck, one of my sons had

joined with four other recent college graduates to form a dot-com company. The five of them rented a house in New Hampshire, slept upstairs, and commuted to work by walking downstairs.

What kind of work were they doing downstairs? They didn't have a business plan. The key phrase was "nimble." They were bright, creative, and flexible. When a profitable opportunity appeared, these five nimble lads would seize it with all ten hands. I knew that these were terrific kids and that hundreds of terrific kids were looking for ways to profit from the Internet. But I still hadn't heard a single word about whether stock prices were too high, too low, or just right.

The next speaker talked about how Alan Greenspan was a wonderful Fed chair. The Federal Reserve decides when to increase the money supply to boost the economy and when to restrain the money supply to stifle inflationary pressures. As a cynic (me) once wrote, the Fed jacks up interest rates to cause a recession whenever they feel it is in our best interests to be unemployed.

It is very important to have the Fed chaired by someone who knows what they're doing. I listened intently and I agreed that Alan Greenspan was an impressive Fed chair. But, once again, I didn't hear anything about whether stock prices were too high, too low, or just right.

I was the last speaker, and I was the grump at this happy party. I looked at stock prices from a variety of perspectives and concluded that not only was it far-fetched to think that the Dow would hit 36,000 anytime soon, but that the current level of stock prices was much too high. My final words were, "This is a bubble, and it will end badly."

I was right—eerily so. The conference was on Saturday, March 11, 2000. The NASDAQ dropped the following Monday and fell by 75 percent over the next three years from its March 10, 2000, peak. AOL fell 85 percent, Yahoo 95 percent. The interesting question is not the coincidental timing of my remarks, but why I was convinced that this was a bubble.

During the dot-com bubble, most investors did not try to gauge whether stocks were reasonably priced. Instead, they watched stock prices go up and they invented explanations to rationalize what was happening. They talked about smart kids and Fed chairs. They looked at processing speeds and website visitors.

They didn't talk about whether stock prices were too high, too low, or just right. This book will explain how to answer that question, which is after all the most fundamental question in investing. The answer—no surprise—is value investing.

SPECULATION VERSUS

INVESTING

Separate and distinct things not to be confused,
as every thoughtful investor knows, are real worth and market price.
—JOHN BURR WILLIAMS

Decades ago, investing was haphazard. Investors figured that a stock was worth whatever people were willing to pay, and the game was to guess what people will pay tomorrow for a stock you buy today. Then John Burr Williams unleashed a revolution by arguing that investors could use something called present value to estimate the intrinsic value of a company's stock.

Think of a stock as a machine that generates cash every few months—cash that happens to be called dividends. The key question is how much you would pay to own the machine in order to get the cash. This is the stock's *intrinsic value*. People who think this way are called *value investors*.

In contrast, *speculators* buy a stock not for the cash it dispenses, but to sell to others for a profit. To a speculator, a stock is worth what somebody else will pay for it, and the challenge is to guess what others will pay tomorrow for the stock you buy today. This guessing game is derisively called the Greater Fool Theory: Buy stocks at inflated prices and hope to sell to even bigger fools at still higher prices.

Legendary investor Warren Buffett has this aphorism: "My favorite holding period is forever." If we think this way, never planning to sell, we force ourselves to value stocks based on the cash they generate, instead of being distracted by guesses about future prices. A Buffett variation on this theme is, "I never attempt to make money on the stock market. I buy on the assumption that they could close the market the next day and not reopen it for five years." If we think this way, we stop speculating about zigs and zags in stock prices and focus on the cash generated by the money machine.

The idea is simple and powerful, but often elusive. It is very hard to buy a stock without looking at what its price has been in the past and thinking about what its price might be in the future. It is very hard to think about waiting patiently for cash to accumulate when it is so tempting to think about making a quick killing by flipping stocks.

People are often lured to the stock market by the ill-conceived notion that riches are there for the taking—that they can buy a stock right before the price leaves the launchpad. This dream is aided and abetted by get-rich-quick gurus peddling fantasies. I once received a letter that began "Dear friend." There's the first red flag: Real friends don't address you as "Dear friend." The letter went on, "IMAGINE turning $1,000 into $34,500 in less than one year!" The letter said that "no special background or education" was needed and that "it's an investment you can make with spare cash that you might ordinarily spend on lottery tickets or the racetrack." Second red flag: I don't buy lottery tickets or bet on horses. Where did they get my name? Why did they think I was a sucker? This was getting embarrassing.

The "secret" was low-priced stocks. To demonstrate the "explosive profit potential," the letter listed twenty low-priced stocks and said that $100 invested in each ($2,000 in all) would have grown in the blink of an eye to $26,611. Not only that, but another stock, LKA International, had gone from 2 cents to 69 cents a share in a few months, which would have turned $1,000 into $34,500. The letter concluded by offering a special $39 report that would give me access to "the carefully guarded territory of a few shrewd 'inner circle' investors."

That was the third red flag. Why would anyone who had a real get-rich-quick system peddle it instead of using it? Why waste precious time selling newsletters for $39? Some self-proclaimed gurus assert that they have made more than enough money and want to share their secrets with others who are as poor as they once were: "If a loser like me can make money, so can a loser like you!" If they are truly rich, why don't they send us money instead of asking for more?

It is preposterous to think that the stock market gives away money. There is a story about two finance professors who see a $100 bill on the sidewalk. As one professor reaches for it, the other says, "Don't bother; if it were real, someone would have picked it up by now." Finance professors are fond of saying that the stock market doesn't leave $100 bills on the sidewalk, meaning that if there were an easy way to make money, someone would have figured it out by now.

There is truth in that, but it is not completely true. Stock prices are sometimes wacky. During speculative booms and financial crises, the stock market leaves suitcases full of $100 bills on the sidewalk. Still, when you think you have found an easy way to make money, you should ask yourself if other investors have overlooked a $100 bill on the sidewalk or if you have overlooked a logical explanation.

Investors make voluntary transactions—some buying and others selling—and a stock won't trade at 2 cents if it is clear that the price will soon be 69 cents. Even if only a shrewd inner circle know that the price will soon be 69 cents, they will buy millions of shares, driving the price today up to 69 cents.

When LKA traded at 2 cents a share, there were an equal number of buyers and sellers, neither side knowing for sure whether the price would be higher or lower the next day or the day after that. The optimists bought and the pessimists sold. The optimists happened to be right this time. But to count on being right every time, buying stocks at their lowest prices and selling at their highest, is foolish.

Probably the most successful stock market investor of all time is Warren Buffett, who made about 20 percent a year over some fifty years. This isn't close to the fantasies concocted by dream peddlers, but it is absolutely spectacular compared to the performance of the average investor, who has made about 10 percent a year.

Some stocks do spectacularly well, just as some lottery tickets turn out to be winners. But it is a delusion to think that you will become an instant millionaire by buying stocks or lottery tickets. A more realistic goal is to make intelligent investments and avoid financial potholes.

The key is to resist the temptation to buy and sell stocks based on wishful thinking about prices. Instead, think of stocks as money machines and think about what you would be willing to pay for the cash they generate over an indefinite horizon. If you do, you will be a value investor—and glad of it.

SEMI-EFFICIENT MARKETS

*The real trouble with this world of ours is not that it is an unreason-
able world, nor even that it is a reasonable one. The commonest
kind of trouble is that it is nearly reasonable, but not quite.
Life . . . looks just a little more mathematical and regular than it is;
its exactitude is obvious, but its inexactitude is hidden;
its wildness lies in wait.*

—G. K. CHESTERTON

I have a small army of former students who alert me to interesting stories I may have missed. One sent me a *Wall Street Journal*
article titled "Clues Abound for the Small Investor to Divine Market
Direction." According to the article:

> The long-term investor can make his decisions based on in-
> formation easily available in his morning newspaper. In-
> deed, Thom Brown, managing director of the Philadelphia
> investment firm of Rutherford, Brown & Catherwood, ad-
> vises investors to simply read a daily newspaper.
>
> "Look for anything that suggests the direction of the
> economy," he says. "Auto sales, for example, give you an idea
> about how willing consumers are to part with their money."
> An expanding economy usually means rising stock prices.

Was this former student passing along a useful tip? Nope. She was
contributing to my extensive collection of silly things said by sensi-

ble people. She added this note, "What everyone knows isn't worth knowing."

THE IDEA OF AN EFFICIENT MARKET

The efficient market hypothesis is that stock prices take into account all relevant information so that no investor can take advantage of other people's ignorance. An efficient market does not require zero profits. After all, even boring bank accounts pay interest. Investors won't buy stocks unless they expect to make some money. Stocks do pay dividends and the average stock investor does make money—about 10 percent a year over the past 100 years. The efficient market hypothesis is that no one can make excessive profits except by being lucky.

The stock market would not be efficient if sales of Ford F-150 pickup trucks jumped dramatically and investors who read about the sales increase in the morning newspaper could buy Ford stock at low prices from investors who didn't know about the sales bump. Market efficiency does not assume that every investor knows about the sales increase—just that enough well-informed and well-financed investors are ready to jump-start Ford's stock price to where it would be if everyone did know the news. Ford's stock price should jump as soon as some investors know of the F-150 surge, and this immediate price bump protects amateurs from selling at outdated prices. An efficient market is a fair game in the sense that no investor can beat the market by knowing something other investors don't know.

ANTICIPATED EVENTS AND SURPRISES

If a toy store's sales increase before Christmas, will its stock price increase too? It depends. When the stock traded in the summer, investors tried to predict holiday sales and they valued the stock based on these predictions. If the forecasts turn out to be correct, there is no reason for the stock price to change on the day that the sales numbers are announced. The price will change, however, if sales turn out to be unexpectedly strong or disappointing.

Stock prices do not rise or fall when events that are expected to happen do happen. Stock prices do change if the unexpected happens. However, by definition, it is impossible to predict the unexpected. Therefore, it is impossible to predict changes in stock prices. That is a pretty good argument. So is its implication.

It is not enough to know that Ford F-150 sales increased last quarter or that auto sales increase when the economy gets stronger. The benchmark to gauge your investment ideas is not,

How is today different from yesterday?

or

How will tomorrow differ from today?

but

How does my prediction of tomorrow differ from what others expect?

When you think you have a good reason for buying a stock, ask yourself if you know something that other investors don't know. If you do, it may be inside information that is illegal to use (for reasons discussed later in this chapter). If you don't, your information is probably already reflected in market prices.

It seems obvious, but sometimes the obvious is overlooked. A longtime financial columnist for the *New York Times* offered this logical, but not very helpful, advice for buying bonds:

> It is obviously good sense to buy bonds when the Federal
> Reserve Banks start lowering interest rates. It is just as obvi-
> ously bad sense to buy them at any time when, two or three

or four months hence, the Fed is certain to start raising money rates and lowering the prices of outstanding bonds.

Anything that has already happened or is certain to happen is surely already embedded in bond prices.

Similarly, you won't get rich following this advice in the Consumers Digest *Get Rich Investment Guide*:

> The ability to track interest rates as they pertain to bonds is made easier by following the path of the Prime Rate (the rate of interest charged by banks to their top clients). If the consensus shown in top business journals indicates that rates are going up, this means that bonds will go down in price. Therefore, when it seems that rates are moving up, an investor should wait until some "peaking" of rates is foreseen.

Seriously, isn't it obvious that easily available information doesn't give you an edge over other investors? What everybody knows isn't worth knowing.

UNCERTAINTY AND DISAGREEMENT

The efficient market hypothesis does not assume that everyone agrees on what a security is worth. Market opinion of IBM in the spring of 1987 provides a particularly dramatic example. At that time, IBM was probably the most widely scrutinized company. Value Line's highly regarded analysts gave IBM stock its lowest rating, placing it among the bottom 10 percent in predicted performance over the next twelve months. At the very same time, Kidder Peabody's widely respected research department gave IBM its highest rating and included IBM in its recommended model portfolio of twenty stocks. This was not an isolated fluke.

On Thursday, November 11, 2010, TheStreet.com posted an article titled "How Nokia's Stock Price Could Double." Three days

later, on Sunday, November 14, Seeking Alpha posted an article titled "Nokia Is Still Overvalued," arguing that a "more realistic" value
would be half of its current price. Nothing substantive happened between November 11 and November 14, yet these two influential
websites had dramatically different views of Nokia stock. That's why
there are buyers and sellers.

For any stock, at the current market price, there are as many buyers as sellers—as many people who think that the stock is overpriced as think it is a bargain. The efficient market hypothesis says
that it is never evident that a stock's price is about to surge or collapse—for if it were, there wouldn't be a balance between buyers and
sellers.

The fact that changes in stock prices are hard to predict does not
imply that stock prices are correct according to some external, objective criterion. Market prices reflect what buyers are willing to pay
and sellers to accept, and both may be led astray by human emotions
and misperceptions. This distinction is crucial for understanding
what the efficient market hypothesis does and does not say.

MARKET TIMING

Most investors try to time their purchases and sales—to buy before
prices go up and sell before they go down. A longtime financial
writer for the *New York Times* offered this attractive goal:

> Since we know stocks are going to fall as well as rise, we
> might as well get a little traffic out of them. A man who buys
> a stock at 10 and sells it at 20 makes 100 percent. But a man
> who buys it at 10, sells it at 14 1/2, buys it back at 12 and sells
> it at 18, buys it back at 15 and sells it at 20, makes 188 percent.

If only it were this easy!

It would be great to jump nimbly in and out of stocks, catching
every rise and missing every drop, but how do we know in advance

whether prices are headed up or down? J. P. Morgan was exactly right when he said that "the market will go up and it will go down, but not necessarily in that order."

I am no fan of frenetic trading; still, there are times when stock prices are seriously out of whack because investors are far too pessimistic or optimistic. Our goal is to recognize compelling times to buy and times to sell. Ironically, the key is *not* to attempt to buy before prices go up and sell before they go down, but to think about whether the money machine is cheap or expensive—to be a value investor. I will explain this paradox in later chapters.

STOCK SELECTION

In contrast to market timing, stock selection is picking stocks that will beat other stocks, a task the efficient market hypothesis says is futile. For example, you might buy stock in a company that announces a large earnings increase and avoid firms that report flat or declining earnings. However, analysts predict earnings long before they are announced and stock prices reflect these predictions. Announcements that are in line with predictions—regardless of whether earnings are predicted to go up or down—have little effect on prices. To pick stocks that will do better than other stocks, based on their earnings, you need to predict which companies' earnings surprises will be good news and which will be bad news. How does one predict surprises?

A former student told me about an interesting project he had worked on. His consulting firm had been hired by the directors of a major consumer-products company to recommend an executive compensation plan. The board wanted the firm, year after year, to be one of the highest-ranked consumer-products companies based on total shareholder return, dividends plus capital gains.

The consulting company immediately recognized the problem with this goal. Do you see it, too?

The consulting company calculated shareholder returns for 160 consumer-products companies over three-year intervals: 1980–1982, 1983–1985, and so on. For each three-year period, they ranked the companies from 1 to 160 based on total shareholder return. They then made a scatter plot with each firm's ranking during one of those three-year periods on the horizontal axis and the ranking during the next three-year period on the vertical axis. The scatter plot in Figure 3-1 is striking, but not for the usual reason. Instead of showing a strong positive or negative correlation, it appears that a blindfolded person threw ink at paper.

That was exactly the point the consulting firm wanted to make. A company's executives may be able to increase a firm's profits, but trying to outperform the stock market year after year is an elusive goal. For a company's stock price to go up more than investors expect, the firm must do better than investors expect. For the stock price to soar every year, the firm must do better than investors expect every year. Good luck with that!

FIGURE 3-1. Shareholder return in adjacent three-year periods

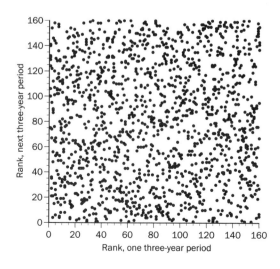

THE PERFORMANCE OF PROFESSIONALS

Another way of testing the efficient market hypothesis is to look at the records of professional investors, who presumably base their decisions on publicly available information. If they consistently beat the market, they apparently have an advantage over amateur investors.

The record of professional investors as a group has been mediocre, at best. In his persuasive book *The New Contrarian Investment Strategy*, David Dreman looked at fifty-two surveys of stocks or stock portfolios recommended by professional investors. Forty of them underperformed the market. Perhaps some professionals are pros and the rest are amateurs pretending to be pros. Nope. There is no consistency in which professional investors do well and which do poorly. A study of 200 institutional stock portfolios found that of those who ranked in the top 25 percent in one five-year period, 26 percent ranked in the top 25 percent during the next five years, 48 percent ranked in the middle 50 percent, and 26 percent were in the bottom 25 percent.

CAN WE DISTINGUISH SKILL FROM LUCK?

Some investors do compile outstanding records. However, consider the coin-calling experiment that I sometimes do in my investment classes. Suppose that there are thirty-two students and that half of them predict heads for the first flip while half of them predict tails. The coin is flipped and lands heads, making the first half right. The sixteen students who were right then predict a second flip, with half saying heads and the other half tails. It comes up tails and the eight students who have been right twice in a row now try for a third time. Half predict heads and half tails, and the coin lands tails again. The four students who were right divide again on whether the next flip will be heads or tails. The result is tails and now we're down to two students. One calls heads and the other tails. It is a heads and we have our winner—the student who correctly predicted five in a row. Are you confident that this student will call the next five flips correctly?

Even monkeys throwing darts and analysts flipping coins sometimes get lucky—an observation that cautions us that past successes are no guarantee of future success. Not only that, even if some analysts are somewhat better than average, stock market volatility makes it very difficult to separate the skilled from the lucky.

Imagine there are 10,000 analysts and 10 percent of them have a 0.60 probability of predicting correctly whether the stock market will go up or down in the coming year. The remaining 90 percent, like monkeys throwing darts, have only a 0.50 probability of making a correct prediction. Call the analysts in the first group skilled and those in the second group lucky.

If we look at their records over a ten-year period, we can expect six of the 1,000 skilled analysts to make correct predictions in all ten years. Among the 9,000 analysts who are merely lucky, nine can be expected to make ten correct predictions. This means that if we choose one of the fifteen analysts who have been right for ten years in a row, there is only a 40 percent chance that we will choose a skilled analyst. This is considerably better than the 10 percent chance of picking a skilled analyst if we ignore their records; but still—and this is the point—past performance is far from a guarantee of future success.

In practice, there is even more uncertainty because we often do not have a complete and accurate record over many years. Some analysts are too young. Others distort their records, perhaps by selectively reporting their successes and omitting their failures. Also, alas, skills are not constant. By the time someone has compiled an impressive track record, energy and insight may be fading.

Some investors surely are more skilled than lucky. However, the records of most are brief, mixed, or exaggerated, and there is no sure way to separate the talented from the lucky and the liars. The stock market is not all luck, but it is more luck than nervous investors want to hear or successful investors want to admit.

INSIDER TRADING

Section 10(b)5 of the 1934 Securities and Exchange Act makes it "unlawful for any person to employ any device, scheme or artifice to defraud or to engage in any act, practice or course of business which operates as a fraud or deceit upon any person."

This law was enacted in response to a variety of fraudulent activities in the 1920s that manipulated stock prices and misled naive investors. For instance, an investment pool could push a stock's price up, up, and up by trading the stock back and forth among members of the pool, and then sell to investors lured by the stock's upward momentum.

Such activities have not disappeared completely. In 1987 a con man was sentenced to two-and-a-half years in prison after he pleaded guilty to conspiracy and fraud in manipulating the prices of two small stocks by buying and selling shares through fifty-three accounts at eighteen brokerage firms.

The U.S. Securities and Exchange Commission (SEC) also uses Section 10(b)5 for a very different purpose—to prosecute perceived insider-trading abuses. Insider information is not even mentioned, let alone defined in the law, but over the years, through a series of court cases, the SEC has created a set of legal precedents. The SEC has also gone after insider traders for related crimes, such as mail or wire fraud, obstruction of justice, and income tax evasion.

The SEC interprets illegal insider trading as that based on important information that has not yet been made public if the information was obtained wrongfully (such as by theft or bribery) or if the person has a fiduciary responsibility to keep the information confidential. Nor can investors trade on the basis of information that they know or have reason to know was obtained wrongfully.

The SEC is unlikely to press charges if it is convinced that a leak of confidential information was inadvertent; for example, a conversation overheard on an airplane. However, courts have consistently ruled that a company's officers and directors should not profit from buying or selling stock before the public announcement of important corporate news. The SEC has also won cases against relatives and friends of corporate insiders, establishing the principle that someone tipped by an insider is an insider, too. In the 1968 Texas Gulf Sulphur case, involving the purchase of stock by company executives and outsiders who had been tipped before the public announcement of an enormous ore discovery, a federal appeals court ruled that "anyone—corporate insider or not—who regularly receives material non-public information may not use that information to trade in securities without incurring an affirmative duty to disclose."

The SEC has frequently won cases based on a different principle—that insider trading is robbery, the theft of information. In 1984, a federal court of appeals upheld the conviction of Anthony Materia, a printing house employee, who had decoded documents (with missing company names) that he was printing relating to mergers and takeovers and then bought shares in the target companies. The court ruled that he violated a duty to his employer and its clients when he "stole information to which he was privy in his work. . . . Materia's theft of information was indeed as fraudulent as if he had converted corporate funds for his personal benefit."

Please don't take chances cheating and hoping to outwit the SEC. It isn't worth it and you don't need to break any laws. You can make more than enough money by being an honest value investor.

HUMAN EMOTIONS

Investment decisions depend not only on known facts, but also human emotions like greed and overconfidence, which lead some investors astray and leave opportunities for others. This is why the stock market is only semi-efficient. Here are three examples.

Confusing a great company with a great stock. We eat in a good restaurant, buy a fun toy, admire attractive clothing, see a wonderful movie, ride in a nice car, and think, "I should buy stock in that company." Before rushing to buy, ask yourself whether you are the only one who knows how wonderful these things are. If not, the stock price probably already reflects the fact that it is a good company. The question is not whether the products are worth buying, but whether the stock is worth buying. If the stock's price is too high, the answer is no.

Later, you will see that the glamour stocks of companies that make great products and generate strong profits are more likely to be overpriced than are the stocks of struggling companies. Who has the courage to buy stock in bad companies? Not many, which is why struggling companies' stocks are often cheap.

Buying hot tips. My family went on a vacation to Costa Rica in 2010 and we met a man named David who bragged that he was paying for his vacation with the profits he was going to make on a stock investment. I asked him about the stock and was not surprised when he said that he had been given a hot tip by his auto mechanic on a stock that had nothing whatsoever to do with cars.

The hot tip was Ecosphere Technologies (ESPH), a small company that owns several environmental technologies, including the Ecos PowerCube, a solar-power generator that can be used in remote locations. David bought 10,000 shares at $1 per share in early March. The price had jumped to $1.65 in late March and his $6,500 profit was enough to pay for his Costa Rica vacation.

The problem was that, year after year, Ecosphere Technologies either lost money or made a small profit. There was nothing to prop up the price except people like David, who were buying the stock based on a hot tip. Figures 3-2 and 3-3 show that there was a huge surge in the stock's price and the volume of trading during the first three months of 2010 (when David bought). Then the price collapsed. Six years later, the price was 3 cents a share.

FIGURE 3-2. ESPH price per share

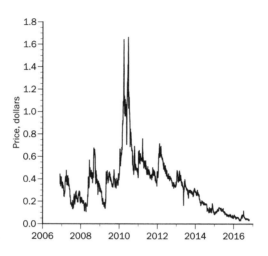

FIGURE 3-3. ESPH daily volume of trading

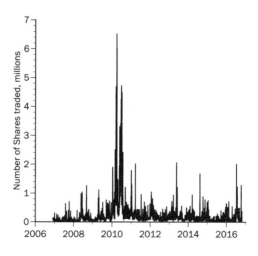

ESPH's stock price had gone up, no doubt fueled by people who heard the hot tips and rushed to buy the stock. There are two problems with hot tips. One is that they may be unfounded rumors, perhaps spread by people who own the stock already and want to sell at a higher price. Second, if there is any truth to the rumors, it may already be embedded in the price.

Chasing trends. I was talking to a friendly guy named Lou at a party and he told me that, because he lives in California, he gets up at five thirty every morning so that he can be at his computer, ready to trade, when the stock market opens at six thirty Pacific Time. He has a software program that alerts him when it notices a stock price going up by some preset amount; for example, one percent since the market opened or one percent in the past hour. Lou watches the price for a few moments and, if he likes what he sees, he buys the stock and holds it until the price goes down enough to persuade him that the run-up is over.

I asked Lou how he was doing and was surprised by his candor: "I lower my tax bill every April." He explained that, on balance, he always seems to have more capital losses than gains and he can use his net capital losses to reduce his taxable income. He said that he is still trying to perfect his timing but, more often than not, he either buys the stock too late (after the run-up is over) or sells too late (after he has lost money).

Lou's explanation is just a roundabout way of saying that chasing trends doesn't work because what a stock price has done in the past is an unreliable predictor of what the price will do in the future.

Sometimes, there are a lot of folks like Lou out there, chasing the same trends. They notice stock prices going up (perhaps because their friends are bragging about how much money they are making) and rush to buy so that they can make money, too. When lots of trend chasers are buying, their lust can push prices higher still, luring more trend chasers. This imitative behavior fuels speculative bubbles—stock prices going up for no reason other than people are buying stock because prices have been going up.

When stock prices stop going up, they go down very fast because there is no reason to buy other than a belief that prices will go up.

THE DELUSION OF CROWDS

Michael C. Jensen, a Harvard Business School professor, wrote, "The vast scientific evidence on the theory of efficient markets indicates that, in the absence of inside information, a security's market price represents the best available estimate of its true value." The idea is that while some investors may substantially overestimate the value of a stock, other investors will err in the other direction, and these errors will balance out so that the collective judgment of the crowd is close to the correct value.

The wisdom of crowds has a lot of appeal. The classic example is a jelly bean experiment conducted by finance professor Jack Treynor. He showed fifty-six students a jar containing 850 jelly beans and asked them to write down how many beans they thought were in the jar. The average guess was 871, an error of only 2 percent. Only one student did better. This experiment has been cited over and over as evidence that the average opinion of the value of a stock is likely to be close to the "correct" value.

The analogy is not apt. As Treynor noted, the student guesses were made independently and had no systematic bias. When these assumptions are true, the average guess will, on average, be closer to the true value than the majority of the individual guesses. That is a mathematical fact. But it is not a fact if those assumptions are wrong. After the initial student guesses were recorded, Treynor advised the students that they should allow for air space at the top of the bean jar and that the plastic jar's exterior was thinner than a glass jar. The average estimate increased to 979.2, an error of 15 percent. The many were no longer smarter than the few. "Although the cautions weren't intended to be misleading," Treynor wrote, "they seem to have caused some shared error to creep into the estimates."

There is a lot of shared error in the stock market. Investor opinions are not formed independently and are not free of systematic biases. Stock prices are buffeted by fads, fancies, greed, and gloom—what Keynes called "animal spirits." Contagious mass psychology causes not only pricing errors, but speculative bubbles and unwarranted panics.

In an investor survey near the peak of the dot-com bubble in 2000, the median prediction of the annual return on stocks over the next ten years was 15 percent. It wasn't just naive amateurs. Supposedly sophisticated hedge funds were buying dot-com stocks just as feverishly as small investors. This was not collective wisdom; this was collective delusion. They didn't see the bubble because they did not want to see it. The actual annual return over the next ten years turned out to be -0.5 percent.

The 2013 Nobel Prize in Economics was given to two economists with very different views of the efficient market hypothesis. As described by Chicago professor Eugene Fama:

> An "efficient" market for securities . . . [is] a market where, given the available information, actual prices at every point in time represent very good estimates of intrinsic values.

Yale professor Robert Shiller has a very different view:

> One form of this argument claims that . . . the real price of stocks is close to the intrinsic value. . . . This argument for the efficient markets hypothesis represents one of the most remarkable errors in the history of economic thought.

Fama believes that markets set the correct price, the price that God herself would set, and that changes in stock prices are hard to predict because they are caused by new information, which, by definition, cannot be predicted.

Shiller's view is that changes in stock prices may be hard to predict because of unpredictable, sometimes irrational, revisions in investor expectations—as if God determined stock prices by flipping a coin. If so, changes in market prices are impossible to predict, but market prices are not good estimates of intrinsic value.

What they both agree on is that it is hard to predict changes in stock prices. It is tempting to think that, as in any profession, good training, hard work, and a skilled mind will yield superior results. And it is especially tempting to think that you possess these very characteristics.

A student did a term paper in my statistics class at Pomona College where 200 randomly selected students were asked if their height, intelligence, and attractiveness were above average or below average compared to other Pomona students of the same gender. The reality is that an equal number are above average and below average. Individual perceptions were quite different. Fifty-six percent of the female students and 49 percent of the males believed their height was above average, well within the range of sampling error. However, 84 percent of the females and 79 percent of the males believed their intelligence was above average; and 74 percent of the females and 68 percent of the males believed their attractiveness was above average.

It is a common human trait, probably inherited from our distant ancestors, to overestimate ourselves. Back then, it was hard to survive in a challenging, often unforgiving world without confidence. Self-confidence had survival and reproductive value and came to dominate the gene pool. These days, we still latch on to evidence of our strengths and discount evidence to the contrary. This is so common that it even has a name: confirmation bias.

We think we can predict the result of a football game, an election, or a stock pick. If our prediction turns out to be correct, this confirms how smart we are. If our prediction does not come true, it was just bad luck—poor officiating, low voter turnout, the irrationality of other investors.

Very few investors think they are below average, even though half are. After all, would people sell one stock and buy another if they thought they would be wrong more often than right? Every decision that works out confirms our wisdom. Every mistake is attributed to bad luck beyond our control.

This overconfidence is why people trade so much, thinking they know more than the investors on the other side of their trades. It is why investors don't hold sufficiently diversified portfolios, believing that there is little chance that the stocks they pick will do poorly. It is why investors hold on to their losers, believing that it is only a matter of time until other investors realize how great these stocks are.

WARREN BUFFETT AND SOME CONTRARIANS

Human sentiments like greed and overconfidence illustrate the crucial difference between *possessing* information and *processing* information. Possessing information is knowing something about a company that others do not know. Processing information is thinking more clearly about things we all know.

Warren Buffett did not beat the market for decades by having access to information that was not available to others, but by thinking more clearly about information available to everyone. Beginning in 1956 with a $100,000 partnership, he earned a 31 percent compound annual rate of return over the next fourteen years, with never a losing year. In 1969, feeling stocks to be overpriced, Buffett left the stock market and dissolved the partnership. The "wizard of Omaha" returned to the stock market in the 1970s, making investments through Berkshire Hathaway, formerly a cloth-milling company. Continuing to earn nearly 20 percent a year, his net worth was $65 billion in 2016.

In the 1980s I debated the efficient market hypothesis with a prominent Stanford professor. I said that Buffett was evidence that the market could be beaten by processing information better than other investors. His response was immediate and dismissive: "Enough monkeys hitting enough keys . . ." He was referring to the classic *infinite monkey theorem*, one version of which states that a handful of monkeys pounding away at typewriters will eventually write every book that humans have ever written. One eternal monkey could do the same; but a very large number of monkeys could be expected to do it sooner. The Stanford professor's argument was that with so many people buying and selling stocks over so many decades, one person is bound to be so much luckier than the rest as to appear to be a genius—when he is really just a lucky monkey.

In a 1984 speech at Columbia University celebrating the fiftieth anniversary of Benjamin Graham and David Dodd's value-investing treatise, *Security Analysis*, Buffett rebutted the lucky-monkey argument by noting that he personally knows eight other portfolio managers who, like Buffett, adhere to the value-investing principles taught by Graham and Dodd. All nine have outperformed the market dramatically for many years. How many monkeys would it take to generate that performance?

Yet many academics are skeptical (or perhaps jealous?). In 2006, Austan Goolsbee, a Chicago Booth School of Business professor who served as chair of the Council of Economic Advisers for President Obama, was interviewed on American Public Media and said:

> I'd tell [Berkshire Hathaway] shareholders to watch their wallets. See, I'm an economist, and it always sticks in my craw when people say Warren has the Midas touch. That's because the one thing that professors pound into young economists is that the only investors who beat the market are ones who get lucky or else take risk.

I am unpersuaded. I have a personal interest in believing that some investors process information better than others, just as some doctors and lawyers do. My belief in Buffett is fortified by the fact that, unlike monkeys, Buffett makes sense. His annual reports are exceptionally wise and well written. They are also his own opinions, not a repackaging of what others are saying.

Too many investors are hostage to a groupthink mentality that values conformity above independent thought. Ironically, institutional groupthink is encouraged by a legal need to be "prudent." Just as no purchasing agent ever got fired for buying IBM equipment, so no money manager has ever been thought imprudent for buying IBM stock. As Keynes observed, "Worldly wisdom teaches that it is better for reputation to fail conventionally than to succeed unconventionally." Who can fault someone who fails when everyone else is failing?

Buffett generally ignores the crowd and makes up his own mind. Other investors have prospered by watching the crowd and doing the opposite. In May 1932, with stock prices at their lowest level in this century, Dean Witter sent a memo to his company's brokers and management saying:

> All of our customers with money must someday put it to work—into some revenue-producing investment. Why not invest it now, when securities are cheap?
>
> Some people say they want to wait for a clearer view of the future. But when the future is again clear, the present bargains will have vanished. In fact, does anyone think that today's prices will prevail once full confidence has been restored?

That's exactly right. Bargains are not going to be found when investors are optimistic, but when they are pessimistic. In Warren Buffett's memorable words, "Be fearful when others are greedy and greedy when others are fearful."

If the herdlike instincts of institutional investors push the prices of glamour stocks to unjustifiable levels, then perhaps the road to investment success is to do the opposite—as J. Paul Getty advised in his autobiography, "Buy when everyone else is selling and hold until everyone else is buying." A deliberate attempt to do the opposite of what others are doing is called a *contrarian* strategy, and it can be applied to individual stocks (buying the least popular stocks) and to the market as a whole (buying when other investors are bearish).

The experts have been notoriously wrong at dramatic market turning points: In recent years, they were optimistic before the dotcom bubble popped in the spring of 2000 and pessimistic before the market bottomed in the summer of 2002. The optimism returned as the market peaked in the summer of 2007, followed by pessimism as the market bottomed in the winter of 2009.

With individual stocks, the favorites often do poorly. A representative example is a study of the recommendations of the twenty "superstar" analysts selected in a poll of institutional investors. Of the 132 stocks they recommended, two-thirds did worse than the S&P 500. The average gain for the 132 stocks picked by the most respected and highly paid security analysts was 9 percent, as compared to 14 percent for the S&P 500. A large institutional buyer of research concluded glumly, "It's uncanny—when they say one thing, start doing the opposite. Usually you are right."

These superstar pros were not throwing darts. They were infatuated with fads, overconfident of their abilities, chasing trends, or seduced by other human misperceptions.

Because of these human emotions, the stock market is only semi-efficient, which is good news for value investors—who don't throw darts, either.

TORTURING DATA

If you torture the data long enough, it will confess.
—Ronald Coase

W hat's so hard about predicting stock prices? Anyone with open eyes can see patterns in stock prices—patterns that are a self-evident foretelling of whether prices are headed up or down.

Thirty years ago, a former student named Jeff called me with exciting news—my lectures on the futility of trying to discern profitable patterns in stock prices were hogwash. Jeff had taken a job with IBM and, in his spare time (ha, ha!), was studying stock prices and had found some clear patterns. He was fine-tuning his system and would soon be rich. He told me that he was going to rent a helicopter and land it on the lawn outside my classroom so that he could march into my investments class triumphantly and tell students the truth.

Every year, I tell the students this story. Then I walk over to a classroom window and look outside to see if Jeff's helicopter is parked outside. I'm still waiting.

THE NATURE OF TECHNICAL ANALYSIS

Technical analysts try to gauge investor sentiment by studying stock prices, trading volume, and various measures of investor sentiment. Technicians do not look at dividends or profits, either for individual companies or for the market as a whole. If they are studying an individual company, they don't even need to know the company's name. It might bias their reading of the charts.

A technical analyst can be compared to a person who watches a computer program draw lines on a monitor and tries to discover a pattern that will predict the next line to be drawn. The lines themselves are all that matters and it would be distracting to think about whether the computer program was written in Java or C++. In the same way, the mood of the stock market can be gauged by watching stock prices; additional news about the economy or specific companies would be distracting. John Magee, who coauthored the so-called bible of technical analysis, boarded up the windows of his office so that his readings of the hopes and fears of the market would not be influenced by the sight of birds singing or snow falling.

A technician's most important tool is a chart of stock prices. The most popular are vertical-line charts, traditionally using daily price data. Each vertical line spans the high and low prices, with horizontal slashes showing the opening and closing prices. A technician adds lines, like the channel in Figure 4-1, to show a trend or other exploitable pattern (to reduce the clutter, I omitted the vertical lines and just show the closing prices).

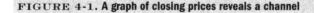

FIGURE 4-1. A graph of closing prices reveals a channel

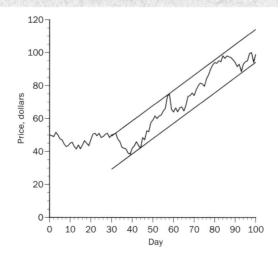

TECHNICAL GURUS

Humans have a natural affinity for professed experts who replace confusion and ambiguity with clarity and decisiveness. Periodically, a technical analyst is elevated to the status of financial guru when astoundingly accurate predictions are reported in the media and devoted followers seek the advice of these celebrities.

For example, Joseph Granville was a flamboyant guru, sometimes enlivening his public speeches with vaudeville skits using a chimpanzee or ventriloquist's dummy and at other times preaching in a prophet's robes:

> The market is a jealous God. It rewards winners and chastises losers. The Holy Bible is a record of winners and losers. The market follows every precept in that Book—if the market does not follow man's ways, what does it follow? God's ways.

His forecasts were so inaccurate in the early 1970s (due, he says, to an addiction to golf) that he abandoned the stock market completely. But then "golfers anonymous" turned his life around and he wrote a book, *How to Win at Bingo*, that sold 500,000 copies. Buoyed by this success and four years of good stock market predictions in the late 1970s, he boasted of having "cracked the secret of markets," promised that he would never make a serious mistake again, and nominated himself for the Nobel Prize in Economics. In his spare time, he predicted that Los Angeles would be destroyed by an 8.3 earthquake in May 1981.

Granville issued a buy recommendation in April 1980 and the Dow jumped 30 points the next day, perhaps propelled by avid subscribers following his advice. In September, he continued to predict a runaway stock market. "Short sellers are about to get the heat, and if you think hell is hot, watch." On January 6, 1981, he abruptly turned bearish; his post-midnight calls to his biggest subscribers telling them to sell all of their stocks (even while his normal market letter advised smaller subscribers to buy) provoked the "Granville crash," a

24-point drop in the Dow on January 7. In his March 7, 1981, news-letter, he declared that the "March Massacre" had begun and that he couldn't possibly be wrong in his prediction that the Dow would fall at least 100 points and possibly 200 points by May 1. In fact, the Dow rose from 965 to 996. His recycled sell recommendation in September 1981 sent tremors through financial markets.

In late September 1981, he appeared on British television, advising investors to sell everything. He predicted that British interest rates would jump from 14 percent to above 17 percent and that the British industrial stock index would sink like a stone, from 480 to 150. British interest rates peaked the next month and headed downward to 12 percent in 1982 and 10 percent in 1983. The stock index bottomed at 474 in October 1981, too, and headed upward, to 580, a year later, then 700 the year after, and then to 900 in 1984. It reached 1000 in 1985 and 1300 in 1986.

Meanwhile, back in the United States, Granville remained bearish throughout 1982–1985, missing one of the greatest bull markets. In 1982 and 1983, he advised his subscribers to sell short; those who did lost 30 percent in 1982 and then another 25 percent in 1983 as the market rose sharply. For 1984 he cited "333 exact parallels with 1929" and predicted that a comparable crash would drive the Dow Jones Industrial Average below 700 by the spring of 1985. The Dow topped 1,300 that spring and Granville stubbornly continued predicting a Second Great Crash.

The *Hulbert Financial Digest*, which tracks the performance of investment newsletters, put Granville dead last over the twenty-five-year period 1980 to 2005, with an annual return of −20 percent while the S&P returned 14 percent a year.

THE DATA MINING TRAP

To many, the value of technical analysis is self-evident. Any reasonably alert person can see well-defined patterns in stock prices. However, investors need a crystal ball, and stock charts provide a rearview mirror. In any set of data, even randomly generated data, it is possible to find a pattern if one looks long enough.

Ransacking data for patterns is called *data mining* and demonstrates little more than the researcher's persistence. Remember this chapter's opening quotation: "If you torture the data long enough, it will confess."

I once sent ten different charts of stock prices (including Figure 4-1) to a technical analyst—let's call him Ed—and asked his help in deciding whether any of these stocks looked like promising investments.

Ed was so excited by the patterns he found in four charts that he overlooked the odd coincidence that all of the price charts started at a price of $50 a share. This was not a coincidence.

These were not real stocks. I created fictitious data from student coin flips. In each case, the "price" started at $50 and then each day's price change was determined by twenty-five coin flips, with the price going up 50 cents if the coin landed heads and going down 50 cents if the coin landed tails. For example, fourteen heads and eleven tails would be a $1.50 increase that day. After generating dozens of charts, I sent ten of them to Ed with the expectation that he would find seductive patterns. Sure enough, he did.

When this ruse was revealed, Ed was disappointed that these were not real stocks, with real opportunities for profitable buying and selling. However, the lesson he drew from this hoax was quite different from what I intended. Ed concluded that it is possible to use technical analysis to predict coin flips!

PATTERNS IN THE STOCK MARKET

Millions of investors have spent billions of hours trying to discover a formula for beating the stock market. It is not surprising that some have stumbled on rules that explain the past remarkably well but are unsuccessful in predicting the future. Many such systems would be laughable, except for the fact that people believe in them.

Analysts have monitored sunspots, the water level of the Great Lakes, and sales of aspirin and yellow paint. Some believe that the market does especially well in years ending in five—1975, 1985, and so on—while others argue that years ending in eight are best. Burton Crane, a longtime *New York Times* financial columnist, reported that a man "ran a fairly successful investment advisory service based in his 'readings' of the comic strips in *The New York Sun.*" *Money* magazine once reported that a Minneapolis stockbroker selected stocks by spreading the *Wall Street Journal* on the floor and buying the stock touched by the first nail on the right paw of his golden retriever. The fact that he thought this would attract investors says something about him—and his customers.

WHY I LOVE THE PACKERS

On Super Bowl Sunday in January 1983, both the business and sports sections of the *Los Angeles Times* carried articles on the Super Bowl stock market predictor. The theory is that the stock market goes up if the National Football Conference (NFC) or a former National Football League (NFL) team now in the American Football Conference (AFC) wins the Super Bowl; the market goes down otherwise. A Green Bay Packer win is good for the stock market; a New York Jets win is bad for stocks.

This theory had been correct for fifteen of the first sixteen Super Bowls, and one stockbroker said that "market observers will be glued to their TV screens . . . it will be hard to ignore an S&P indicator with an accuracy quotient that's greater than 94 percent." Washington (an NFC team) won, the stock market went up, and the Super Bowl Indicator was back in the news the next year, stronger than ever. The Super Bowl system worked an impressive twenty-eight out of thirty-one times through 1997, but then failed eight of the next fourteen years.

The stock market has nothing to do with the outcome of a football game. The accuracy of the Super Bowl Indicator is nothing more than an amusing coincidence fueled by the fact that the stock market usually goes up and the NFC usually wins the Super Bowl. The correlation is made more impressive by the gimmick of counting the Pittsburgh Steelers, an AFC team, as an NFC team. The excuse is that Pittsburgh once was in the NFL; the real reason is that Pittsburgh won the Super Bowl several times when the stock market went up. Counting Pittsburgh as an NFC team twists the data to support this cockamamie theory.

The *New York Times* reversed the direction of the prediction. Instead of using the Super Bowl to predict the stock market, why not use the stock market to predict the Super Bowl? Why not? It's no more ridiculous than the original Super Bowl Indicator. The *Times* reported that, if the Dow increases between the end of November and the time of the Super Bowl, the football team whose city comes second alphabetically usually wins. (Hint: Why do you suppose they chose the end of November for the starting date, as opposed to January 1, a month before the game, a year before the game, or another logical date?)

The performance of the Super Bowl Indicator has been mediocre since its discovery—which is unsurprising since there was nothing behind it but coincidence. What is genuinely surprising is that many people do not get the joke. The man who created the Super Bowl Indicator intended it to be a humorous way of demonstrating that correlation does not imply causation. He was flabbergasted when people started taking it seriously!

THE FOOLISH FOUR

In 1996, two brothers, Tom and David Gardner, wrote a wildly popular book with the beguiling name, *The Motley Fool Investment Guide: How the Fools Beat Wall Street's Wise Men and How You Can Too.* Hey, if fools can beat the market, so can we all.

The Gardners recommended the Foolish Four Strategy. They claimed that during the years 1973–1993, this strategy had an annual average return of 25 percent and concluded that it "should grant its fans the same 25 percent annualized returns going forward that it has served up in the past."

Here's their recipe for investment riches:

1. At the beginning of the year, calculate the dividend yield for each of the thirty stocks in the Dow Jones Industrial Average. For example, on December 31, 2013, Coca-Cola stock had a price of $41.31 per share and paid an annual dividend of $1.12 per share. Coke's dividend yield was $1.12/$41.31 = 0.0271, or 2.71 percent.

2. Of the thirty Dow stocks, identify the ten stocks with the highest dividend yields.

3. Of these ten stocks, choose the five stocks with the lowest price per share.

4. Of these five stocks, cross out the stock with the lowest price.

5. Invest 40 percent of your wealth in the stock with the next lowest price.

6. Invest 20 percent of your wealth in each of the other three stocks.

No, I'm not making this up.

Any guesses why this strategy is so complicated, verging on baffling? Data mining perhaps?

Steps 1 and 2 are plausible. There is a long-established investment strategy called the Dogs of the Dow that favors buying the Dow stocks with the highest dividend yields, and this sensible strategy has been reasonably successful.

But beyond this kernel of a borrowed idea, the Foolish Four

Strategy is pure data mining. Step 3 has no logical foundation since a stock's price depends on how many shares the company has outstanding. If a firm were to double the number of shares, each share would be worth half as much. There is no reason why a Dow stock with more shares outstanding (and a lower price per share) should be a better investment than a Dow stock with fewer shares outstanding (and a higher price per share). Berkshire Hathaway (which is not in the Dow) has *very* few shares outstanding and consequently sells for a mind-boggling price of nearly $200,000 per share. Yet it has been a great investment.

What about step 4? Why, after selecting the five stocks with the lowest prices (as if a low price is good), would we cross out the stock with the lowest price? Why indeed.

And steps 5 and 6? Why invest twice as much money in the next lowest priced stock as in the other three stocks? We all know the answer. Because it worked historically. Period.

Shortly after the Gardners launched the Foolish Four Strategy, two skeptical finance professors tested it using data from the years 1949–1972, just prior to the period that had been data-mined by the Gardners. It didn't work. The professors also retested the strategy during the years that were data-mined by the Gardners, but with a clever twist. Instead of choosing the portfolio on the first trading day in January, they implemented the strategy on the first trading day of July. If the strategy has any merit, it shouldn't be sensitive to the starting month. But, of course, it was.

In 1997, only one year after the introduction of the Foolish Four, the Gardners tweaked their system and renamed it the UV4. Their explanation confirms their data mining: "Why the switch? History shows that the UV4 has actually done better than the old Foolish Four." It is hardly surprising that a data-mined strategy doesn't do as well outside the years used to concoct the theory. The Gardners admitted as much when they stopped recommending both the Foolish Four and UV4 strategies in 2000.

The Foolish Four strategy was indeed foolish.

CONVERGENCE TRADES

In the 1980s, an investment advisory firm with the distinguished name Hume & Associates produced *The Superinvestor Files*, which were advertised nationally as sophisticated strategies that ordinary investors could use to reap extraordinary profits. Subscribers were mailed monthly pamphlets, each about fifty pages long and stylishly printed on thick paper, for $25 each plus $2.50 for shipping and handling.

In retrospect, it should have been obvious that if these strategies were as profitable as advertised, the company could have made more money by using the strategies than by selling pamphlets. However, gullible and greedy investors overlooked the obvious and, instead, hoped that the secret to becoming a millionaire could be purchased for $25, plus $2.50 for shipping and handling.

One Superinvestor strategy was based on the gold-silver ratio (GSR), which is the ratio of the price of an ounce of gold to the price of an ounce of silver. In 1985, the average price of gold was $317.26 and the average price of silver was $5.88, so the GSR was 317.26/5.88 = 54, which meant that an ounce of gold cost the same as 54 ounces of silver.

In 1986 Hume wrote:

> The [GSR] has fluctuated widely just in the past seven or eight years, dipping as low as 19-to-1 in 1980 and soaring as high as 52-to-1 in 1982 and 55-to-1 in 1985. But, as you can also clearly see, it has always—ALWAYS—returned to the range between 34-to-1 and 38-to-1.

Figure 4-2 confirms that the GSR fluctuated around the range of 34 to 38 during the years 1970 through 1985.

FIGURE 4-2. The GSR 1970-1985

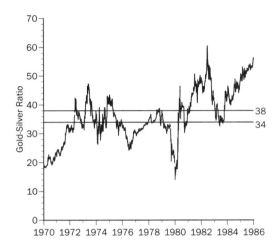

The GSR strategy is to sell gold and buy silver when the GSR is un-usually high and to do the opposite when the GSR is unusually low. Using futures contracts to make these trades creates the potential for astonishing profits.

There is no logical reason why an ounce of gold should cost the same as 36 ounces of silver. As it turned out, after the GSR went above 38 in 1983, it did not come back until twenty-eight years later, in 2011. Futures contracts multiply losses as well as gains, and a 1983 bet on the GSR would have been disastrous.

Figure 4-3 shows that the years when the GSR hovered around 34 to 36 were a temporary fluke, not the basis for a super strategy.

Modern computers can ransack large databases looking for more subtle and complex patterns, but the problem is the same. If there is no underlying reason for the discovered pattern, there is no reason for deviations from the pattern to self-correct.

The moral is simple: Don't bet the bank on historical patterns that have no logical basis.

FIGURE 4-3. The GSR 1970-2010

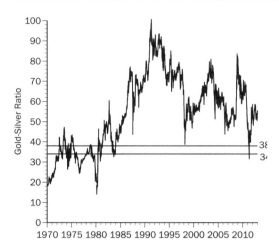

COMPUTERIZED TRADING SYSTEMS

Computerized trading systems remove all human judgment. The computers are programmed to track stock prices, other economic and noneconomic data, and news stories, looking for patterns that precede stock price movements. For example, the computers might notice that after the number of stocks going down in price during the preceding 140 seconds exceeds the number going up by more than 8 percentage points, the S&P 500 usually rises.

The computer files this indicator away and waits. When this signal appears again, the computer moves fast, buying thousands of shares in a few seconds and then selling these shares seconds later. Done over and over, day after day, a profit of a few pennies (or even a fraction of a penny) in a few seconds on thousands of shares can add up to real money. The technology magazine *Wired* gushed that these automated systems are "more efficient, faster, and smarter than any human."

True, these programs process data faster than any human, but they are no smarter than the humans who write the code that guides the computers. If a human tells a computer to look for potentially profitable patterns—no matter whether the discovered pattern makes sense—and to buy or sell when the pattern reappears, the computer will do so—whether it makes sense or not. Indeed, some of the human brains behind the computers boast that they don't understand why their computers decide to trade. After all, their computers are smarter than them, right? Instead of bragging, they should be praying.

On May 6, 2010, the U.S. stock market was hit by what has come to be known as a "flash crash." Investors that day were nervous about the Greek debt crisis, and an anxious mutual fund manager tried to hedge his portfolio by selling $4.1 billion in S&P 500 futures contracts. The idea was that if the market dropped, the losses on this fund's stock portfolio would be offset by profits on its futures contracts. This seemingly prudent transaction somehow triggered the computers. The computers bought many of the futures contracts the fund was selling, then sold them seconds later. Futures prices started falling and the computers were provoked into a trading frenzy as they bought and sold futures contracts among themselves, like a hot potato being tossed from hand to hand.

Nobody knows exactly what unleashed the computers. Remember, even the people behind the computers don't understand why their computers trade. In one fifteen-second interval, the computers traded 27,000 contracts among themselves, half the total trading volume, and ended up with a net purchase of only 200 contracts at the end of this fifteen-second madness. The trading frenzy spread to the regular stock market, and the flood of sell orders overwhelmed potential buyers. The Dow Jones Industrial Average fell nearly 600 points (more than 5 percent) in five minutes. Market prices went haywire, yet the computers kept trading. Procter & Gamble (P&G), a rock-solid blue-chip company, dropped 37 percent in less than four minutes. Some computers paid more than $100,000 a share for Apple, Hewlett-Packard, and Sotheby's. Others sold Accenture and other major stocks for less than a penny a share. The computers had no common sense. They blindly bought and sold because that's what their algorithms told them to do.

The madness ended when a built-in safeguard in the futures market suspended all trading for five seconds. Incredibly, this five-second time-out was enough to persuade the computers to stop their frenzied trading. Fifteen minutes later, markets were back to normal and the temporary 600-point drop in the Dow was just a nightmarish memory.

There have been other flash crashes since and there will most likely be more in the future. Oddly enough, Procter & Gamble was hit again on August 30, 2013, on the New York Stock Exchange (NYSE) with a mini flash crash, so called because nothing special happened to other stocks on the NYSE and nothing special happened to P&G stock on other exchanges.

Inexplicably, nearly 200 trades on the NYSE, involving a total of about 250,000 shares of P&G stock, occurred within a one-second interval, triggering a 5 percent drop in price, from $77.50 to $73.61, and then a recovery less than a minute later. One lucky person happened to be in the right place at the right time and bought 65,000 shares for a quick $155,000 profit. Why did it happen? No one knows. Remember, humans aren't as smart as computers.

Fortunately, value investors are inoculated from the perils of technical analysis, since value investors do not try to predict stock prices. Value investors buy a stock because it is an inexpensive money machine, generating bountiful cash, it is hoped, over many, many years.

5

BAUBLES AND BUBBLES

When beggars and shoeshine boys, barbers and beauticians can tell you how to get rich, it is time to remind yourself that there is no more dangerous illusion than the belief that one can get something for nothing.
—BERNARD BARUCH

Early in my teaching career, a student named Jon told me about an exciting investment he was making. All through high school he had been collecting postage-stamp plate blocks. At the time, stamps were printed fifty stamps to a sheet and a plate block was the four stamps in a two-by-two block next to the sheet's serial number.

Plate blocks were rare because no one had ever thought to save them. Then, unexpectedly, plate blocks became a collectible. Prices rose rapidly and Jon joined others in the gold rush. Every time a new stamp came out, Jon went to his local post office and bought several plate blocks. Sometimes, he bought complete fifty-stamp sheets in case these, too, became collectible. He kept his stamps in mint condition by storing them in protective plastic sleeves in binders. He proudly told me that he had several thousand dollars "invested."

I told Jon that this was speculation, not investing, because his stamps didn't generate any income. Jon insisted that it was an investment because prices had been going up. Indeed, the plate-block market was doing better than the stock market. Seeing that I was getting nowhere, I said, "Twenty years from now, let me know how it works out."

Roughly twenty years later I got a large envelope in the mail from Jon. He told me about his career as a portfolio manager and thanked me for the class he had taken from me. The postage on the envelope consisted of dozens of stamps, shown in Figure 5-1. The plate-block market had collapsed and this was Jon's way of saying that I was right.

When Jon tried to liquidate his stamp collection, dealers offered him $9 for every $10 of face value. Nobody wanted to buy the stamps for anything other than mailing letters and dealers didn't want to tie their money up in inventory that wasn't moving. Jon was stubborn, so he kept his stamps and was liquidating his collection letter by letter.

FIGURE 5-1. The risks of speculation

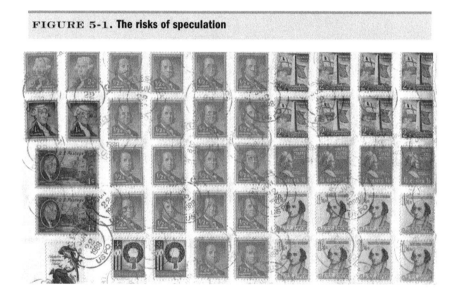

Baseball cards are another collectible. For many years, baseball cards were advertising giveaways or sold with cigars, cigarettes, and bubble gum. Children traded cards, played games with them, and stuck them in their bicycle spokes to make motorcycle sounds. Then grown-ups decided that baseball cards were a collectible, too valuable to be touched, let alone played with. They were convinced that they could get rich buying baseball cards for pennies and selling them a few years later for dollars.

Eventually, the market for new cards crashed. However, old cards are still considered valuable—simply because they are rare. In 2007 a collector paid $2.8 million for a 1909 Honus Wagner card that had originally been included in a cigarette pack. Wagner reportedly did not smoke and asked the company not to distribute the cards because he did not want children to buy cigarettes. Only about 200 cards were printed and, of these, only fifty or so were distributed. At the time of the 2007 auction, it was thought that only three cards had survived, but more have since surfaced.

Does this card's rarity make it worth millions of dollars? No. Baseball cards have no intrinsic value because they generate no cash whatsoever. Yet some people believe that rare cards have value because they are rare. It's sort of like people being famous for being famous. There is no rational explanation. Rarity does not make something valuable.

A former student sent me a collection of cards that are rarer than baseball cards that are thought to be worth thousands of dollars. These are economics trading cards distributed by the economics club at the University of Michigan, Flint. Each card has a picture of a famous economist on the front and some lifetime statistics on the back. The James Tobin card (see Figure 5-2) says he was born in Champaign, Illinois, in 1918, and received his bachelor's degree and PhD from Harvard in 1939 and 1947 (interrupted by military duty during World War II).

FIGURE 5-2. James Tobin trading card

There is a summary of his research and a memorable quotation:

> I studied economics and made it my career for two reasons. The subject was and is intellectually fascinating and challenging, particularly to someone with taste and talent for theoretical reasoning and quantitative analysis. At the same time it offered the hope, as it still does, that improved understanding could better the lot of mankind.

If you are interested, make me an offer. Remember, this card is VERY rare.

Some people believe in the Latin saying, *Res tantum valet quantum vendi potest*: A thing is worth only what someone else will pay for it. That's like many of the quotations attributed to former baseball player and manager Yogi Berra; for example, "It's not over until it's over." It is literally true, but so circular as to be meaningless. Yes, something is worth what someone is willing to pay for it, if by "worth" you mean the price people pay is the price they are willing to pay. Investors think differently. As John Burr Williams said, "A stock is worth only what you can get out of it."

What do you get out of looking at a postage stamp or a baseball card or any other so-called collectible? A collector who paid $250,000 for an early *Batman* comic explained that he keeps the comic in an airtight bag in a bank vault: "I've been toying with the idea of reading it, but I haven't yet."

BEANIE BABIES

Beanie Babies are stuffed animals with a heart-shaped hang tag. The beanie name refers to the fact that these toys are filled with plastic pellets ("beans"). Around 1995, the same time the dot-com bubble was inflating, Beanie Babies came to be viewed as collectibles because buyers expected to profit from escalating Beanie Baby prices by selling these silly bears to an endless supply of greater fools.

Delusional grown-ups stockpiled Beanie Babies, thinking that they would pay for their retirement or their kids' college education. Ah, good plan.

What is the intrinsic value of a Beanie Baby? It doesn't pay dividends. It doesn't pay anything! You can't even play with a Beanie Baby. To preserve its value as a collectible, a Beanie Baby must be stored in an airtight containers in a cool, dark, smoke-free environment. Yet the hopeful and the greedy paid hundreds of dollars for Beanie Babies that originally sold in toy stores for a few dollars. They saw how much prices had increased in the past and assumed the same would be true in the future. They had no reason for believing this, but they wanted to believe.

Figure 5-3 shows the Princess Beanie Baby honoring Diana, the Princess of Wales. The Princess sold for $500 in 2000. Then the bubble popped. I bought this bear on the internet in 2008. The shipping cost more than the bear.

FIGURE 5-3. Is this Beanie Baby worth $500?

PONZI SCHEMES

If you mail a letter to a person in another country, you can enclose an international reply coupon that can be exchanged for postage stamps in that country and used to mail a letter back to you. It is like enclosing a self-addressed stamped envelope, but gets around the problem of the sender having to buy foreign postage stamps. It is the polite thing to do, but also the source of the most famous swindle in history.

In 1920, a Massachusetts man named Charles Ponzi promised to pay investors 50 percent interest every forty-five days. Compounded eight times a year, the effective annual rate of return would be 2,463 percent! He said that his profits would come from taking advantage of the difference between the official and open market price of Spanish pesos. He would buy Spanish pesos cheap in the open market, use these pesos to buy international reply coupons, and then trade these coupons for U.S. postage stamps at the higher official exchange rate. If everything worked as planned, he could buy 10 cents' worth of U.S. postage stamps for a penny. (It was not clear how he would convert these stamps into cash.) In practice, he received $15 million from investors and appears to have bought only $61 in stamps.

If he didn't invest any money, how could he afford to pay a 50 percent return every forty-five days? He couldn't. But he could create a temporary illusion of doing so. Suppose that a person invests $100, which Ponzi spends on himself. If Ponzi now finds two people to invest $100 apiece, he can give the first person $150, and keep $50 for himself. Now, he has forty-five days to find four people willing to invest $100 so that he can pay each of the two previous investors $150 and spend $100 on himself. These four can be paid with the money from eight new investors, and these eight from sixteen more.

THE FALLACY

Ponzi's legacy is the *Ponzi scheme*. In a Ponzi scheme, money from new investors is paid to earlier ones, and it works as long as there are enough new investors. The problem is that the pool of fish is exhausted surprisingly soon. The twenty-first round requires a million new people and the thirtieth round requires a billion more. At some point, the scheme runs out of new people and those in the last round (the majority of the investors) are left with nothing. A Ponzi scheme merely transfers wealth from late entrants to early entrants (and to the person running the scam).

Ponzi's scam collapsed after eight months when a Boston newspaper discovered that during the time that he supposedly bought $15 million in postage coupons, the total amount sold worldwide came to only $1 million. Ponzi promised that he could pay off his investors by starting a company and selling stock to other investors. Massachusetts officials were unpersuaded. They sent Ponzi to jail for ten years.

A Ponzi scheme is also called a pyramid deal, since its workings can be visualized by imagining a pyramid with the initial investors at the top and the most recent round on the bottom; the pyramid collapses when the next round doesn't materialize. Even though it seems obvious that no one will make money unless others lose money, greed blinds participants to the likelihood that they will be among the losers.

INVESTMENTS THAT WERE
TOO GOOD TO BE TRUE

Ponzi schemes are illegal frauds, but they usually disguise their true nature by promising to channel investors' money to a unique investment or to a fabulous money manager. Our best protection is sober reflection and common sense. If it looks too good to be true, it probably isn't true. But greed is a powerful emotion and often tramples common sense. One of the most notorious cases involved Bernie Madoff.

For more than a decade, Madoff told investors—many of them Jewish charitable organizations—that he was earning double-digit returns year after year using a "split-strike conversion" strategy that involves buying stock and put options and writing call options. This is actually a conservative strategy that is unlikely to generate double-digit returns. Perhaps even more suspiciously, Madoff reported negative returns in only seven months over a fourteen-year period. Skeptics looked at the ups and downs in the S&P and concluded that Madoff's performance claims were mathematically impossible. To true believers, this added to his mystique. One of his clients raved, "Even knowledgeable people can't really tell you what he's doing."

What he was doing was running a Ponzi scheme, the largest ever. In December 2008, Madoff was having severe liquidity problems and confessed to his sons that it was "one big lie," a Ponzi scheme that was collapsing. His sons reported his confession to the government. Madoff was arrested and, four months later, pleaded guilty to eleven felonies. He admitted that he had not made any real investments for nearly two decades and that there was a $65 billion shortfall between what his clients thought they had in their accounts and what they actually had. Once the lawyers had been paid, investors got back $10 billion less than their original investment.

Madoff was sentenced to 150 years in prison and sent to a federal facility in North Carolina. He told a relative, "It's much safer here than walking the streets of New York."

SPECULATIVE BUBBLES AND PANICS

From time to time, investors are gripped by what, in retrospect, seems to have been mass hysteria. The price of something climbs higher and higher, beyond all reason, but it's a speculative bubble because nothing justifies the rising price except the hope that it will go higher still. Then, suddenly, the bubble pops, buyers vanish, and the price collapses. With hindsight, it is hard to see how people could have been so foolish and paid such crazy prices. Yet, at the time of the bubble, it seems foolish to sit on the sidelines while others become rich.

Some people, including Nobel laureate Eugene Fama, do not think that bubbles can even occur. They argue that since markets always set the correct prices, whatever prices those markets set must be correct.

It is hard to take this circular argument seriously if we define a bubble as a situation in which the price cannot be justified by an asset's intrinsic value, but is instead propelled by a belief that the price will keep rising. When a Beanie Baby sold for $500, was that not a bubble? What rational explanation are we overlooking?

In 2013 Fama accepted that a bubble is "an extended period during which asset prices depart quite significantly from economic fundamentals." Yet, he danced around this definition when he argued the following:

> The word "bubble" drives me nuts, frankly, because I don't think there's anything in the statistical evidence that says anybody can reliably predict when prices go down. So if you interpret the word "bubble" to mean I can predict when prices are going to go down, you can't do it. . . .
>
> I believe markets work. And if markets work those things shouldn't be predictable. If I can predict that housing prices will go down, if the market's working properly, they should go down now. . . . If the market's working properly, the information should be in the prices.

The argument that prices sometimes go far above intrinsic value does not require that we know *when* prices will crash. Indeed, the essence of a bubble is that people do not know when it will pop.

Fama is correct in arguing that if people know that prices will go down tomorrow, prices will go down today. But he is wrong in arguing that bubbles must be predictable. And he is wrong in arguing that the fact that price changes are hard to predict proves that prices are always equal to intrinsic values. Price changes might be hard to predict because they are swayed by irrational, unpredictable emotions.

THE SOUTH SEA BUBBLE

In 1720, the British government gave the South Sea Company exclusive trading privileges with Spain's American colonies. None of the company's directors had ever been to America, nor had they any concrete plans to trade anything. Nonetheless, encouraged by the company's inventive bookkeeping, English citizens rushed to invest in this exotic venture. As the price of the South Sea Company's stock soared from £120 on January 28 to £400 on May 19, then £800 on June 4, and £1,000 on June 22, some people became rich and thousands rushed to join their ranks. It was said that you could buy South Sea stock as you entered Garraway's coffeehouse and sell it for a profit on the way out.

Soon con men were offering stock in even more grandiose schemes and were deluged by frantic investors not wanting to be left out. It scarcely mattered what the scheme was. One promised to build a wheel for perpetual motion. Another was formed "for carrying on an undertaking of great advantage, but nobody is to know what it is." The shares for this mysterious offering were priced at £100 each, with a promised annual return of £100; after selling all of the stock in less than five hours, the promoter left England and never returned. Yet another stock offer was for the "nitvender" or selling of nothing. Yet, nitwits bought nitvenders. When the South Sea Bubble burst, fortunes and dreams disappeared.

As with all speculative bubbles, there were many believers in the

Greater Fool Theory. While some suspected that prices were unreasonable, the market was dominated by people believing that prices would continue to rise, at least until they could sell to the next fool in line. In the spring of 1720, Sir Isaac Newton said, "I can calculate the motions of the heavenly bodies, but not the madness of people," and sold his South Sea shares for a £7,000 profit. But later that year, he bought shares again, just before the bubble burst, and lost £20,000. When a banker invested £500 in the third offering of South Sea stock, he explained that "when the rest of the world are mad, we must imitate them in some measure." After James Milner, a member of the British Parliament, was bankrupted by the South Sea Bubble, he explained that "I said, indeed, that ruin must soon come upon us but . . . it came two months sooner than I expected."

Yes, no one knows for certain when a bubble will pop, but that does not mean that a bubble is not a bubble. The price of nitvender stock was no more related to economic fundamentals than was the price of the Princess Beanie Baby.

THE DOT-COM BUBBLE

It is hard to imagine life without the internet—without email, Google, and Wikipedia at our fingertips. When the electricity goes out or we go on vacation, internet withdrawal pains can be overwhelming. Cell phones only heighten our addiction. Do we really need to be online and on call 24/7? Must we respond immediately to every email, text, and tweet? Do we really need to know what our friends are eating for lunch? Apparently we do.

Back in the 1990s, when computers and cell phones were just starting to take over our lives, the spread of the internet sparked the creation of hundreds of online companies, popularly known as dot-coms. Some dot-coms had good ideas and matured into strong, successful companies. But many did not. In too many cases, the idea was simply to start a company with a dot-com in its name, sell it to someone else, and walk away with pockets full of cash. It was so Old Economy to have a great idea, start a company, make it a successful business, and turn it over to your children and grandchildren.

One study found that companies that did nothing more than add .com, .net, or the word "internet" to their names more than doubled the price of their stock. Money for nothing!

A dot-com company proved it was a player not by making a profit but by spending money—preferably other people's money. (I'm not joking!) One rationale was to be the first-mover by getting big fast. (A popular saying was "Get large or get lost.") The idea was that once people believe that your website is the place to go to buy something, sell something, or learn something, you have a monopoly that can crush the competition and reap profits.

It is not a completely idiotic idea. It sometimes even works. (Think Amazon.) Often it doesn't. Can you name the first-movers in the personal computer revolution? (Apple survived, but Commodore, Kaypro, and Tandy are answers to trivia questions.)

The fundamental problem is that there were thousands of dot-com companies and there isn't room for thousands of monopolies. Of the thousands of companies trying to get big fast, very few can ever be monopolies.

Most dot-com companies had no profits. If investors had thought about stocks as money machines and noticed how little cash was being generated, they would have been skeptical rather than delirious. Instead, wishful investors thought up new metrics for the so-called New Economy to justify ever higher stock prices. They argued that instead of being obsessed with something as old-fashioned as profits, we should look at a company's sales, spending, and number of website visitors. Companies responded by finding creative ways to give investors what they wanted. Investors want more sales? I'll sell something to your company and you sell it back to me. No profits for either of us, but higher sales for both of us. Investors want more spending? Order another thousand Aeron chairs. Investors want more website visitors? Give stuff away to people who visit your website. Buy Super Bowl ads that advertise your website. Two dozen dot-com companies ran ads during the January 2000 Super Bowl game, at a cost of $2.2 million for thirty seconds of ad time, plus the cost of producing the ad. Companies didn't need profits. They needed traffic.

One measure of traffic was eyeballs, the number of people who visited a page; another was the number of people who stayed for at least three minutes. Even more fanciful was hits, the number of files requested when a web page is downloaded from a server. Companies put dozens of images on a page, and each image loaded from the server counted as a hit. Incredibly, investors thought this meant something important. They should have been thinking about money machines.

Stock prices tripled between 1995 and 2000, an annual rate of increase of 25 percent. Dot-com stocks rose even more. The tech-heavy NASDAQ index more than quintupled during this five-year period, an annual rate of increase of 40 percent. Someone who bought $10,000 of AOL stock in January 1995 or Yahoo when it went public in April 1996 would have had nearly $1 million in January 2000.

In 1999, a small internet company called NetJ.com filed an SEC statement that was brutally candid: "The company is not currently engaged in any substantial business activity and has no plans to engage in any such activity in the foreseeable future." A modern nitv-ender! And yet the price rose from $0.50 a share to $3.50 a share in six months. A company that doesn't do anything or plan to do anything was valued at $22.9 million—not much for a real company, but a lot for a do-nothing company.

In March 2000, the *Wall Street Journal* ran a front-page story that reminded me of Bernard Baruch's comment about barbers and beauticians. At Bill's Barbershop in Dennis, Massachusetts, a shop I've been to, the locals talked about dot-com stocks while they watched stock prices dance on television. One regular said, "You get three or four times in your life to make serious bucks. If you miss this one,

you're crazy." Another agreed: "I don't think anything could shake
my confidence in the market. Even if we do go down 30 percent,
we'll just come right back."

Dot-com entrepreneurs and stock market investors were getting
rich and they wanted to think that it would never end. But, of course,
it did.

THE 36K NONSENSE

Chapter 1 recounted my warnings, delivered at a March 11, 2000,
conference, on the Glassman-Hassett prediction that the Dow
Jones Industrial Average would more than triple, from below 12,000
to 36,000.

How did I know that the 36K prediction was nonsense? I looked
at their reasoning. The total return from a stock is the dividend
yield (the dividend D divided by the price P) plus the capital gains g
(the percentage change in the price).

$$R = \frac{D}{P} + g$$

Suppose that a representative stock at the time was selling for $12 a
share and paid an annual dividend of $0.18. The dividend yield would
be 1.5 percent:

$$\frac{D}{P} = \frac{\$0.18}{\$12.00} = 0.015$$

Glassman-Hassett assumed that, in the long run, dividends and
stock prices will grow by 5 percent a year, which is perfectly reasonable and implies a total stock return of 1.5 + 5.0 = 6.5 percent. They
noted that, at the time, the interest rate on long-term Treasury
bonds was 5.5 percent.

Now the trouble starts. Glassman-Hassett argued that investors
should be happy to hold stocks if the anticipated returns were only

5.5 percent, the same as Treasury bonds, because stocks are safer than Treasury bonds—as evidenced by the fact that stocks, on average, have done better than Treasury bonds in the past. Not only that, because stocks are safer, they reasoned that investors should hold stocks happily if the anticipated returns were less than 5.5 percent.

Nonetheless, they made the "conservative" assumption that stocks should be priced to give a 5.5 percent return, consisting of a 0.5 percent dividend yield plus 5.0 percent growth. For the dividend yield to fall from 1.5 percent to 0.5 percent, the stock price has to be three times as high ($36 rather than $12):

$$\frac{D}{P} = \frac{\$0.18}{\$36.00} = 0.005$$

Thus, they concluded that stock prices should triple, from $12 to $36 (or, in the case of the Dow, from 12,000 to 36,000).

The crucial assumption is clearly that investors would be satisfied with the same anticipated returns on stocks and bonds because stocks are as safe, or safer, than bonds. However, the fact that stocks have beaten bonds in the past does not guarantee that stocks will beat bonds in the future. The extraordinary twentieth-century performance of the U.S. stock market was, most likely, a surprise—and we can't count on another hundred years of pleasant surprises.

Their model is also internally inconsistent. Glassman and Hassett argued that because stocks always outperform bonds, stocks should be priced to do the same as bonds—in which case, stocks won't outperform bonds.

The second inconsistency involves what happens in their model if the Treasury rate goes up to, say, 6 percent, which it did a few months after their book *Dow 36,000* appeared. For the anticipated stock return to increase from 5.5 percent to 6 percent, the dividend yield would have to double from 0.5 percent to 1.0 percent. For this to happen, the stock price would have to fall 50 percent, from $36 to $18:

$$\frac{D}{P} = \frac{\$0.18}{\$18.00} = 0.01$$

How can any sane person argue that stocks are as safe as bonds if a half-percentage-point increase in interest rates causes stock prices to fall 50 percent? Nor can we rely on a hypothetical "long run" to save the day for stocks. Their model implies that if interest rates increase permanently, stocks will be a permanently disastrous investment.

A value investor would have recognized the dot-com bubble for what it was—a bubble. The 12,000 value of the Dow gave a 1.5 percent dividend yield and a predicted 6.5 percent stock return, a slim one percent risk premium over bonds. I argued at the time that a reasonable risk premium should be higher and stock prices should be lower—much lower—though I didn't know when the dot-com bubble would burst.

I reached the same conclusion using a different model (which is explained in Chapter 6).

After the dot-com bubble popped, the *Wall Street Journal* made another visit to Bill's Barbershop. Bill was now sixty-three years old and his retirement portfolio had been decimated. His $834,000 was down to $103,000, which was $50,000 less than his initial investment: "It means that I'm looking at another ten years of work, instead of being retired," he said. Bill had given up playing the stock market. Now, he was playing blackjack and poker at a Connecticut casino and said, "I do better there than I do in the market." Which isn't saying much.

INTRINSIC VALUE

Investors should buy stocks as if they were groceries instead of perfume.
—BENJAMIN GRAHAM

When we buy groceries, clothing, or a television, we ask not only whether the food is tasty, the clothing attractive, and the television well built, but how much it costs. Is it worth the price? When we buy stock, we should ask the same question—not whether it is issued by a good company, but whether the price is right. Is it worth the cost? The relevant question is not whether Amazon is a better company than Target, but whether Amazon stock, at $800 a share, is a better buy than Target stock at $80 a share.

What is a share of stock worth? We do not buy stock to eat, wear, or watch at night. We buy stock for the cash it generates: the dividends. This insight is the basis of value investing.

Value investors buy stock with the expectation that, even if they never sell the stock, they will be satisfied with the dividends they expect to receive. Value investors don't invest in postage stamps, baseball cards, or Beanie Babies because they don't generate income. John Burr Williams, a Harvard economist temporarily turned poet, wrote:

A cow for her milk
A hen for her eggs
And a stock, by heck
For her dividends.

> An orchard for fruit
> Bees, for their honey
> And stock, besides,
> For their dividends.

It would be a mistake "to buy a cow for her cud or bees for their buzz."

If a city slicker comes to your farm and offers a low price for your cow, you ignore him. You bought the cow for the milk, not to sell to city slickers. If the city slicker returns the next day and offers a ridiculously high price, more than the milk is worth, you take advantage of his ignorance.

In the same way, Benjamin Graham created an imaginary Mr. Market, a person who comes by every day offering to buy the stock you own or to sell you more shares. Sometimes, Mr. Market's price is reasonable. Other times, it is silly. There is no reason for your assessment of your stock to be swayed by Mr. Market's prices, though you may sometimes take advantage of his foolishness.

MR. MARKET IS FICKLE, AND THAT'S A GOOD THING

Figure 6-1 shows the daily Dow Jones Industrial Average from August 26, 2015, to August 25, 2016. I am writing this on August 26, 2016, so the figure reflects the most recent fifty-two-week period I have available. I scaled the Dow to equal 100 on August 26, 2015, so that percentage changes can be gauged by comparing the daily prices to 100.

The Dow was up about 15 percent over this fifty-two-week period, but its volatility is even more interesting. The Dow went up 12 percent in the five weeks between September 28, 2015, and November 3, 2015, then fell 14 percent during the next three months, followed by a 16 percent increase in the two months after that.

FIGURE 6-1. Dow Jones Industrial Average, August 26, 2015, to August 25, 2016

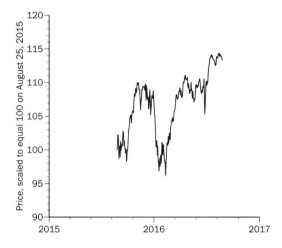

The Dow is an average of the prices of thirty prominent blue-chip stocks. In the words of Dow Jones & Company, these are "substantial companies—renowned for the quality and wide acceptance of their products or services—with strong histories of successful growth." The intrinsic value of these bluest of blue-chip companies surely did not go up or down by double-digit amounts every few months. Yet their stock prices did.

And this is the *average* of the prices of thirty blue-chip stocks. Swings in individual stock prices can be even wilder. Pick any of the Dow stocks at random and look at its high and low prices over the preceding fifty-two weeks. Seriously, take a break from reading this book and find a list of the thirty Dow stocks. Pick one at random. Then go to a finance website and look at the fifty-two-week high and low prices for this stock. Now ask yourself if it is reasonable that the real value of this company would vary so much in one year's time.

I did the same exercise. I used a random number generator to pick a number between 1 and 30. The number selected was 21, so I looked at Nike, the twenty-first stock in the Dow list when the company names are arranged alphabetically. The high price was $67.16, on November 27, 2015; the low price was $51.89 on June 27, 2016. According to Mr. Market, Nike had lost a quarter of its value in seven months.

But wait, there's more. Figure 6-2 shows Nike's price between August 26, 2015, to August 25, 2016, scaled to equal 100 on August 26, 2015. There are several 20-percentage-point swings in the price of Nike stock, although the intrinsic value of the company surely did not go up, down, up, down by 20 percent in a manner of months—not to mention the 5 to 10 percent zigs and zags from one week to the next. On February 1, Mr. Market said that Nike was worth $99 billion. A week later, Mr. Market announced that Nike was now worth $85 billion. Two weeks later, Mr. Market changed his mind, now proclaiming that Nike was again worth $99 billion. Mr. Market is nuts.

FIGURE 6-2. Nike, August 26, 2015, to August 25, 2016

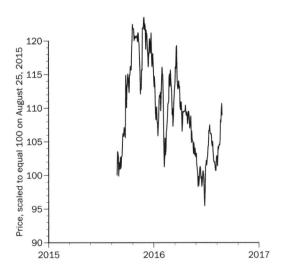

There are two takeaways. First, Mr. Market is very volatile, border-ing on unstable. His opinion of what a company is worth can vary much more than the company's real value. Second, Mr. Market's fickleness may create rewarding opportunities for value investors looking to buy good stocks at bargain prices. Instead of bemoaning Mr. Market's fickleness, we should embrace it.

THE PRESENT VALUE OF DIVIDENDS

John Burr Williams and Benjamin Graham were both teaching us to form our own opinions of what a stock is worth, based on the income it generates, not on the daily fluctuations in stock prices. Similarly, Warren Buffett suggested that we think of stocks as disguised bonds so that we will value stocks by looking at their dividends the same way we value bonds by looking at their coupons.

Let's assume, as do John Burr Williams, Benjamin Graham, and Warren Buffett, that we plan to hold the stock forever. Even though this is not literally true, it forces us to think about the cash generated by the company instead of guessing whether Mr. Market's price tomorrow will be higher or lower than his price today.

Consider a stock that will pay a $10 dividend one year from today. (Companies usually pay dividends quarterly; for simplicity, we assume annual dividends.) How much would you pay for this $10? Somewhat less than $10, because if you had the $10 today, you could invest it for a year and have more than $10. This is the *time value of money*: A dollar today is worth more than a dollar tomorrow.

Looking at other ways you might invest your money, you may decide that you do not want to buy this $10 dividend unless it gives you a 5 percent return. If so, the highest price you are willing to pay is $9.52 because that would give you your 5 percent required return. Paying $9.52 for a $10 dividend is a 48-cent profit, which is a 5 percent return on your $9.52 investment:

$$\frac{\$10.00 - \$9.52}{\$9.52} = \frac{\$0.48}{\$9.52} = 0.05 \text{ (5 percent)}$$

The $10 dividend one year from now is worth $9.52 to you today.

If your required return were 10 percent, you would be willing to pay $9.09 today for a $10 dividend a year from now because your profit would be 91 cents, a 10 percent return on your $9.09 investment:

$$\frac{\$10.00 - \$9.09}{\$9.09} = \frac{\$0.91}{\$9.09} = 0.10 \text{ (10 percent)}$$

The higher your required return, the less the dividend is worth. This makes sense. The only way you can get a higher return from a $10 dividend is if you can buy it for a lower price.

The math is more complicated for dividends further into the future, but the principle is the same. The *present value* of future cash is how much you are willing to pay today for cash that you have to wait to receive in the future.*

A former student who is now a fund manager told me that if you understand present value, you'll understand 90 percent of investing. That's an exaggeration, but like all good exaggerations, there is truth to it. An understanding of present value is indispensable for informed investment decisions.

The right way to think about a prospective investment is to consider the cash it will generate and then discount this cash by a required return that takes into account the time value of money. This simple idea is the cornerstone of value investing.

Because you are acting as if you are going to hold a stock forever and receive dividends forever, the stock's intrinsic value is the present value of these dividends. The intrinsic value does not depend on predictions about what the stock's price will be tomorrow or a year from now.

The only market price that matters is today's price. A stock is worth buying if Mr. Market's price today is lower than the stock's intrinsic value, and the bigger the gap, the bigger the appeal.

---

*Here's the math. The present value of $1 received n years from now is $\$1/(1 + R)^n$, where R is the required return.

To implement the intrinsic-value model, we need to specify the future dividends and a required return, what Williams called an investor's "personal rate of interest." The required return for stocks surely depends on the returns available on other investments, such as Treasury bonds. Suppose that the interest rate on Treasury bonds is 5 percent. Stocks are riskier than Treasury bonds because stock dividends are less certain than Treasury coupons. Risk-averse investors will consequently have a higher required return. How much higher? Some investors, looking back over the last 100 years, see that the average return on U.S. stocks has been some 5 to 7 percent higher than the average return on Treasury bonds and conclude that the risk premium going forward must be around 5 to 7 percent. However, we shouldn't use after-the-fact returns to estimate before-the-event preferences, because U.S. stock returns over the past several decades probably turned out to be much higher than investors anticipated at the time.

A study of the twentieth-century performance of stock markets in thirty-nine different countries found that the U.S. stock market beat all the rest. It seems unlikely that investors worldwide knew that the twentieth century would turn out to be America's century and the U.S. stock market would turn out to be the winner. If they had known that, they would have bought U.S. stocks instead of other stocks. It is more likely that the remarkable performance of the U.S. stock market was a pleasant surprise to investors who owned U.S. stocks.

The question going forward is how much of a risk premium you require. If long-term Treasury bonds pay 5 percent, would you be satisfied with a 12 percent anticipated return from stocks? Most likely. What about 10 percent? Or 8 percent? It's your call and it has nothing to do with how well the U.S. stock market has done over the past hundred years.

THE CONSTANT-GROWTH MODEL

Investors often predict future dividends by assuming that dividends grow at a steady rate each year. In this case, a stock's intrinsic value (the present value of all its future dividends) is given by an equation derived by John Burr Williams, which I call the JBW equation:

$$V = \frac{D}{R - g}$$

The intrinsic value V is equal to the current dividend D, divided by the shareholders' required return R minus the dividend growth rate g. Suppose the dividend is $5 and the required return is 10 percent. If dividends grow at 5 percent, the intrinsic value is $100:

$$V = \frac{\$5}{0.10 - 0.05}$$
$$= \$100$$

Dividends never grow at a perfectly constant rate, but the JBW equation is a reasonable approximation with logical implications.

First, it makes sense. Suppose you buy the stock for $100. The initial $5 dividend is a 5 percent return on your $100 investment. If dividends grow by 5 percent, the dividend will be $5.25 next year and the stock's value will be $105:

$$V = \frac{\$5.25}{0.10 - 0.05}$$
$$= \$105$$

You get a 5 percent dividend and a 5 percent increase in the stock's value, which gives you a 10 percent total return. Year after year, the dividend and value grow by 5 percent, keeping the dividend yield at 5 percent and increasing the value of your investment by 5 percent. Year after year, you get a 10 percent return.

Think about this for a moment, because it is very important and yet not always fully appreciated. If you buy a stock with, say, a 3 per-cent dividend yield, and the dividends grow by 5 percent a year, a reasonable estimate of your long-run return is 8 percent. The JBW equation makes no assumptions about future stock prices; it assumes that you never sell. However, the model is internally consistent in that if you do sell and market prices grow at the same rate as dividends, your total return, dividends plus capital gains, will equal your required return.

THE VALUE OF GROWTH

The JBW equation also demonstrates how important the growth rate is to the value of a stock. At a 10 percent required return, a stock paying a $5 dividend has an intrinsic value of $50 if there is no growth and an intrinsic value of $100 with 5 percent growth. The intrinsic values for other growth rates are shown in Table 6-1.

Growth makes a big difference because of the power of compounding. The difference between zero and 5 percent growth may not sound like much; but fifty years down the road, the first company will still be paying a $5 dividend while the second pays a $57 dividend.

TABLE 6-1. Value of $5 dividend with a 10 percent required return

Growth Rate, %	Value, $
0	50
1	56
2	63
3	71
4	83
5	100
6	125
7	167
8	250

This logic explains the lure of growth stocks, companies with high anticipated growth rates. The logic works in reverse, too. Sometimes, a company with bright prospects announces an earnings increase and its stock price free-falls downward. Why? Because the announced increase in earnings was not as large as had been anticipated, and small differences in growth rates can make a big difference to the value of a company's stock. In Table 6-1, a scaling down of growth prospects from 8 percent to 6 percent cuts the intrinsic value in half.

A particularly dramatic example happened to Oracle, a software powerhouse, on December 9, 1997. Analysts had been expecting Oracle's second-quarter sales to be 35 percent higher than a year earlier and its profits to be 25 percent higher. After the market closed on December 8, Oracle reported that its second-quarter sales were only 23 percent higher than a year earlier and its profits were only 4 percent higher. The next day, 171.8 million Oracle shares were traded, more than one-sixth of all Oracle shares outstanding, and the stock's price fell 29 percent, reducing Oracle's total market value by more than $9 billion.

As is so often the case, Mr. Market overreacted. The annual return on Oracle stock over the next sixteen years, through December 31, 2013, was 15.8 percent, compared to 4.1 percent for the S&P 500. A $10,000 investment in Oracle the day after its 1997 crash would have grown to $105,000 compared to $19,000 for the S&P 500.

A more prolonged example involved Disney, a favored growth stock that fell from a high of $122 on January 19, 1973, to $17.50 on December 17, 1974, even while its earnings were increasing. Its 1973 earnings of $1.64 a share were 16 percent *above* 1972's $1.41 earnings, but below analysts' optimistic $1.80 to $2.00 predictions. Even the revised predictions of $1.95 for 1974 proved to be optimistic, as earnings only increased slightly, to $1.66. Recession, inflation, and the energy crisis took their toll, but worst of all was the fear that Disney had changed from a glamorous growth stock into something a bit more mature and much less exciting.

This, too, proved to be an overreaction. If you had invested $10,000 in Disney on December 31, 1974, at a slightly recovered price of $21.375, you would have earned 15.5 percent a year through December 31, 2013, and your investment would have been worth $2.77 million, compared to 8.8 percent and $270,000 for the S&P 500.

More recently, on January 24, 2013, Apple reported a record quarterly profit of $13.1 billion, selling 28 percent more iPhones and 48 percent more iPads than a year earlier, but the stock dropped more than 12 percent, reducing its market value by $50 billion. Apple had sold a record 47.8 million iPhones, but this was less than the consensus forecast of 50 million. Earnings per share were *higher* than forecasted ($13.81 versus $13.44), and so was revenue ($54.7 billion versus $54.5 billion), but investors were used to Apple clobbering forecasts. A bit of a paradox here. If analysts expected Apple to beat their forecasts, why didn't they raise their forecasts? In any case, Mr. Market was scared and the price plunged. Will this, too, prove to be an overreaction?

While the value of growth cannot be doubted, the uncertainty in valuing rapidly growing companies is what kept Benjamin Graham away from IBM and other, more temporary highfliers. Thinking the same way, Warren Buffett has always had an aversion to speculative tech stocks and a fondness for boring companies that generate profits reliably: Benjamin Moore, Burlington Northern, Dairy Queen, Fruit of the Loom, GEICO, See's Candies, Coca-Cola, Kraft, Procter & Gamble. When Buffett bought Apple stock in 2016, this did not mean that he had changed his mind about growth stocks. Instead, it signaled that he now viewed Apple as a money machine, a mature company with dependable profits and an attractive stock price.

There is an old Wall Street saying, "A bargain that stays a bargain isn't a bargain," suggesting that buying a stock for a price less than its intrinsic value is not a good investment if the price doesn't increase afterward. Investors who focus on intrinsic value don't think that way. Remember Warren Buffet's aphorism, "My favorite holding period is forever." Intrinsic-value investors are not dismayed if the price doesn't go up, because they buy stocks for income, not price appreciation. In fact, if the price goes down and the income projections haven't changed, they will buy more. In market panics, value investors say, "Wall Street is having a sale." They back up a truck and fill it with bargains.

ECONOMIC EVENTS AND THE STOCK MARKET

The two main economic drivers of the stock market are the state of the economy (boom or recession) and interest rates. When the economy is strong, profits surge and dividends follow close behind. When recession hits, profits slump and dividends grow slowly, or even drop. When interest rates go up or down, so do the required returns used to determine the intrinsic value of stocks. Higher required returns reduce intrinsic values; lower required returns increase intrinsic values. This is why higher interest rates are bad news for the stock market and lower interest rates are good news.

It is often thought, wrongly, that the only reason interest rates affect the stock market is because they affect the economy—making it more or less expensive for firms to borrow money to expand and for households to borrow money to buy things. For example, in March 1986, a seasoned market observer wrote:

> The force driving stock prices up is declining interest rates (and oil prices). Well, interest rates decline when lenders have lots of money but borrowers don't have lots of need for it; that is, when business is slow. Like now. Every new statistic—retail sales off a bit, unemployment up a bit—indicates that the economy is only so-so. Which wouldn't be so bad if the outlook for the economy were better. But it's not. Despite lower interest rates, business doesn't seem in a hurry to invest in new plants and equipment. . . .

What does it all mean? Only that the economy will putter along—no disaster but no great glory either—and the stock market will probably take a sharp decline.

He was seemingly oblivious to the fact that, even if the economy just putters along, lower interest rates, all by themselves, make stocks more valuable because they increase the present value of future dividends. As it turned out, the market did not take a sharp decline. The S&P 500 rose 26 percent over the next twelve months.

The evidence is everywhere, but most obviously in big market moves. The 1973–1974 stock market crash ended when interest rates peaked, and the 1985–1986 stock market surge coincided with a 3-percentage-point drop in long-term interest rates. The unemployment rate was near double-digit levels in 2009, 2010, and 2011, but there was a stock market boom fueled by the Fed reducing interest rates to keep the economy from collapsing.

ECONOMIC VALUE ADDED

If a company has strong earnings but doesn't pay dividends, it is clearly worth something, but the present value of the nonexistent dividends is zero. We might assume that the company will eventually pay dividends, like Microsoft, Apple, and countless other companies that never paid dividends—until they did. Value investors might predict a future date when the company will start paying dividends and predict how big the dividend will be and how rapidly it will increase. Then they could calculate the present value of these distant dividends. Not an easy task! And what about companies like Berkshire Hathaway that generate enormous profits but may never pay a dividend, reasoning that they can help their shareholders more by using the money to continue making profitable investments?

I will discuss two value-investor alternatives in Chapter 7, based on models created by Robert Shiller and John C. Bogle. Another appealing approach is called economic value added (EVA). Suppose that a firm has $100 million in assets and earns $15 million, a 15 percent return on its assets. So far, so good. Some profits are better than no profits. However, economic value added depends on whether earnings are higher than shareholders' required earnings. If shareholders require a 10 percent return, required earnings are $10 million and the firm's $15 million in actual earnings provides an economic value added of $5 million. If, on the other hand, the shareholders' required return is 20 percent, there is a $5 million shortfall. Instead of adding value, the firm is subtracting value.

Economic value added makes a lot of sense because it asks and answers the right questions—and it makes no assumptions about Mr. Market's prices. The clincher is that, for firms that do pay dividends, economic value added gives the same intrinsic value as the dividend-discount model! The advantage of the EVA model is that it can be used for firms that do not pay dividends.

In the spring of 2000, Yahoo stock was one of the things I considered when assessing whether we were in a bubble. At that 36K conference, I noted that Yahoo's stock price was $475 a share at the start of the year. Unlike most dot-coms, Yahoo was profitable, earning $55.8 million. Still, this was only 20 cents a share. Yahoo's price-earnings ratio (P/E) was a mind-boggling 2,375.

Yahoo didn't pay a dividend and there were no dividends in the foreseeable future, so the dividend-discount model couldn't be used to value its stock.

Could Yahoo's price be justified by plausible assumptions? Here's where economic value added comes in handy. With $1.24 billion in assets, a 10 percent shareholder required return implies required profits of $124 million. Yahoo's actual $55.8 million profit in 1999 was $68.2 million less than required. Instead of economic value added, Yahoo had economic value *subtracted* of $68.2 million. To justify its $125 billion market value, Yahoo would have needed an annual EVA of $1.3 billion in 2000, $2.6 billion in 2001, $3.9 billion in 2002, and so on forever.

This is an interesting number because Walmart's 1999 economic value added was $1.3 billion. So, to be worth its market value, Yahoo would have to be as profitable as Walmart in 2000, twice as profitable in 2001, three times as profitable in 2002, and so on.

It is hard to escape the conclusion that Yahoo was deliriously overvalued. The market soon came to its collective senses and Yahoo stock fell off the proverbial cliff (see Figure 6-3). Yahoo's stock plummeted 90 percent over the twelve months following the 36K conference in the spring of 2000.

In the spring of 2000, value investors could not predict what Yahoo's stock price would be in the next few months or years, but they were confident that Yahoo's bubbly stock price made it an extremely unattractive value investment.

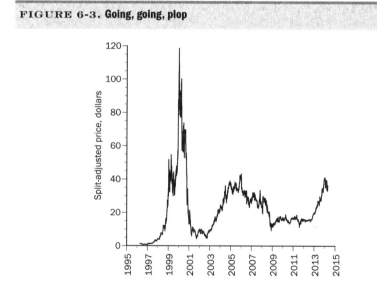

FIGURE 6-3. Going, going, plop

PRECIOUS-METAL IRAS

We've all heard and seen advertisements urging us to invest our individual retirement accounts (IRAs) in gold, silver, and other precious metals:

Gold carries the unique distinction of always maintaining its intrinsic value, which means gold has never been worth zero.

Don't rely on stocks, bonds, and other paper-based investments valued according to others' opinions.

Precious metals protect your investment and ensure that you are not putting your future in the hands of a volatile stock market.

Nothing brings peace of mind like knowing your retirement assets are precious metals stored in a fortified bank vault.

The Taxpayer Relief Act of 1997 allows people to invest their IRAs in precious metals. Many precious-metal companies try to persuade people to do so. These arguments, taken from their advertisements, are unpersuasive. "Never worth zero" is hardly an assurance that the value won't drop precipitously. Yes, stock prices depend on the opinions of others, but so do precious-metal prices. Yes, stock prices are uncertain, but so are precious-metal prices.

Figure 6-4 shows the daily price of gold back to the 1970s, when governments abandoned the fixed exchange rate of $35/ounce. The price hit a high of $843 in January 1980, then fell over the next twenty years to $252 in June 1999. Then the price surged upward to a peak of $1,896.50 in September 2011, before falling 45 percent to $1,050.60 in December 2015.

And yet, after all these booms and busts, newspaper, magazine, radio, television, and internet ads continue to tout gold as a safe investment. Perhaps the most dangerous part of this nonsense is that IRAs are intended to maintain the living standards of retired people. It sounds cruel, but the main financial risk during retirement is outliving one's wealth and having to live in poverty. It is little comfort to retirees to know that their IRAs will never go all the way to zero.

FIGURE 6-4. Daily gold prices

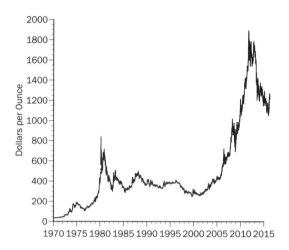

The most salient fact about gold is that it has *no* intrinsic value, because it generates no cash whatsoever. In fact, it has a negative intrinsic value to the extent that investors must pay storage and security fees to safeguard it. In a 1998 speech at Harvard, Warren Buffett said that gold "gets dug out of the ground in Africa or someplace. Then we melt it down, dig another hole, bury it again, and pay people to stand around guarding it. It has no utility. Anyone watching from Mars would be scratching their head." In his 2011 letter to Berkshire Hathaway shareholders, Buffett estimated that if we were to collect the world's gold stock and melt it into a giant 170,000-ton cube, it would be about sixty-eight feet on a side and fit inside a baseball field easily. At the 2011 price of $1,127 per ounce, it would be worth about $9.6 trillion.

For that $9.6 trillion, we could instead buy all U.S. cropland, which generates $200 billion in revenue each year, plus sixteen companies the size of ExxonMobil, each earning $40 billion, and still have $1 trillion left over to buy other revenue-generating assets. Buffett concludes with his usual wisdom and wit:

A century from now the 400 million acres of farmland will have produced staggering amounts of corn, wheat, cotton, and other crops—and will continue to produce that valuable bounty, whatever the currency may be. Exxon Mobil will probably have delivered trillions of dollars in dividends to its owners and will also hold assets worth many more trillions (and, remember, you get 16 Exxons). The 170,000 tons of gold will be unchanged in size and still incapable of producing anything. You can fondle the cube, but it will not respond.

Value investors do not buy metals—no matter how precious—because metals do not generate cash; they are not money machines.

INVESTMENT BENCHMARKS

My favorite definition of a growth stock is
"a stock that somebody is trying to sell you."
—Burton Crane

Astock's intrinsic value equals the present value of its divi-dends, but value investors look beyond dividends to a firm's earnings and assets. Earnings are important because these give firms the means to pay dividends, and assets are important because these are the source of earnings. Dividend-price ratios, earnings-price ratios, and asset-price ratios are sensible financial benchmarks, but none are infallible.

THE EARNINGS-PRICE RATIO

A stock's earnings-price ratio (E/P), or earnings yield, is a rough es-timate of a stock's rate of return. If a stock sells for $100 a share and the company earns $10 a share, it seems as though the shareholders have earned $10, which is a 10 percent return on their investment. If so, earnings yields should be related closely to the interest rates on Treasury bonds.

Figure 7-1 shows the S&P 500 earnings yield and the interest rate on long-term Treasury bonds back to 1871. There does not appear to be a consistent relationship. One thing that does stand out is how volatile earnings yields have been compared to interest rates, a reflection of the collective euphoria and hysteria that periodically seizes the stock market. Mr. Market is fickle.

FIGURE 7-1. The S&P 500 earnings yield (E/P) and long-term Treasury rate (R), 1871-2015

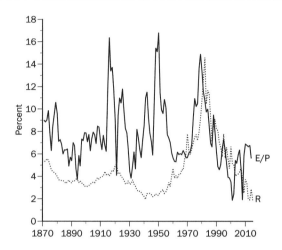

The earnings yield was well above the Treasury rate up until the 1960s. Figure 7-2 zooms in on the years since 1960. Over the last fifty years, these two series have been more closely aligned, but they hardly move in unison. Sometimes they even move in opposite directions. After 2010, the Treasury rate dropped while the earnings yield rose, creating a substantial gap between the two.

The problem with interpreting the earnings yield as the shareholders' return is that stockholders receive dividends, not earnings. Getting a $10 dividend is a lot different from reading about $10 in earnings in the annual report.

If a company pays a $5 dividend out of its $10 earnings, stockholders should consider the fate of the remaining $5. If these retained earnings are squandered, the $5 might as well not have been earned in the first place. For a dollar of retained earnings to be worth

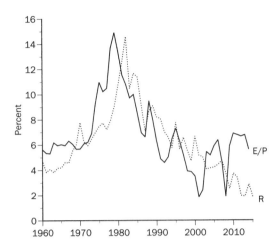

FIGURE 7-2. The S&P 500 earnings yield (E/P) and long-term Treasury rate (R), 1960–2015

a dollar to shareholders, the firm must earn a return equal to the shareholders' required return. If the firm earns less than the required return, a dollar of retained earnings is worth less than a dollar. If the firm earns more than the required return, a dollar of retained earnings is worth more than a dollar. This is why Berkshire Hathaway doesn't pay dividends. Its managers believe that their investments will earn more than their shareholders' required return.

The more general point is that the earnings–price ratio is an imperfect measure of the stockholders' return. Earnings are important because they are the source of dividends. However, earnings are the means to the end, not the end itself.

THE DIVIDEND-PRICE RATIO

Some investors use the dividend yield, the ratio of dividends per share to price (D/P), as a measure of the shareholders' return. In our example, investors see the stock's $5 dividend and $100 price, and they estimate the stock's return to be 5 percent. However, this calculation only makes sense if the dividend stays at $5 indefinitely. A $5 dividend, year after year, on a $100 investment is, indeed, a 5 percent return. However, most firms grow with the economy and their earnings and dividends grow, too.

Figure 7-3 shows the history of the S&P 500 dividend yield and the interest rate on long-term Treasury bonds. As with the earnings yield, there is no consistent relationship. It is very interesting, though, that the dividend yield was always above the bond rate before 1958 and persistently below afterward, until they converged in 2009.

In 1950, for example, stocks had a dividend yield of nearly 9 percent when long-term Treasury rates were only 2 percent. Investors either woefully underestimated the likelihood that dividends would grow over time, providing a double-digit return from stocks, or they were so afraid of stocks that they required double-digit returns to persuade them to leave the safety of 2 percent Treasuries. The former explanation is more plausible. What a great time to be a value investor!

FIGURE 7-3. The S&P 500 dividend yield (D/P) and long-term Treasury rate (R), 1871–2015

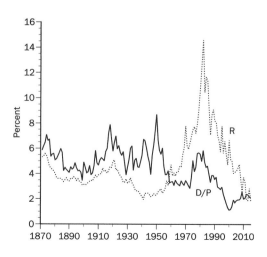

A BETTER ALTERNATIVE

The earnings yield looks at profits rather than dividends. The dividend yield ignores the future growth of dividends. A better rule of thumb is to use the insight provided by the JBW equation that was introduced in Chapter 6: The total return equals the dividend yield plus the growth rate of dividends:

$$R = \frac{D}{P} + g$$

We can apply this equation to the overall market by calculating the current dividend yield for the S&P 500 and making an assumption about the long-run growth of dividends, which is perhaps equal to the long-run growth of the economy. This total return estimate—the dividend yield plus the dividend growth rate—can be compared to the interest rate on long-term Treasury bonds plus whatever risk premium seems appropriate. In 1950, for example, a 9 percent dividend yield plus a 5 percent growth rate implies a 14 percent total return, R = 0.09 + 0.05 = 0.14, far above the 2 percent interest rate on long-term Treasury bonds. Value investors were, no doubt, ecstatic about an anticipated 14 percent annual return.

The comparison was much closer in 2013, when the dividend yield and long-term Treasury rate were both around 2 percent. Now, a 5 percent projected growth rate gives stocks a 5 percent margin over Treasuries (7 percent versus 2 percent), which might not be enough for value investors requiring more than a 5 percent risk premium. I was satisfied with a 5 percent premium and wrote a blog saying so.

THE PRICE-EARNINGS RATIO

A stock's price-earnings ratio is obtained by dividing the price per share by the annual earnings per share. The price-earnings ratio,

P/E, is the inverse of the earnings yield, E/P, and its mechanical usage to gauge whether stocks are cheap or expensive is subject to the same cautions.

Many investors have long considered a P/E ratio of 10 as normal and the purchase of a stock with a P/E ratio less than 10 a sound investment. For example, Burton Crane, a *New York Times* financial writer from 1937 to 1963, observed that "most of us over the age of forty, unless we are completely without market knowledge, subconsciously think of [dividend] yields of 6 per cent and price-earnings ratios of 10 as about right."

Figure 7-4 shows that the price-earnings ratio for the S&P 500 has varied considerably, falling to a low of close to 5 in some years and topping 20 in others. The average value has been a P/E ratio of 14.9. The P/E spikes in 2001 and 2008 were due to economic recessions that caused earnings to fall by more than 50 percent. Stock prices fell, too, but not as far as earnings because investors believed that the recession would not last long. With earnings down a lot and prices down a little, the P/E went up.

FIGURE 7-4. The S&P 500 price-earnings ratio, 1871–2015

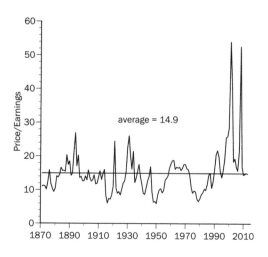

A LOW P/E IS NOT NECESSARILY A BARGAIN

Crane correctly cautioned that "no market is cheap because the price-earnings ratio is low and no market is dear because the ratio is high." Mechanical rules ignore perfectly logical reasons why individual stocks or the market as a whole may be cheap even if the P/E ratio is high and expensive even though the P/E is low.

The intrinsic value of a stock is higher if earnings (and dividends) are expected to grow faster. Intrinsic values are also higher if interest rates are low. Thus, the market P/E tends to be high when investors are bullish on the economy and/or interest rates are low.

The same is true of individual stocks. Figure 7-5 shows P/E ratios and five-year earnings growth predicted by professional security analysts for the Dow Jones Industrial stocks. Investors were willing to pay more for faster-growing companies.

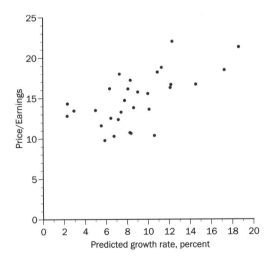

FIGURE 7-5. Dow stocks' predicted five-year growth and P/E ratios, January 2014

There are two other factors to consider: short-run fluctuations in earnings and creative accounting. If earnings are depressed temporarily by an economic recession or corporate misfortune, a stock's price may stay relatively firm as current earnings sag, driving the P/E ratio skyward. In these circumstances, the P/E ratio is unusually high because earnings are abnormally low. In the reverse situation, the P/E will fall if investors perceive a temporary bulge in earnings to be due to extraordinary good luck. Similarly, if investors believe that the firm has used dubious accounting procedures to boost reported earnings, the P/E ratio will be deceptively small because earnings are fictitiously large.

The bottom line is that there is no reason to think that the market's P/E should be some magic number like 10 or 14.9. There is even less reason to think this should be true of individual stocks.

USING P/ES FOR INVESTMENT DECISIONS

Although it is unwise to base investment decisions on P/E rules carved in stone—for example, buy when the P/E is below 7, sell when it is above 15—price-earnings ratios can still be used to help value investors make informed investment decisions. We will look at a model developed by John C. Bogle, the founder and former chairman of Vanguard. Although his procedure can be used for individual securities and for short horizons, Bogle cautions that there are "two lessons that I have learned in more than a few decades in the investment field. First, the performance of individual securities is unpredictable, period. Second, the performance of portfolios of securities is unpredictable on any short-term basis."

Thus he recommends using his approach for portfolios (such as the S&P 500) over ten-year horizons. Bogle assumes that intrinsic value is equal to the present value of the cash generated, and that dividends and earnings grow at the same rate. For an investor with a ten-year horizon, this cash consists of the dividends over the next ten years and stock prices ten years from now.

Bogle's clever insight is that stock prices ten years from now depend on two factors: the growth in earnings and the change in the

P/E ratio that the market uses to value these earnings. If earnings double, the stock price will double. If the P/E ratio doubles, the stock price will double. If earnings and the P/E both double, the stock price will quadruple.

This insight also helps us understand why growth stocks are doubly vulnerable. A stock's price is, by definition, its earnings per share multiplied by its price-earnings ratio. If earnings turn out to be lower than expected, this will reduce the stock price. If the P/E falls because of the disappointing earnings, this will reduce the stock's price. That's a double blow to the growth stock's price.

To implement Bogle's model, we need to predict the growth rate of earnings and the change, if any, in the price-earnings ratio. We can then estimate the implied rate of return using this simple approximation:

$$\frac{\text{stock}}{\text{return}} = \frac{\text{dividend}}{\text{yield}} + \frac{\text{annual growth}}{\text{of earnings}} + \frac{\text{annual change}}{\text{in P/E}}$$

Bogle gives this example for the S&P 500 in the 1980s. At the start of the decade, the dividend yield was 5.2 percent and the P/E was 7.3. Earnings grew at a 4.4 percent rate during this decade and the P/E at the end of the decade was 15.5, an annual growth rate of 7.8 percent. Thus the annual rate of return on the S&P 500 during the 1980s was approximately 17.4 percent:

$$\text{return} = \frac{\text{dividend}}{\text{yield}} + \frac{\text{annual growth}}{\text{of earnings}} + \frac{\text{annual change}}{\text{in P/E}}$$

$$= \quad 5.2\% \quad + \quad 4.4\% \quad + \quad 7.8\%$$

$$= \quad 17.4\%$$

Table 7-1 shows the components of the annual returns for each decade from 1900 through 2010. Stocks did great in the 1950s, 1980s, and 1990s because of extraordinary increases in the P/E ratio. The below-average stock returns in the 1960s, 1970s, and 2000s, in contrast, reflected a falling price-earnings ratio. Overall, the average change in the P/E has been essentially zero. In the long run, half of the return from stocks has been from dividends and half from earnings growth—nothing from changes in the P/E.

TABLE 7-1. Components of S&P 500 returns, annual percentages

	Dividend Yield	Earnings Growth	P/E Growth	Total Return
1900s	3	5	1	9
1910s	4	2	−3	3
1920s	6	6	3	15
1930s	5	−6	0	−1
1940s	5	10	−6	9
1950s	7	4	9	20
1960s	3	6	−1	8
1970s	4	10	−8	6
1980s	5	4	8	17
1990s	3	8	7	18
2000s	1	1	−3	−1
Average	5	4	0	9

SEEING THE DOT-COM BUBBLE

In March 2000, the S&P 500 was four times higher than a decade earlier, a 16 percent annual rate of increase. Add in dividends and investors had made close to 20 percent a year. Easy money! A survey asked investors what annual rate of return they expected over the next ten years. The median answer was 15 percent.

One reason I was convinced that the dot-com boom was a dot-com bubble was an application of Bogle's model. In the spring of 2000, the S&P 500 had a dividend yield of 1.3 percent and a P/E of 30. Interest rates were 6.4 percent on ten-year Treasury bonds.

Because the future is uncertain, it is a good idea to consider a variety of scenarios. In my investments class, I used Bogle's model to estimate stock returns over the next ten years for the four scenarios in Table 7-2.

TABLE 7-2. Four scenarios, March 2000

	Earnings Growth, %	P/E in 2010	P/E Growth, %	Total Return, %
Pessimistic	4	10	–10	–5
Historical	5	15	–7	–1
Optimistic	6	35	2	9
Delirious	7	60	7	15

The historical baseline assumed that dividends and earnings would grow by 5 percent a year, as they had over the previous decade, and that the price-earnings ratio would return to its historical average of 15. If so, the shareholders' annual return would be negative (–1 percent). More pessimistic scenarios implied worse.

The unemployment rate had fallen from 5.6 percent in 1990 to 4.0 percent in March 2000, and it seemed unlikely that the economy would grow faster than it had during the previous decade. An optimistic scenario of 6 percent growth and the P/E rising to 35 would give a 9 percent shareholder return, not much more than the 6.4 percent interest rate on Treasury bonds and a whole lot less than the 15 percent that investors anticipated.

To get that 15 percent return, investors needed to make seemingly delirious assumptions, such as the earnings growth rate rising to 7 percent and the P/E doubling to 60. What would happen when this preposterous future did not materialize and investors learned that stocks were not easy riches? I told my students to expect investors to head for the exits, and most to get trampled.

SEEING THROUGH THE DOOM-AND-GLOOM

The stock market did crash and euphoria turned into hysteria. In December 2008, I was interviewed on a local television show. The S&P 500 was down 40 percent from March 2000 and dot-com stocks were down more—much more. The unemployment rate was 7.8 percent and rising as the economy hurtled into the Great Recession. Who would be crazy enough to buy stocks? I raised my hand.

Here are some excerpts from my interview:

> We're in an economy that's sick. Everyone is depressed. Everyone is gloomy. Everyone is worried about the future. And yet you gotta think about the prices, how far stock prices have fallen. So, today, you have dividend yields that are close to 4 percent, Treasury bonds are paying 3 percent. Remember back in 2000, Treasury bonds were paying 5 percent more than dividend yields. Now it's the other way around. Dividend yields are above Treasury bonds. You have price-earnings ratios that are down to 13 or 14.
>
> It reminds me a lot of the 1973–74 crash, which you and I both lived through, and it was just a fearful, fearful time, but 1974 in retrospect was a great time to buy stocks. And then you had the 2000 internet bubble and the crash, 2001–2002, and people were getting out of the market and said they would never go back. In retrospect, 2002 was a great time to buy stocks. . . .
>
> I would say that the worst possible thing to do now if you are in the market is to say I've gotta sell everything, I can't afford to lose any more money. What you're doing is you're just locking in your losses.
>
> You and I—we don't know what stock prices are going to be tomorrow, or next week, or next month, but . . . we can say with great confidence . . . this economy will be much bigger, much stronger ten years from now than it is today, and

stock prices will be much higher. And, so, this is a time to be buying, not a time to be panicking. . . .

I'm really excited. I was so gloomy in 2000 and I was so pumped up in 1974 and I was so pumped up in 2002, and I'm pumped up again. I feel like this is a buying opportunity that only comes around a half dozen times in a lifetime.

We're not yet ten years into December 2008's future, but the market did recover nicely, with the S&P 500 doubling over the next five years.

SHILLER'S CYCLICALLY ADJUSTED EARNINGS

Nobel laureate Robert Shiller has a sensible way of dealing with short-term fluctuations in earnings. First, he calculates real, inflation-adjusted earnings for the S&P 500. Then he calculates the average value of these inflation-adjusted earnings over the preceding ten years. Figure 7-6 shows that this ten-year average—which he calls cyclically adjusted earnings—smooths out earnings fluctuations caused by temporary booms and recessions.

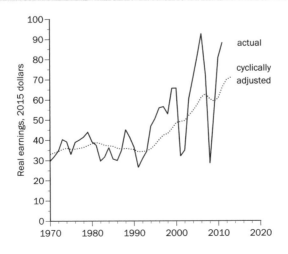

FIGURE 7-6. Actual and cyclically adjusted earnings

Shiller calculates a cyclically adjusted P/E ratio (CAPE) by dividing the inflation-adjusted value of the S&P 500 by cyclically adjusted
earnings. Figure 7-7 shows the actual and cyclically adjusted P/Es for
the S&P 500.

FIGURE 7-7. Actual and cyclically adjusted price-earnings ratio

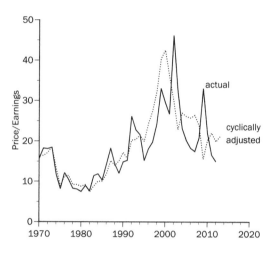

This reasonable procedure has the virtue of averaging out booms
and busts. However, the cyclically adjusted P/E still has some of the
same issues as unadjusted P/Es in gauging whether stocks are cheap
or expensive. One is that growth matters. The cyclically adjusted
P/E may be unusually high, but still perfectly reasonable, if earnings
over the next ten years are expected to be much higher than earnings over the previous ten years.

Also, interest rates matter. When interest rates are low, P/E
should be high, too. Shiller uses a graph, like the one in Figure 7-8,
to demonstrate the inverse relationship between the cyclically adjusted P/E and the interest rate on ten-year Treasury bonds. As interest rates came down from their double-digit levels in the early
1980s, the price-earnings ratio went up.

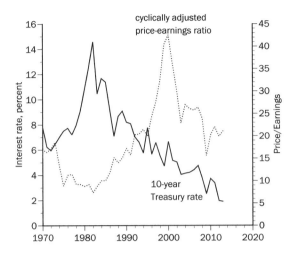

FIGURE 7-8. Ten-year Treasury rate and cyclically adjusted price-earnings ratio

Although the price-earnings ratio P/E is more familiar than the earnings yield E/P, the positive relationship between interest rates and the earnings yield is easier to see than is the negative relationship between interest rates and the price-earnings ratio. Figure 7-9 shows that the cyclically adjusted earnings yield (CAEP) and ten-year Treasury rate have tended to move up and down together.

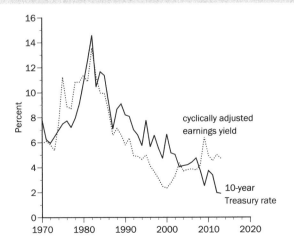

FIGURE 7-9. Ten-year Treasury rate and cyclically adjusted earnings yield

DID THE STOCK MARKET MAKE A MISTAKE?

The interest rates in Figures 7-8 and 7-9 are not adjusted for inflation. Suppose a one percent increase in the rate of inflation were to
increase interest rates and stock dividends, earnings, and prices by
one percent. Dollar interest rates would be one percent higher, but
inflation-adjusted interest rates and the earnings-price ratio would
be constant. These assumptions are surely too simple. Nonetheless,
it is reasonable that the earnings yield is more closely related to inflation-adjusted interest rates than to dollar interest rates.

In the spring of 1979, Franco Modigliani and Richard Cohn made
the provocative argument that investors in the 1970s mistakenly believed earnings yields should go up and down with dollar interest
rates rather than inflation-adjusted interest rates.

A telling example is Benjamin Graham, who recommended a
maximum P/E ratio of 15 in the early 1960s, when interest rates on
long-term, high-grade corporate bonds were around 4.5 percent, but
halved his maximum P/E to 8 in 1974, with corporate bond rates
above 9 percent.

Modigliani and Cohn argued that because of this market-wide
mistake, stock prices were about half what they should have been,
which made earnings yields twice what they should have been.

To investigate this argument, I calculated the real inflation-
adjusted interest rate each year by using the change in the consumer
price index over the next year. For example, I adjusted the dollar interest rate in January 2000 by using the change in the consumer
price index between January 2000 and January 2001. This is an imperfect measure of investors' inflation expectations, but maybe it is
not systematically biased.

Figure 7-10 compares these real interest rates with Shiller's cyclically adjusted earnings yield. What immediately leaps out of this figure is how close they were between 1981 and 2009, and how far apart
they were in the 1970s. A comparison of Figures 7-9 and 7-10 confirms the Modigliani-Cohn argument. In the 1970s, investors evi-

dently compared earnings yields with dollar interest rates rather than real interest rates. If this was a mistake, stock prices were much too low in the 1970s.

FIGURE 7-10. Inflation-adjusted ten-year Treasury rate and cyclically adjusted earnings yield

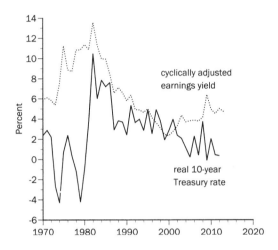

Although Modigliani and Cohn cautioned that mispriced stocks need not be correctly priced anytime soon, 1979 would have been a very good time to buy stock, as the return from doing so would have been 32 percent in 1980 and 18 percent compounded annually for the entire 1980s.

Part of the reason for the booming market was the drop in interest rates in the 1980s, but part of the reason was that investors made a colossal mistake in the 1970s. This is one of those occasions, like speculative bubbles and panics, where the presumption that markets know best is battered and bruised. It wasn't a slight mispricing. It was a blunder that left truckloads of $100 bills on the sidewalk.

THE GROWTH TRAP

Decades ago, many investors gauged a stock's attractiveness by its dividend yield. Indeed, as Figure 7-3 shows, up until 1958 the average dividend yield almost always exceeded the interest rate on Treasury bonds, indicating that investors attached little importance to dividend growth. As late as 1950, the average dividend yield was nearly 9 percent while the yield on Treasury bonds was only 2 percent. The JBW equation teaches us that growth, too, is important. If a stock has a 9 percent dividend yield and the dividend will grow by 5 percent a year, the annual rate of return is 14 percent, not 9 percent.

As the value of growth was increasingly recognized in the 1950s and 1960s, rising stock prices pushed dividend yields below bond yields. By the early 1970s, investors seemed to be interested *only* in growth, especially the premier growth stocks labeled the Nifty 50. This myopia led them to pay what, in retrospect, were ridiculous prices for growth stocks.

THE NIFTY 50

In the early 1970s, the attention of institutional investors was focused on a small group of "one decision" stocks that were so appealing that they should always be bought and never sold, no matter what the price. Value investors know that it is always a bad idea to buy or sell stocks without considering the price, and this time was no exception.

Among these select few were IBM, Xerox, Disney, McDonald's, Avon, Polaroid, and Schlumberger. In each case, earnings had grown by at least 10 percent a year over the past five to ten years, and no reason for a slowdown was in sight. Each company was a leader in its field, with a strong balance sheet and profit rates close to 20 percent.

David Dreman recounted the dreams of missed opportunities that danced in investors' heads:

> Had someone put $10,000 in Haloid Xerox in 1960, the year the first plain copier, the 914, was introduced, the investment would have been worth $16.5 million a decade later. McDonald's earnings increased several thousand times in the 1961–66 period, and then, more demurely, quadrupled again by 1971, the year of its eight billionth hamburger. Anyone astute enough to buy McDonald's stock in 1965, when it went public, would have made fortyfold his money in the next seven years. An investor who plunked $2,750 into Thomas J. Watson's Computing and Tabulating Company in 1914 would have had over $20 million in IBM stock by the beginning of the 1970s.

The unfortunate consequence of this fixation on the Nifty 50 was the belief that there is never a bad time to buy a growth stock, nor is there too high a price to pay. A money manager infatuated with growth stocks wrote, "The time to buy a growth stock is now. The whole purpose in such an investment is to participate in future larger earnings, so *ipso facto* any delay in making the commitment is defeating." This is suspiciously similar to the Greater Fool Theory and contradicts the main tenet of value investing—that stocks, like groceries, should never be bought without regard for price. IBM is a fine company, but is its stock worth $1,000 a share? Any price, no matter how high?

The subsequent performance of many of the Nifty 50 was disappointing; yet, even today, some money managers believe that you can't go wrong with a good growth stock, no matter what price you pay. Michael Lipper, president of Lipper Analytical Services, was very blunt: "[Suppose] an investor's timing was exquisitely wrong and he bought a growth stock at its peak. If he held that stock until the top of the next market cycle, such an investor would be better off with a growth stock than a value play."

Not necessarily. Avon was a hot growth stock in 1973 when it sold for $140 a share, sixty times earnings. In 1974, the price collapsed to $19; twelve years later, in 1986, it was selling for $25 a share. Polaroid sold for $150 in 1972 (an astounding 115 times earnings), $14 in 1974, and $42 in 1986, before going bankrupt in 2001. Xerox hit $172 in 1972 (sixty times earnings), $49 in 1974, $27 in 1982, and $49 in 1986. An investor with exquisitely wrong timing would have been better off putting money under the mattress, not to mention buying reasonably priced stocks.

These were not isolated cases. Many glamour stocks that were pushed to extraordinary P/E ratios in the 1970s did substantially worse than the market over the next several decades.

There is some uncertainty about the exact composition of the Nifty 50, with one *Forbes* article referring to a Morgan Guaranty Trust list and several other *Forbes* articles referring to a Kidder Peabody list. If any group of stocks can be clearly counted among the stocks of the Nifty 50 legend, it is the twenty-four stocks that appear on both lists.

A student and I looked at the performance of these Terrific 24 stocks over the twenty-nine-year period from December 1972 through December 2001. Figure 7-11 shows that eighteen of them underperformed the S&P 500 and that those stocks with the highest P/Es were most likely to underperform. These stocks should be renamed the *Terrible 24*.

An investor who bought these twenty-four stocks at the end of 1972 would have had 50 percent less wealth at the end of 2001 than an investor who bought the S&P 500.

There are two reasons why growth stocks are sometimes disappointing. First, investors appraising a stock with their hearts instead of their minds see temporary growth and think they have found permanent growth. Second, some growth is worthless and some firms create an appearance of growth to boost the price of their stock. We will look at each of these pitfalls in turn.

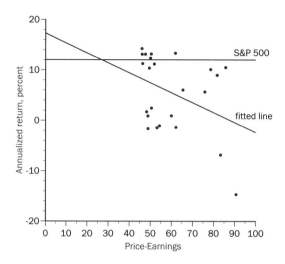

FIGURE 7-11. Return vs. P/E for the Terrible 24

THE DANGERS OF INCAUTIOUS
EXTRAPOLATION

Benjamin Graham was wary of growth stocks because growth pro-jections are so often based on little more than simple-minded ex-trapolations: "It must be remembered that the automatic or normal economic forces militate against the indefinite continuance of a given trend. Competition, regulation, the law of diminishing re-turns, etc. are powerful foes to unlimited expansion."

The value of a growth stock lies in the distant future, and it is risky to extrapolate a few years of impressive growth into several de-cades of stunning growth. Many ludicrous examples have been con-cocted to dramatize the folly of incautious extrapolation. A study of British public speakers over the past 350 years found that the aver-age sentence length had fallen from seventy-two words per sentence for Francis Bacon to twenty-four for Winston Churchill. If this trend continues (famous last words), the number of words per sen-tence will soon hit zero and then go negative.

It is also an incautious extrapolation to assume that a firm's extraordinary profits will continue indefinitely.

WORTHLESS GROWTH

Growth *per se* is not valuable. A company that reduces current dividends in order to grow bigger always increases the firm's earning growth (as long as profits are positive) but doesn't increase the intrinsic value of its stock unless the profit is larger than the shareholders' required return.

Here is a great example of how growth is not necessarily valuable. Consider a mutual fund that invests in Treasury bills—all Treasury bills all the time—paying 4 percent interest. If the fund pays all the interest to its shareholders, they earn a 4 percent return and the fund has a zero percent growth rate. Now suppose the fund switches to a growth philosophy by paying out half the interest to its shareholders and using the other half to buy more Treasury bills. The fund is growing now, but shareholders are no better off—because all the firm did is buy Treasury bills that investors could have purchased themselves.

CREATING AN ILLUSION OF GROWTH

Another trap for investors who focus myopically on earnings growth is that companies can manufacture growth by acquiring companies with low P/E ratios. For a simple example, consider the two firms in Table 7-3, each with $100 million in assets and one million shares outstanding. Smith earns a 10 percent profit on its assets and shareholders require a 10 percent return on their stock. Hwang earns a 20 percent return on its assets and shareholders require a 20 percent return. Both companies pay all of their earnings out as dividends. Both are no-growth companies and each has a total market value of $100 million, $100 a share.

Now assume that Smith merges with Hwang by issuing a million new shares of stock that are traded one-for-one to the Hwang shareholders. The two companies continue to operate exactly as before, the only difference being that their balance sheets are combined. The results are in the last column in Table 7-3. Since there are no changes in their operations or in current and future earnings, the market value of the combined companies should be the sum of the market values of the two separate firms, $100 million + $100 million = $200 million, and the per-share price should stay at $100.

TABLE 7-3. The merger of Smith and Hwang.

	Smith	Hwang	Smith & Hwang
Total shares, millions	1	1	2
Total assets, millions	$100	$100	$200
Assets/share	$100	$100	$100
Total earnings, millions	$10	$20	$30
Earnings/share	$10	$20	$15
Total dividends, millions	$10	$20	$30
Dividends/share	$10	$20	$15
Price/share	$100	$100	$100 (?)
Price/earnings	10	5	6.67 (?)

Yet, from the standpoint of Smith, earnings per share have jumped 50 percent, from $10 to $15. Conversely, from the standpoint of Hwang, earnings per share have fallen 25 percent, from $20 to $15. If the merged company is named Smith, investors might compare last year's $10 earnings with this year's $15, decide Smith is now a growth company, and apply a higher price-earnings ratio, pushing the price above $150 a share. Then Smith will be even better positioned to manufacture more earnings growth by acquiring more low-P/E companies. If, on the other hand, the new company is named Hwang, investors may compare this year's $15 earnings with last year's $20 and flee a disaster in the making. Both conclusions are wrong. The lesson is simple: Value investors should look at the reasons for earnings growth.

BOOK VALUE

The book value of a firm is the net worth shown on the accountants' books. It is commonly calculated on a per-share basis, total assets minus liabilities, divided by the number of shares outstanding.

Book values are generally based on the cost of a firm's assets, depreciated over time for presumed wear and tear. However, a firm's value to shareholders is the cash that it generates, not the cost of its assets. A firm that loses money year after year is of little value to shareholders even if it costs billions to construct its money-losing buildings and equipment. (Imagine a tomato farm on top of Mount Everest.) Conversely, a high-technology company operating out of a garage can be worth millions of dollars even though its garage is only worth thousands.

TOBIN'S Q

James Tobin argued that we should look at how financial markets value a firm relative to the replacement cost of its assets:

$$q = \frac{\text{market value of firm}}{\text{replacement cost of firm's assets}}$$

Tobin's q is larger or smaller than 1 depending on whether the firm's profits are larger or smaller than the shareholders' required return on their stock. If this sounds like economic value added, you're right.

If a firm's profits are persistently larger than shareholders' required return, economic value added is positive and Tobin's q is larger than 1. If profits are less than shareholders' required return, economic value added is negative and Tobin's q is less than 1.

Tobin argues that a firm should invest in new buildings and equipment if the stock market will value the investment at more than its cost (that is, if its q ratio is greater than 1). Put more plainly, the appropriate question a firm should ask is whether, if the firm were to sell shares in its expansion, it could raise enough money to cover the cost.

The persuasive logic can be illustrated by a home builder's calculation. It only makes sense to build homes if the potential market value exceeds the construction cost. The same reasoning applies to all corporate investment. A firm should compare the cost of its investments with the value that financial markets will place on these investments. If the market value is larger than the cost (q greater than 1), shareholders want the firm to make this investment, gladly giving up a dollar of dividends in exchange for a two-dollar increase in the value of their stock.

If a firm's market value is less than the replacement cost of its assets (q less than 1), the firm is worth more dead than alive, and it should sell its assets and distribute the proceeds as dividends. Shareholders prefer two dollars of dividends to one dollar of market value.

WHAT DETERMINES Q?

How can assets be valued in financial markets at other than their replacement cost? Assets are of value to shareholders only to the extent they generate profits. It matters not at all that a factory cost $1 billion to build if it doesn't make a dime of profits. For a factory to be worth what it costs shareholders, it must earn the shareholders' required return.

Consider a restaurant that would cost $1 million to build and earn a constant 20 percent annual profit, $200,000, forever. All earnings are paid out as dividends. How much will investors pay for a $200,000 annual dividend? If Treasury bonds pay 5 percent, perhaps stock in a risky restaurant is priced to yield 10 percent. Using the JBW equation in Chapter 6 with no growth, the restaurant's value is $2 million:

$$V = \frac{\$200,000}{0.10} = \$2,000,000$$

Valued at $2 million, the $200,000 annual dividend gives investors their 10 percent required return. The market value of the restaurant is twice its cost of construction (q = 2) and the restaurant is worth building because its 20 percent profit is larger than the investors' 10 percent required return.

If, on the other hand, the investors' required return is 25 percent, then the market value is only $800,000:

$$V = \frac{\$200,000}{0.25} = \$800,000$$

Now q = 0.8 and the restaurant is not worth building. Investors require a 25 percent return on their stock, but the restaurant earns only 20 percent on its cost. The stock must be valued at less than cost to give investors their requisite return.

USING Q TO PREDICT THE MARKET

A *New York Times* article titled "A New Way to Measure an Exhausted Bull" began: "Is the q ratio signaling that the end is near for this great bull market? The what? If you're an economist, you didn't even ask the second question." The article went on to point out that q was 1.7 at that time and quoted a British consulting firm: "Professor Tobin received a Nobel prize for his work, and the U.S. stock market may thus be said to be making a bet of approximately $3 trillion that he should return his laurels. I expect him to be justified in keeping them."

This bearish consultant evidently believed that market values were too high because they were 1.7 times replacement cost, rather than equal to replacement cost. The $3 trillion figure was the difference between market value and replacement cost.

However, Tobin's q need not equal 1. The value of q could be 1.7, or even higher, if profit rates are higher than shareholder required returns. In our restaurant example, there is a compelling reason why q equals 2 and no reason why it should equal 1.

It turned out that the bull market was not exhausted. After the *New York Times* article appeared, the S&P went up 26 percent over the next twelve months and doubled over the next three years. Tobin's q helps us understand why the stock market goes up or down, but it is not necessarily a tool for picking $100 bills up off the sidewalk.

VALUE STOCKS

There is considerable evidence of abnormal returns from "value" stocks that have low prices relative to dividends, earnings, and book value. Mechanical rules are no guarantee of success, but these valuation metrics have the virtue of cultivating a contrarian approach to investing. Value investing and contrarian investing are often two sides of the same coin. When investors are fearful and contrarian investors look to pounce, stock prices are low relative to dividends, earnings, and book value, and these bargain prices attract value investors. Greed, on the other hand, which is a sell sign for contrarian investors, fuels high stock prices that scare off value investors.

Eugene Fama and others who believe that the market never makes a mistake argue that the abnormal returns from value strategies must be risk premiums. Therefore, value strategies must be risky—even if the only evidence we have of their riskiness is that they are profitable. Skeptics dismiss this reasoning as circular and argue that animal spirits and other market noise create profitable opportunities for contrarians and value investors.

THE DOGS OF THE DOW

Michael B. O'Higgins was an early and enthusiastic advocate of a strategy with the memorable name: the Dogs of the Dow. At the beginning of each year, calculate the dividend yield (dividend divided by price) for each of the thirty stocks in the Dow Jones Industrial Average and invest in the ten stocks with the highest dividend yields. These stocks are evidently out of favor, in that their prices are low relative to dividends—hence the label Dogs of the Dow. Writing in 1991, O'Higgins reported that the Dogs had outperformed the market for decades.

One explanation is the contrarian idea that investors overreact to bad news and their overreaction causes stock prices to fall too far, so that out-of-favor stocks are bargains. Another explanation is that a bird in the hand is worth two in the bush; that is, it is better to have a dividend in your pocket than dreams of capital gains at the end of a rainbow. Or perhaps it is just a coincidence uncovered by ransacking the data.

If it is just data mining, then it should do poorly with fresh data. In the twenty years after the Dogs of the Dow theory was first reported, the strategy had an annual return of 10.8 percent, the same as the Dow as a whole, but better than the S&P 500's 9.6 percent. Solid, but not spectacular. Perhaps the Dogs of the Dow are not as far out of favor as are dogs not in the Dow.

LOW PRICE-EARNINGS RATIOS

Several studies have found that stocks with low P/Es outperform stocks with high P/Es. For instance, Benjamin Graham divided the Dow Jones Industrials into the ten highest, ten middle, and ten lowest P/E ratios. For every five-year holding period between 1937 and 1969, the low P/E stocks outperformed the middle P/E stocks, which outperformed the high P/E stocks. If $10,000 had been invested and reinvested every five years in the ten stocks with the lowest P/E ratios at that time, it would have grown to more than $100,000 by 1969, more than twice the amount accumulated by investing and reinvesting in the ten highest P/E stocks.

LOW PRICE-BOOK RATIOS

Another plausible identifier of out-of-favor stocks is the ratio of the stock price to book value. One study calculated the ratio of market value to book value for the S&P 500 on January 1 of each of the forty-five years from 1950–1994. The years were then divided into two categories, depending on the beginning-of-year ratio of market value to book value: 1) the twenty-two years with the highest ratios and 2) the twenty-two years with the lowest ratios. (The median year was discarded.) The years with low beginning-of-year price-book ratios had an average return of 20 percent, the years with high price-book ratios 6 percent.

Similar results have been found for individual stocks. Even Fama, perhaps the most enthusiastic proponent of the efficient market hypothesis, has admitted that stocks with low price-book ratios beat the market. His explanation is unconvincing. He argues that because markets are efficient (might as well assume what you are trying to prove), low price-book stocks must have risks that we do not understand but investors fear.

A more persuasive explanation is that Mr. Market's prices fluctuate more than intrinsic values. When Mr. Market's prices are high
relative to benchmarks like dividends, earnings, and book value, his
prices are probably too high. When Mr. Market's prices are low relative to these benchmarks, they are probably too low.

SMALL CAPITALIZATION STOCKS

It is not profitable for large institutions to do expensive research on
small companies because any attempt to buy a substantial number
of shares will drive the price upward and a later sale will force the
price down. If small stocks are neglected, they might also be cheap.

Several studies have found that firms with a small total market
value, called small capitalization or small-cap firms, have significantly outperformed larger companies. One study considered the
performance of ten portfolios revised annually by dividing 2,000
stocks into ten groups based on their total market value at the time.
The subsequent annual rates of return, neglecting transaction costs,
are in Table 7-4 and show that small-cap portfolios consistently outperformed large-cap portfolios.

TABLE 7-4. Annual rates of return, by firm size

Group	Median Value, $millions	Average Return, %
1 (small)	5	33
2	11	24
3	19	23
4	31	20
5	47	19
6	74	18
7	119	16
8	209	14
9	435	13
10 (large)	1,103	10

Fama has acknowledged that small-cap stocks have outperformed large caps. And he has again reached for the unconvincing explanation that small-cap stocks must be riskier than large-cap stocks; we just don't know how to measure these risks.

SCUTTLEBUTT

Philip Fisher touted "scuttlebutt"—talking to a company's managers, employees, customers, and suppliers and to knowledgeable people in the industry in order to identify able companies with good growth prospects. In an efficient market, if it is well known that a company is great, its stock should trade at a price that reflects its greatness. However, Fisher's scuttlebutt might be justified by the argument that Wall Street is fixated with numbers and it takes more than numbers to identify a great company.

Since 1983, *Fortune* magazine has published an annual list of the most-admired companies based on surveys of thousands of executives, directors, and securities analysts. The top 10 (in order) in 2016 were Apple, Alphabet (Google), Amazon, Berkshire Hathaway, Walt Disney, Starbucks, Southwest Airlines, FedEx, Nike, and General Electric.

I looked at the performance of a stock portfolio of *Fortune*'s top-10 companies from 1983 through 2015. In one set of calculations, the trading day for the *Fortune* portfolio was the official publication date, which is a few days after the magazine goes on sale. I also looked at trading days one to four weeks after the publication date. On the trading day each year, the *Fortune* portfolio was reinvested in that year's ten most admired companies.

The *Fortune* strategy beat the S&P 500 soundly, with respective annual returns of 15 percent versus 10 percent. It is unlikely that this difference is some sort of risk premium since the companies selected as America's most admired are large and financially sound and their stocks are likely to be viewed by investors as very safe. By the usual statistical measures, they were safer. Nor is the difference in returns due to the extraordinary performance of a few companies. Nearly 60 percent of the *Fortune* stocks beat the S&P 500.

This is a clear challenge to the efficient market hypothesis since *Fortune*'s list is readily available public information. I have no compelling explanation for this anomaly. Perhaps Fisher was right. The way to beat the market is to focus on scuttlebutt—intangibles that don't show up in a company's balance sheet—and the *Fortune* survey is the ultimate scuttlebutt.

THE CONSERVATION OF VALUE

The idea is there, locked inside.
All you have to do is remove the excess stone.
—MICHELANGELO

Mergers, stock splits, stock dividends, cash dividends, share repurchases, stock sales. Many potentially confusing corporate actions seem difficult to assess. Which are good for shareholders? Which are bad? Which are meaningless?

Once again, John Burr Williams helps clarify our reasoning, this time with his Law of the Conservation of Investment Value: The value of a firm depends on the cash it generates, regardless of how that cash is packaged or labeled. Nothing is gained or lost by combining two income streams or by splitting income in two and calling one part one thing and the rest something else. Many seemingly important corporate decisions are, in fact, nonevents that do not leave $100 bills on the sidewalk.

STOCK SPLITS

A *Business Week* article was titled "How to Double Your Shares Without Spending a Dime." The secret is to buy a stock before it splits 2-for-1, doubling the number of shares you own. Sounds great, right?

Just be sure to buy the stock before it splits. In the *Sopranos* television show, Carmela has been nagging Tony to buy a stock. Finally, Tony says, "Let's buy that stock." Carmela makes a face: "It split. It's too late, we missed it."

If it's so great for shareholders, why don't all companies split their stock? The answer is that stock splits do nothing at all for shareholders. A stock split increases the number of shares, true enough, but it reduces the value of each share proportionately. The real mystery is why companies split their stock.

Consider a company with one million shares valued at $60 apiece, or a total market value of $60 million. If the stock splits 2-for-1, with no change in the company's operations, its aggregate market value should stay at $60 million, implying a $30 per-share market value: A doubling of the shares halves the value of each.

If stock splits are nonevents, why do firms bother? One explanation is that if a company allows its price to rise to $200, $500, or $1,000 a share, some investors cannot afford buy it. Periodic splits that keep the price per share under $100 keep the stock affordable.

In a market dominated by large institutions, the affordability argument is a bit strained and sometimes preposterous. American Telnet, a television production firm, went public in March 1979 at 50 cents a share. By August 1980, the firm had yet to sell a television show and the price had sagged to 43 3/4 cents. At this point, the firm split its stock 5-for-1 so that, according to its president, the stock would be "more affordable." Given the structure of brokerage commissions, however, it doesn't make sense to buy just one share of an 8-cent stock, and there is no real difference between buying 1,000 shares at 40 cents each or 5,000 shares at 8 cents each.

A somewhat more satisfactory reason for stock splits is that, traditionally, blue-chip stocks have traded in the $20 to $100 range, and some companies like to stay in that range. If a stock's price goes up to $80 and the firm declares a 2-for-1 split, reducing the price back to $40, the split signals to investors that the board of directors is confident that the run up was justified—not mindless speculation that, when it has run its course, will cause the price to collapse to below $20, where lesser stocks trade.

A stock that falls below $20 could do a reverse split—for example, a 1-for-2 split that halves the number of shares and doubles the price. However, resorting to this tactic would be a damaging admission by the company's board that the firm's prospects are not bright enough to increase the price soon.

On April 23, 2014, with Apple stock trading at $524.75, Apple announced a 7-for-1 split. Apple generally has very good reasons for doing what it does, so many investors thought that the highly unusual choice of a 7-for-1 split reflected the company's belief that the stock price would soon approach $700, which would be $100 after the split. They were right. Four months later, Apple popped through $100.

For American Telnet, a logical explanation for the 5-for-1 split is that splitting its stock down to the penny range may attract speculators who habitually restrict their attention to penny stocks. In sharp contrast, Berkshire Hathaway, run by Warren Buffett, has never split, even when its shares cost more than $100,000 apiece. In a Christmas card to a friend, Buffett wrote, "May you live until B-H splits."

In 1996, with Berkshire Hathaway selling for $33,000 a share, outsiders planned to buy Berkshire shares and resell them to investors in $1,000 pieces through unit investment trusts. Not wanting small investors to have to pay sales charges and other administrative expenses that such trusts would entail, Berkshire Hathaway issued Class B shares—dubbed "Baby Berkshires"—each without voting rights and worth one-thirtieth of the regular Class A shares. In January 2010, Class B shares were split 50-to-1, making each worth 1/1,500 the value of Class A shares. On January 10, 2014, Berkshire A closed at $171,322 a share and Berkshire B closed at $114.97 a share.

STOCK DIVIDENDS

A stock dividend is a stock split, only smaller. If a company declares a 5 percent stock dividend, stockholders receive five additional shares for every 100 shares they hold, which is effectively a 21-for-20 stock split. The conservation-of-value principle implies that the value of each share falls by 5 percent, leaving shareholders no better or worse off than before.

Nonetheless, *Barron's Finance and Investment Handbook* made this silly claim:

> From the corporate point of view, stock dividends conserve cash needed to operate the business. From the stockholder point of view, the advantage is that additional stock is not taxed until sold, unlike a cash dividend.

This claim is misdirected and misleading. Companies and their shareholders may well want to retain earnings to finance expansion. But there is no need to declare a stock dividend to do so. The company can expand as planned, and it doesn't matter at all whether the company leaves the number of shares unchanged, declares a 2-for-1 split, or declares a 21-for-20 split (a 5 percent stock dividend).

As with any stock split, the question is why bother? A stock dividend costs the firm the expenses of administering it and doesn't give shareholders anything. If stockholders feel better off having received a stock dividend, they apparently did not notice the offsetting dip in the value of each share, perhaps because a small price change is lost among the daily fluctuations in stock prices.

Andrew Tobias, a keen observer of the stock market, offers a similar explanation for why companies declare stock dividends:

> The only difference between a stock dividend and a stock split is that, being a very small split, it is hoped that no prospective buyers will notice that it has taken place. . . . Sometimes it actually works.

By this logic, stock dividends are like candy-bar inflation: The company shrinks the bar and hopes that consumers will continue to pay full price. If so, Mr. Market is truly dumb.

Writing in the *Harvard Business Review*, a finance professor argued that stock dividends are real events and they are bad:

> What about stock dividends, which are theoretically used as a way of sharing profits while conserving cash? . . . As I see it, the trouble with this approach is that shares outstanding increase at a compound rate. It's a 5% stock dividend this year, but next year it's 5% of 105%, and so forth. This pattern holds down growth in earnings per share.

Once again, the conservation-of-value principle guides us to the truth. Stock dividends are nonevents. Yes, stock dividends (like stock splits) reduce earnings per share, but they also increase the number of shares, leaving earnings per shareholder constant.

What this finance professor's bogus argument really demonstrates is another reason why we should not worship earnings per share. There are lots of ways that companies can increase earnings per share without benefitting shareholders:

1. Invest in marginally profitable ventures.

2. Acquire companies with low price-earnings ratios.

3. Do a reverse stock split.

A 1974 *Wall Street Journal* editorial criticized the myopic focus of many corporate executives on earnings per share:

> A lot of executives believe that if they can figure out a way to boost reported earnings, their stock prices will go up even if the higher earnings do not represent any underlying economic change. In other words, the executives think they are smart and the market is dumb. . . .
>
> The market is smart. Apparently the dumb one is the

corporate executive caught up in the earnings-per-share mystique.

A handbook on management consulting printed this editorial and then stated, "Unfortunately, our experience shows that many corporate managers still worship earnings per share, and thus are still betting that the market is dumb."

REAL DIVIDENDS

Dividends are paid to those who own the company's shares on the *record date*. For instance, the board of directors might declare a $1 dividend to be paid on March 1 to those who own stock on the record date of February 15. To allow for the processing of transactions, the NYSE and most other exchanges use an *ex-dividend* (excluding dividend) date two business days before the record date; those who buy the stock ex-dividend do not receive the dividend.

The Get Rich Investment Guide published by Consumers Digest offered this moneymaking tip:

> Obviously, one strategy is to know when the stock will go ex-dividend and buy a day or two before the cutoff. Then you can receive the dividends, and you can sell the shares as soon as you have [received the dividend].

So, $100 bills are lying on the sidewalk for anyone who can figure out when a stock goes ex-dividend? That doesn't seem difficult, so there must be a flaw in this strategy. The flaw is that a stock's price falls when it goes ex-dividend.

Consider a company with one million shares valued at $100. If the company pays a $1 dividend, the aggregate market value of the company falls from $100 million to $99 million, because its assets have been reduced by the $1 million it paid in dividends. The price of each share should drop to $99. Someone who buys the stock for $100 before it goes ex-dividend gets the $1 dividend, but can only sell the stock for $99. (I'm ignoring other, unpredictable price changes.)

If dividends are nonevents, why bother? Some shareholders may welcome using dividends to pay their bills, but they could always sell some of their stock. This is a classic puzzle in finance—why do companies pay dividends? One answer is that cash dividends are clear and unambiguous proof that the firm really is making money. Firms can use creative accounting to create an illusion of profits, but you can't fake dividends. Firms that pay dividends are making real profits, not imaginary ones.

DIVIDEND REINVESTMENT PLANS

Many companies have dividend reinvestment plans that allow shareholders to use their dividends to buy additional shares of stock. Shareholders avoid brokerage fees and the company raises cash without paying fees to an underwriter. It sounds like win-win but it isn't because shareholders must pay taxes on dividends they don't receive.

Consider again a firm with one million shares priced at $100 a share, and suppose the company pays a $1 dividend and all shareholders participate in a dividend reinvestment plan. What happens? The total number of shares increases by one percent, and the value of each share declines proportionately. Each shareholder continues to own the same fraction of the company's shares as before. The only difference is that shareholders must pay income taxes on dividends they didn't get. It is as if the company sent a notice to its shareholders every three months: "The company is doing fine; please send money to the IRS."

STOCK REPURCHASES AND SALES

A legendary fund manager wrote, "If a company buys back half its shares and its overall earnings stay the same, the earnings per share have just doubled." The obvious flaw is that the firm may have to liquidate half its assets to buy back half its stock. How can earnings stay the same if the firm gets rid of half its assets?

Consider a company with 20 million shares outstanding, each valued at $20 (an aggregate market value of $400 million). This firm has $20 million in cash to distribute to its shareholders. One alternative is to pay a $1 dividend per share; another is to purchase one million shares at $20 apiece.

Table 8-1 shows the consequences for this company. Either way, the $20 million payout reduces the firm's total value from $400 million to $380 million. If the firm pays a $1 dividend, there is a $1 drop in its stock price and shareholder wealth is unchanged. If the firm repurchases shares, the number of shares declines by one million, leaving the price at $20 and again making shareholders no better or worse off.

TABLE 8-1. A Stock repurchase is equivalent to a dividend

	Initial Position	After $1 Dividend	After 1-Million Share Repurchase
Shares, millions	20	20	19
Price per share	$20	$19	$20
Total value, millions	$400	$380	$380

Remember that we are comparing purely financial transactions in order to show that share repurchases are equivalent to dividend payments. Repurchases would increase the stock price if the firm bought the stock with money that would otherwise be wasted on unprofitable ventures. But it is the abandonment of the money-losing projects that raises the price of the stock, not the decision to distribute the proceeds through repurchases instead of dividends.

A comanager of the Federated Strategic Value Dividend Fund gave this answer to the query, "Why isn't it better for companies to engage in stock buybacks [instead of paying dividends]?":

> A dollar of dividends, albeit highly taxed, is still a check in the mail. A share repurchase goes off into the ether and never benefits Main Street. It's just money that could've come to you that didn't.

True, a dividend puts cash in shareholders' pockets, but they can always get cash by selling some of their shares—in essence, a shareholder-determined dividend policy.

Taxes give share repurchases a clear advantage over dividends. Shareholders pay taxes on dividends, but they do not pay capital gains taxes unless they realize their gains by selling—and, even then, they don't pay taxes on the entire sale, only the capital gain (if any). A dividend gives shareholders no alternative but to take the cash and pay taxes. With a share repurchase, shareholders have a choice. Either they can sell shares and pay taxes on the capital gains, or they can let their investment ride.

If a share repurchase is like a dividend, issuing new shares must be equivalent to reducing dividends. It is.

Our conclusion is that except for the benefits from avoiding taxes on dividends, a stock repurchase is equivalent to paying dividends and a stock sale is equivalent to reducing dividends.

STOCKS AS A HEDGE AGAINST INFLATION

Investors ought to find protection from inflation by stockpiling things going up in price. If the price of soup is going up, buy soup before the price goes up. But it is impossible to store some things, such as medical services, and expensive to store others, such as

automobiles. Some assets are beyond the budgets of most investors—Iowa farmland, Arizona shopping centers, Dallas skyscrapers.
Perhaps one way to invest in real assets that may appreciate with inflation is to buy stock in companies that own land, buildings, and
other tangible assets.

In the long run, dividends, earnings, and stock prices have increased faster than consumer prices. From 1900 to 2015, the consumer price index increased at an average annual rate of 3 percent
while the S&P 500 stock index increased by 5 percent a year. If we
add in dividends, investors have averaged more than a 6 percent annual real (inflation-adjusted) return from stocks.

In the short run, however, increases in the rate of inflation have
not increased stock prices reliably. Figure 8-1 compares the high-
inflation 1970s with the low-inflation 1960s. In each decade, real
output increased by 30 percent. In the 1960s, consumer prices rose
by 25 percent and stock prices nearly doubled. In the 1970s, consumer prices doubled and stock prices were virtually unchanged,
causing the real value of stocks to fall by 50 percent.

Many investors who suffered through the inflationary 1970s drew
the understandable conclusion that inflation is bad for the stock
market. However, the facts do not support this simplistic belief any
more than they support the equally simple belief that inflation is
good for the market. Figure 8-2 is a scatter diagram of the annual
rate of inflation and the return on stocks (dividend plus capital gain)
each year from 1926 to 2015. The correlation is a meaningless 0.01.
In the long run, stock prices have increased more than consumer
prices. In the short run, there is no relationship between the inflation and stock returns.

One explanation is that stockholders are not buying assets. They
are buying the profits that come from assets, and after-tax profits do
not move in lockstep with inflation.

FIGURE 8-1. Inflation-adjusted S&P 500, 1950–1990

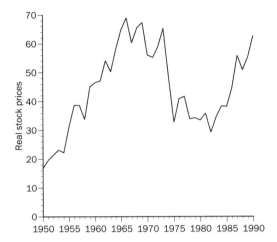

FIGURE 8-2. Annual stock returns and inflation, using data for 1926–2015

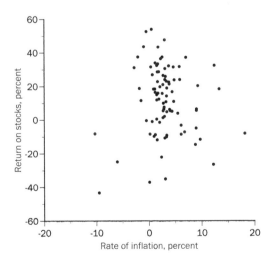

ACCOUNTING FOR INFLATION

After-tax corporate profits often suffer during inflationary periods because taxes are levied on profits calculated according to more or less standard accounting principles, and some of these principles don't make much sense during inflations. For instance, accountants spread out the cost of buildings, machines, and equipment with an annual depreciation expense that, in theory, reflects what it costs to replace things as they wear out. In practice, depreciation expenses are based on original costs, which is like figuring labor costs on the basis of wages twenty years ago. The result is that inflation causes capital costs to be understated and profits to be overstated so that businesses, particularly those with lots of buildings, machines, and equipment, pay higher taxes.

On the other hand, conventionally measured profits are misleadingly low during inflations to the extent they ignore capital gains on corporate assets and liabilities. Just as households profit when they borrow at a fixed interest rate to buy a house whose value increases during an inflation, so do corporations that borrow to buy buildings and equipment. Yet such gains are not included in reported profits unless the firm sells its real estate or retires its debt.

A relatively straightforward approach for valuing stock during inflationary periods is to remember that investors are not buying some accountant's reckoning of profits but the actual cash, the dividends, that stocks provide. Figure 8-3 shows real, inflation-adjusted dividends for the S&P 500 from 1950 to 2015. After growing at a 3.4 percent annual rate from 1950 to 1966, real dividends peaked in 1966 and declined sharply in the early 1970s. It wasn't until 1989 that real dividends returned to the level reached in 1966. The 1970s were the most inflationary decade in memory, and dividends did not keep up with consumer prices.

If real dividends had kept growing at 3.4 percent annually during the inflationary 1970s, dividends would have been 70 percent higher in 1980. Real dividends have spurted higher since 2000, even though the annual rate of inflation has only been about 2 percent.

Yes, dividends have gone up faster than inflation in the long run. No, dividends do not reliably rise and fall with inflation.

FIGURE 8-3. Inflation-adjusted S&P 500 dividends, 1950–2015

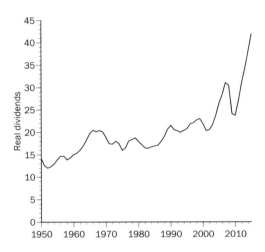

WE'RE ONLY HUMAN

There is nothing so disastrous as a rational
investment policy in an irrational world.
—JOHN MAYNARD KEYNES

Sears is a legendary American success story. Sears began as a mail-order catalog selling everything from watches and toys to cars and ready-to-assemble houses and evolved into the nation's largest retailer. Sears was in the Dow Jones Average for seventy-five years, but struggled in the 1990s to compete with discount retailers like Walmart, Target, and Home Depot. Sales and profits fell, and Sears stock price dropped nearly 50 percent between June and November 1999. Home Depot, on the other hand, was opening a new store every fifty-six hours. Its tools competed directly with the legendary Craftsman tools from Sears, and it was winning the battle. Home Depot's stock rose 50 percent between June and November 1999. On November 1, 1999, Home Depot replaced Sears in the Dow Jones Industrial Average.

Sears stock subsequently outperformed Home Depot. It wasn't a fluke and it wasn't that Home Depot had been jinxed by being included in the Dow. It had everything to do with how stock prices are affected by human emotions that can leave $100 bills on the sidewalk. Let's look at several examples.

ANCHORING

Anchoring is a general human tendency to rely on a reference point when making decisions. A student did a term paper in one of my statistics classes in which randomly selected students were asked one of these two questions:

> The population of Bolivia is 5 million.
> Estimate the population of Bulgaria.

> The population of Bolivia is 15 million.
> Estimate the population of Bulgaria.

Those who were told that Bolivia's population was 15 million tended to give higher answers than did those told that Bolivia's population was 5 million. Several similar questions confirmed this pattern. People use the known "fact" as an anchor for their guess.

When we buy a car, we tend to judge whether we are getting a good deal by comparing the final negotiated price to the dealer's initial price, no matter how unrealistic the initial price. Thus, a good salesman starts the haggling with a high price.

In real estate, many people use the price they paid for their home as an anchor for its current value: "Our house can't be worth $300,000; we bought it for $400,000." This anchoring causes some homeowners to behave in ways that are, well, irrational.

Figure 9-1 shows that the average price of condominiums in Boston nearly tripled between 1982 and 1988 and then fell by almost 35 percent over the next five years.

People who paid low prices for their condos in the early 1980s could make profits selling in the early 1990s, but people who bought in the late 1980s would have losses. A study found that sellers facing losses tended to ask higher prices for their condos. Not surprisingly, their high-priced condos went unsold. These condo owners were using their purchase price as an anchor for what their condos were worth and were so averse to taking a loss that they would rather not sell.

FIGURE 9-1. Boston condominium prices, 1982-1993

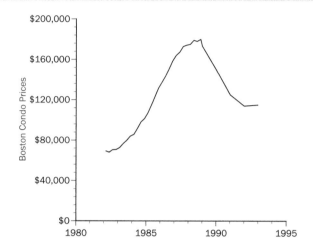

This behavior was not rational. There is no reason why condos purchased during a time of high prices are worth more than condos purchased during a time of low prices. It certainly makes no differ-ence to buyers. If it makes a difference to sellers, they pay for their irrationality by not being able to sell their condos.

People also use anchoring to gauge whether interest rates are high or low. A family I know (I'll call them Greg and Jane Landon) bought their first house in Eugene, Oregon, in 1971. Figure 9-2 shows that going back to at least 1920, mortgage rates had never been above 6 percent until they broke the 6 percent barrier in 1966 and hit 7.5 percent in 1971.

Greg thought they should wait to buy a home until mortgage rates went back to "normal" levels; that is, below 6 percent. Greg was using past mortgage rates as an anchor to gauge what mortgage rates should be.

But interest rates aren't governed by physical laws, like gravity or magnetism, that force them to behave in easily predictable ways. Just because mortgage rates had been 6 percent in the past doesn't mean they will be 6 percent in the future. Jane persuaded Greg that they should buy a home to call their own. Greg grimaced and they

FIGURE 9-2. The Landons buy their first home, when mortgage rates are high

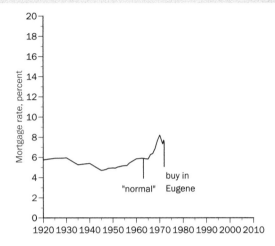

borrowed at 7.5 percent to buy a starter home. (In real estate, that's a euphemism for *small*.)

Seven years later, in 1978, they moved to Houston, Texas, and mortgage rates were now 9.6 percent (see Figure 9-3).

FIGURE 9-3. The Landons buy their second home, when mortgage rates are even higher

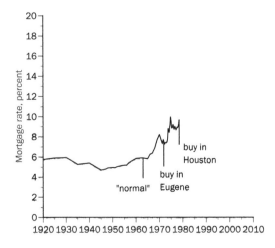

Greg was even more certain that they should wait for mortgage rates to return to normal. But the value of their Oregon home had doubled and, at that time, sellers had to pay a 35 percent capital gains tax on the profit they made from their homes, unless they purchased a new home—in which case the capital gain was rolled over and the tax was deferred, perhaps indefinitely. So Greg gritted his teeth and they bought a home in Houston with a 9.6 percent mortgage.

Three years later, in 1981, they moved to Seattle. Now they would have to pay capital gains taxes on their Eugene and Houston homes unless they bought another house. Unfortunately, mortgage rates were now above 17 percent (Figure 9-4).

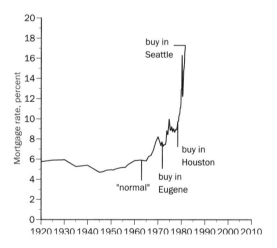

FIGURE 9-4. The Landons buy their third home, when mortgage rates are higher still

Fortunately, Greg's new company had an employee mortgage plan that would lend them money at 8.7 percent. Greg was much happier with 8.7 percent than with 17 percent, but he thought they would be even better off if they waited for mortgage rates to return to normal. The deciding factor was the annoying capital gains tax they would have to pay if they didn't buy. So, they bought a home in Seattle with an 8.7 percent mortgage.

Finally, in 2003 mortgage rates fell below 6 percent (Figure 9-5). Mortgage rates had returned to normal, just as Greg had predicted! But it took forty years. If the Landons had waited to buy a home until mortgage rates went back to 6 percent, they would have missed out on the best investments they made in their entire lives: their homes in Eugene, Houston, and Seattle.

One moral of this story is, don't try to time the real estate market. Another is to watch out for anchors that might sink you.

FIGURE 9-5. Mortgage rates finally return to normal

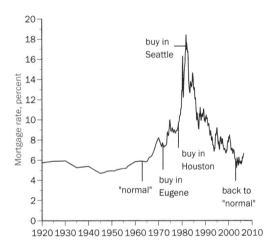

SUNK COSTS

You buy a colossal ice cream sundae for a special price but, halfway through, you're feeling sick. Do you finish the sundae because you want to eat what you paid for? The relevant question is not how much you paid, but whether you would be better off eating the rest of the ice cream or throwing it away.

You have season tickets to college football games in the Midwest. Come November, the team sucks and the weather is worse. Do you go to games because you already paid for the tickets? The relevant question is whether you would be happier at the game or somewhere else.

There is nothing to be gained and much to be lost by moping about things you can't change. Things that can't be changed are called *sunk costs*. The ice cream sundae you bought but would get sick finishing is a sunk cost. So are tickets to a miserable football game. So is the price you paid for a stock. Yet many investors are reluctant to sell losers, despite the tax benefit, because selling for a loss is an admission that they made a mistake buying the stock in the first place.

In the early 1980s a famous Yale professor boasted to a friend of mine that he made 25 percent a year during the terrible bear market in the 1970s. Surely, my friend asked, you must have bought some stocks that went down? He nearly fell out of his chair laughing when the Yale professor replied, "Yes, but I haven't sold them yet!" Then my friend realized that the professor was not trying to be funny.

The price you pay for a stock is a sunk cost. We should think about whether a stock is cheap or expensive at its current price, not whether the price is higher or lower than the price we paid, but it is hard to forget that sunk cost.

A BREAKEVEN MENTALITY

Daniel Kahneman and Amos Tversky observed that betting on long shots at horse races picks up toward the end of the day, presumably because people are looking for a cheap opportunity to win back what they lost earlier in the day. They argued that a "person who has not made peace with his losses is likely to accept gambles that would be unacceptable to him otherwise."

Two students and I looked at the strategies used by experienced

Texas Hold 'Em poker players. We found that most played looser after a big loss (betting so that they could stay in with hands they would normally fold). They evidently remembered their big losses and were eager to win back what they had lost.

Is this riskier play punished? It seems likely that experienced players generally use sound strategies, and that any changes are a mistake. That's what happened. Players who played looser after a big loss were less successful than they were with their normal playing style.

If investors are like poker players, they may be tempted to make long-shot investments to recoup losses. A February 2009 article in the *Wall Street Journal* reported that many investors were responding to their stock market losses by making increasingly risky investments:

> The financial equivalent of a "Hail Mary pass"—the desperate attempt, far from the goal line and late in a losing game, to fling the football as hard and as high as you can, hoping it will somehow come down for a score and wipe out your deficit.

Try not to let a breakeven mentality lure you into Hail Mary investments.

REGRESSION TO THE MEAN

Horace Secrist had a distinguished career as a professor of economics at Northwestern University. He wrote thirteen textbooks and was director of Northwestern's Bureau of Economic Research. In 1933, in the depths of the national economic tragedy that became known as the Great Depression, he published a book that he hoped would explain the cause, provide solutions, and secure his legacy.

Secrist and his assistants spent ten years collecting and analyzing data for seventy-three different industries, including department stores, clothing stores, hardware stores, railroads, and banks. He compiled annual data for the years 1920 to 1930 on several metrics of business success, including the ratios of profits to sales and profits to assets. For each ratio, he divided the companies in an industry into quartiles based on the 1920 values of the ratio: the top 25 percent, the second 25, the third 25, and the bottom 25. He then calculated the average ratio from 1920 to 1930 for the stocks in each 1920 quartile. He found that the companies in the top two quartiles in 1920 were more nearly average in 1930, and that the companies in the bottom two quartiles in 1920 were also more nearly average in 1930.

He had evidently discovered a universal economic truth. American business was converging to mediocrity. His book documenting his discovery was titled *The Triumph of Mediocrity in Business*. The book was a statistical tour de force, 468 pages long, with 140 tables and 103 charts, supporting his remarkable discovery.

Then a brilliant statistician named Harold Hotelling wrote a devastating review that politely but firmly demonstrated that Secrist had wasted ten years proving nothing at all. What Secrist became famous for was being fooled by regression toward the mean.

THE STATISTICAL FALLACY

I once did some research with a student on regression to the mean in baseball. Not 468 pages, but at least we recognized regression when we saw it. A referee for the journal that published our paper wrote:

> There are few statistical facts more interesting than regression to the mean for two reasons. First, people encounter it almost every day of their lives. Second, almost nobody understands it.
>
> The coupling of these two reasons makes regression to the mean one of the most fundamental sources of error in

human judgment, producing fallacious reasoning in medicine, education, government, and, yes, even sports.

Yes, we encounter regression to the mean almost every day and, yes, almost nobody understands it. This is a lethal combination—as Secrist discovered.

To understand regression, suppose that 100 people are asked twenty questions about world history. Each person's "ability" is what his or her average score would be on a large number of these tests. Some people have an ability of 90, some 80, and some near zero.

Someone with an ability of 80 will average 80, but is not going to get 80 percent correct on *every* test. Imagine a test bank with zillions of questions. By the luck of the draw, a person with an ability of 80 will know the answers to more than 80 percent of the questions on one test and to fewer than 80 percent on another test. A person's score on any single test is an imperfect measure of ability.

What, if anything, can we infer from someone's test score? A key insight is that a person whose test score is high relative to the others who took the test probably also had a high score relative to his or her own ability. Someone who scores in the 90th percentile could be someone of more modest ability (perhaps the 85th, 80th, or 75th percentile in ability) who did unusually well, or someone of higher ability (perhaps the 95th percentile in ability) who did poorly. The former is more likely because there are more people with ability below the 90th percentile than above it.

If this person's ability is, in fact, below the 90th percentile, then when this person takes another test, his or her score will probably also be below the 90th percentile. Similarly, a person who scores well below average is likely to have had an off day and should anticipate scoring somewhat higher on another test. This tendency of people who score far from the mean to score closer to the mean on a second test is an example of regression toward the mean.

Regression does not imply that everyone will soon get the same score on history tests, only that scores fluctuate around ability.

SECRIST'S FOLLY

In the same way, Secrist's study of successful and unsuccessful companies involved regression toward the mean. In any given year, the most successful companies are likely to have had more good luck than bad and to have done well not only relative to other firms, but also relative to their own long-run profitability. The opposite is true of the least successful companies. This is why the subsequent performance of the top and bottom companies is usually closer to the average company. At the same time, their places at the extremes are taken by other companies experiencing fortune or misfortune. These fluctuations do not mean that all companies will soon be mediocre. As Hotelling put it, Secrist "really prove[d] nothing more than that the ratios in question have a tendency to wander about."

REGRESSION IN THE STOCK MARKET

In *Against the Gods*, a bestselling, prize-winning book, Peter Bernstein wrote:

> The track records of professional investment managers are also subject to regression to the mean. There is a strong probability that the hot manager of today will be the cold manager of tomorrow, or at least the day after tomorrow, and vice versa. . . . [T]he wisest strategy is to dismiss the manager with the best track record and to transfer one's assets to the manager who has been doing the worst; this strategy is no different from selling stocks that have risen the furthest and buying stocks that have fallen furthest.

Bernstein is wise, but this is not wisdom. The idea that the best will be worst and the worst will be best is the gambler's fallacy that good luck makes bad luck more likely. It is false and it is not regression to the mean. Regression occurs because the managers with the best track records probably benefited from good luck and are consequently not as far above average in ability as they seem. If there is any skill to stock picking, the person with the best track record can be expected to outperform the person with the worst record, but not by as much next year as last year. If stock picking is all luck, you may as well pick managers randomly—or save money by not using a manager at all—but there is no reason to choose the worst manager.

SHRUNKEN EARNINGS PREDICTIONS ARE BETTER PREDICTIONS

There is regression to the mean in stocks, as well as managers. A natural tendency in the stock market, where investors hope to invest in the next IBM, Walmart, or Google, is to see a year or two of rapidly increasing earnings and assume many years of similar rapid growth. Regression teaches us that a company with earnings up by 20 percent this year (or over the past few years) is more likely to have experienced good luck than bad luck and, most likely, will regress toward the mean in the future, disappointing overly optimistic investors.

Something very similar is true of predicted earnings. The most optimistic predictions are more likely to be overly optimistic than to be excessively pessimistic, so the companies with the most optimistic forecasts probably won't do as well as predicted.

Two colleagues and I investigated this reasoning. Regression relates to relative values. Our guiding principle was that firms whose growth rates are predicted to be far from the mean will probably have growth rates closer to the mean. So, we adjusted the analysts' forecasts by shrinking them toward the average forecast for all companies. Our adjusted forecasts were more accurate than the analysts' forecasts 70 percent of the time, which is better than a 2-to-1 margin.

We didn't use spreadsheets to predict market share, revenue, expenses, and the like. We didn't even look at the company names. We just downloaded the forecast earnings growth rates and shrunk them toward the overall mean, using a marvelous statistical formula known as Kelley's equation, and we out-predicted the professional predictors.

If investors are paying attention to these professional analysts (or making similar predictions themselves), stock prices are likely to be too high for companies with optimistic forecasts and too low for those with pessimistic forecasts—mistakes that will be corrected when earnings regress to the mean. If this conjecture is correct, stocks with relatively pessimistic earnings predictions may outperform stocks with relatively optimistic predictions.

Five portfolios were formed each year based on the analysts' predicted earning growth for the current fiscal year. The most optimistic portfolio consisted of the 20 percent of the stocks with the highest predicted growth. The most pessimistic portfolio contained the 20 percent with the lowest predicted growth. The stock returns were then calculated for each portfolio over the next twelve months. A similar procedure was used for the year-ahead earnings forecasts, but the stock returns were calculated over the next twenty-four months.

Table 9-1 shows the results. The pessimistic portfolios trounced the optimistic portfolios. It is hard to imagine that this trouncing reflects some kind of risk premium. The pessimistic portfolios were actually safer.

The most plausible explanation is that the market's insufficient appreciation of regression to the mean is leaving $100 bills on the sidewalk.

TABLE 9-1. Five portfolio returns, percent

	Most Optimistic	Optimistic	Middle Group	Pessimistic	Most Pessimistic
Current-year Average return	11	15	15	16	18
Std. deviation	5.3	4.3	3.9	3.5	4.4
Year-ahead Average return	23	27	32	35	37
Std. deviation	5.4	4.7	4.2	3.9	3.8

DOW DELETIONS

The Dow Jones Industrial Average is an average of the prices of thirty blue-chip stocks that represent the most prominent companies in the United States. An Averages Committee periodically changes the stocks in the Dow, sometimes because a firm merges with another company or is taken over by another company. More often, though, a company has some tough years and is no longer considered to be a blue-chip stock. Such fallen companies are replaced by more successful companies; for example, a thriving Home Depot replaced a struggling Sears in 1999.

When a faltering company is replaced by a flourishing company, which stock do you think does better subsequently—the stock going into the Dow or the stock going out? If you take regression into account, the stock booted out of the Dow probably will do better than the stock that replaces it.

This is counterintuitive because it is tempting to confuse a great company with a great stock. LeanMean may have a long history of strong, stable profits. But is it a good investment? The answer depends on the stock's price. Is it an attractive investment at $10 a share? $100? $1,000? There are prices at which the stock is too expensive. There are prices at which the stock is cheap. No matter how good the company, value investors need to know the stock's price before deciding whether it is an attractive investment.

Regarding Dow additions and deletions, the question for value investors is not whether the companies going into the Dow are doing better than the companies they are replacing, but which stocks are better investments. The stocks going into and out of the Dow are all familiar companies that are closely watched by thousands of investors. In 1999, investors were well aware of the fact that Home Depot was doing great and Sears was doing poorly. Their stock prices surely reflected this knowledge. That's why Home Depot's stock was up 50 percent, while Sears was down 50 percent.

However, the regression argument suggests that the companies taken out of the Dow are generally not in as dire straits as their recent performance suggests and that the companies replacing them are generally not as stellar as they appear. If so, stock prices will often be unreasonably low for the stocks going out and undeservedly high for the stocks going in. When a company that was doing poorly regresses to the mean, its stock price will rise. When a company that was doing spectacularly regresses to the mean, its price will fall. This argument suggests that stocks deleted from the Dow will generally outperform stocks added to the Dow.

Sears was bought by Kmart in 2005, five-and-a-half years after it was kicked out of the Dow. If you bought Sears stock just after it was deleted from the Dow, your total return until its acquisition by Kmart would have been 103 percent. Over the same five-and-a-half-year period, an investment in Home Depot, the stock that replaced Sears, would have lost 22 percent. The S&P 500 index of stock prices during this period had a return of −14 percent. Sears had an above-average return after it left the Dow, while Home Depot had a below-average return after it entered the Dow. (The Kmart-Sears combination has been ugly, but that's another story.)

Is this comparison of Sears and Home Depot an isolated incident or part of a systematic pattern of Dow deletions outperforming

Dow additions? There were actually four substitutions in 1999. Home Depot, Microsoft, Intel, and SBC replaced Sears, Goodyear Tire, Union Carbide, and Chevron. Home Depot, Microsoft, Intel, and SBC are all great companies, but all four stocks did poorly over the next decade.

Suppose that on the day the four substitutions were made, November 1, 1999, you had invested $25,000 in each of the four stocks added to the Dow, for a total investment of $100,000. This is your Addition Portfolio. You also formed a Deletion Portfolio by investing $25,000 in each of the stocks deleted from the Dow.

After ten years, the S&P 500 was down 23 percent. The Addition Portfolio did even worse, down 34 percent. The Deletion Portfolio, in contrast, was up 64 percent.

Maybe 1999 was an unusual year and substitutions made in other years turned out differently? Nope. In 2006 I did a study with two of my students of all fifty changes in the Dow back to October 1, 1928, when the Dow 30-stock average began; we found that deleted stocks did better than the stocks that replaced them in thirty-two cases and did worse in eighteen cases. A portfolio of deleted stocks beat a portfolio of added stocks by about 4 percent a year, which is a huge difference compounded over seventy-eight years. A $100,000 portfolio of added stocks would have grown to $160 million by 2006; a $100,000 portfolio of deleted stocks would have grown to $3.3 billion. The companies doing so poorly that they were booted out of the Dow have been better investments than the darlings that replaced them.

Our findings contradict the efficient market hypothesis since changes in the composition of the Dow are widely reported and well known. Once again, it seems that the market's neglect of regression is leaving $100 bills on the sidewalk.

WOULD A STOCK BY ANY OTHER TICKER
SMELL AS SWEET?

Several companies have shunned the traditional name-abbreviation convention and chosen ticker symbols that are memorable for their cheeky cleverness. Southwest Airlines' choice of LUV as its ticker symbol was related to its efforts to brand itself as an airline "built on love." Southwest is based at Dallas Love Field and has an open-seating policy that reportedly can lead to romance between strangers who sit next to each other. Its onboard snacks were originally called "love bites" and its drinks "love potions," and a Southwest spokesman boasted about the number of romances that started on Southwest flights: "At times, we feel that we are the love brokers of the sky."

Perhaps a clever ticker symbol is an indicator that a firm's managers are smart and creative, with a sense of humor. On the other hand, wary investors may interpret a clever symbol as a silly marketing ploy by a company that feels it must resort to gimmicks to attract investor attention. Perhaps a clever symbol is a signal of desperation rather than intelligence.

Another possibility is that clever ticker symbols matter because they are memorable. There is considerable evidence that human judgments are shaped by how easily information is processed and remembered:

1. Objects shown for longer periods of time or with greater background contrast are rated more favorably.

2. Statements like "Osorno is in Chile" are more likely to be judged true if written in colors that are easier to read.

3. Aphorisms that rhyme are more likely to be judged true; for example, "Woes unite foes" versus "Woes unite enemies."

These arguments suggest that ticker symbols that are easily processed and recalled might be rated favorably. For example, an investor might look at pet-related companies and come across VCA Antech, which operates a network of animal hospitals and diagnostic laboratories. A ticker symbol VCAA might pass unnoticed. But the actual ticker symbol, WOOF, is memorable. Perhaps a few days, weeks, or months later, this investor decides to invest in a pet-related company and remembers the symbol WOOF. (In a weird coincidence, it was a former student of mine who thought up the ticker WOOF.)

Two students and I looked at whether ticker symbols matter. Because cleverness is in the eye of the beholder, we used a survey to identify ticker symbols that people consider witty. First, we sifted through 33,000 ticker symbols for past and present companies, looking for ticker symbols that might be considered noteworthy. Ninety-three percent of our selections coincided. We merged the lists and discarded ticker symbols that were simply an abbreviation of the company's name (BEAR for Bear Automotive Service Equipment and GLAD for Gladstone Capital) and kept symbols that showed ingenuity (GRRR for Lion Country Safari parks and MOO for United Stockyards).

We distributed 100 surveys with our culled list of 358 ticker symbols, the company names, and a brief description of each company's business. We intentionally excluded seasoned investment professionals whose choices might have been influenced by the investment performance of the companies on the list.

For each trading day from the beginning of 1984 (when clever ticker symbols started becoming popular) to the end of 2005, we calculated the daily return for a portfolio of the clever-ticker stocks that received the most votes in our survey. Figure 9-6 shows that the clever-ticker portfolio lagged behind the market portfolio slightly until 1993 and then spurted ahead. Overall, the compounded annual returns were 24 percent for the clever-ticker portfolio and 12 percent for the market portfolio.

FIGURE 9-6. Clever-ticker portfolio relative to market

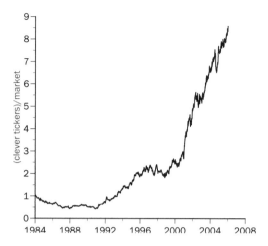

The market-beating performance was not because the clever-ticker stocks were concentrated in one industry. Our eighty-two clever-ticker companies span thirty-one of the eighty-one industry categories used by the U.S. government, with the highest concentration being eight companies in eating and drinking places, of which four beat the market and four did not. Nor was it due to the extraordinary performance of a small number of clever-ticker stocks: 65 percent of the clever-ticker stocks beat the market.

We do not know why these stocks did so well. Perhaps a clever ticker is a useful barometer of the managers' ability, which reveals itself over time as the firm repeatedly exceeds investors' expectations. Or perhaps a clever ticker matters because it is memorable and has a subtle but persistent influence on investors who buy the stock. Either way, it's an unexpected $100 bill on the sidewalk.

IF HUMANS AREN'T AS SMART AS COMPUTERS

If humans are, well, human with human emotions, frailties, and inconsistencies, should we turn our investment decisions over to computers? Computers don't have emotions, and well-written software doesn't have inconsistencies. True enough, but computers don't have common sense, either. Computers can identify statistical patterns but cannot gauge whether there is a logical basis for the discovered patterns.

When a statistical correlation between gold and silver prices was discovered in the 1980s, how could a computer possibly discern whether there was a sensible basis for this statistical correlation? In the 1990s, Long-Term Capital Management was bankrupted by a number of bets on correlations that did not have a persuasive explanation; for example, relationships among various French and German interest rates. A manager later lamented that "we had academics who came in with no trading experience and they started modeling away. Their trades might look good given the assumptions they made, but they often did not pass a simple smell test."

Humans do make mistakes, leaving profitable opportunities for others, but humans also have the potential to recognize those mistakes and to avoid being seduced by patterns that lead computers astray.

Part II will give several detailed examples of how value investors can use the principles discussed in Part I to be successful investors.

VALUE INVESTING
APPLIED

THE RIGHT ATTITUDE

Human behavior flows from three main sources:
desire, emotion, and knowledge.

—PLATO

Some people think you can't go wrong buying stocks, at least in the long run. Others think that stocks are like a trip to Vegas, where most people return home with less money than they came with. Both are wrong. The stock market is more nuanced than these simplistic caricatures. Historically, investors have, on average, made a lot of money, but there is no guarantee how future investors will do.

Table 10-1 shows the average annual returns from short-term Treasury bills, long-term Treasury bonds, and the stocks included in the S&P 500 index. The standard deviation is a measure of the volatility of the annual returns about the historical average. The table uses a peculiar starting year (1926) simply because that's as far back as these data go.

TABLE 10-1. Annual returns 1926–2015, percent

	Treasury Bills	Treasury Bonds	Stocks
Average annual return	4	6	12
Standard deviation	3	10	20

The average annual return on the stocks in the S&P 500 has been 12 percent, which is not only positive but much higher than the average returns from Treasury bills or bonds. An investment of $10,000 is worth $931,000 after forty years if it earns a 12 percent annual return, but only worth $103,000 with a 6 percent return.

Stocks have also been volatile, with an annual standard deviation twice that of Treasury bonds. Figure 10-1 confirms visually what the standard deviation tells us numerically—the stock market fluctuates a lot from year to year. Stock returns also seem random in that there is no evident pattern.

FIGURE 10-1. Annual returns from S&P 500 stocks since 1926

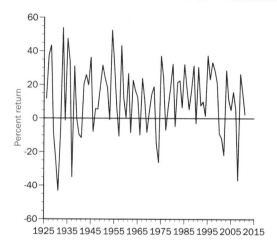

As Figure 10-1 shows, the stock market often rises or falls more than 20 percent in a year. Stock prices also fluctuate wildly month to month, week to week, and even daily. On October 19, 1987, stock prices fell by more than 20 percent in a single day, sending many investors to the sidelines, convinced that the stock market is too risky. That was a costly overreaction. The market bounced back and investors who have been invested in stocks since October 19, 1987, have done *much* better than have those who left the market.

The S&P 500 also conceals the turbulence in individual stocks. A stock can double or be worthless in minutes.

A financial author once wrote:

> An exhaustive computer survey, conducted a few years ago at the University of Chicago, showed that the average annual profit (before taxes) on any New York Stock Exchange investment held for one month or longer—regardless of what the company was, when the shares were purchased or when they were sold—was 9.3 percent.

The 9.3 number would now be 12 percent, but that's not the biggest problem with this claim. The stock market doesn't go straight up and all stocks don't do equally well. The return depends on the stock and when it is bought and sold.

Figure 10-2 shows the daily prices of two popular stocks, Apple and Washington Mutual Saving Bank (commonly known as WaMu) between 1983 and 2003. In March 1983, WaMu was $14 a share and Apple was $42. The zig-zags in Figure 10-2 show that both stocks fluctuated greatly over the next twenty years, with Apple going above $140 in 2000 and below $20 in 2003. Meanwhile, WaMu was above $40 in 2003, triple its value twenty years earlier.

FIGURE 10-2. A tale of two stocks

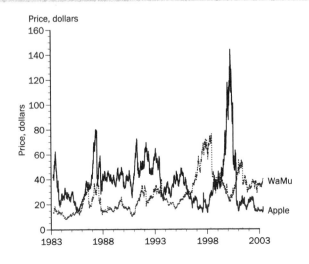

WaMu was on its way to becoming the nation's largest saving and loan association. In 2003 WaMu's CEO boasted:

> We hope to do to this industry what Wal-Mart did to theirs, Starbucks did to theirs, Costco did to theirs and Lowe's-Home Depot did to their industry. And I think if we've done our job, five years from now you're not going to call us a bank.

He was right. Five years later, people didn't call WaMu a bank. They called it bankrupt. In fact, the biggest bank bankruptcy ever.

WaMu's growth was fueled by loans to people who other banks considered too risky, and its downfall came from losses on these sub-prime loans and then a run on the bank as nervous depositors withdrew $16.7 billion over a ten-day period. The federal government took control of WaMu and sold what was left of the wreckage to JPMorgan Chase for $1.9 billion.

Meanwhile, Figure 10-3 shows that Apple jumped and slumped, hitting $190 in 2008 and falling below $80 in 2009. Apple topped $700 in September 2012 and dropped below $400 seven months later. Wheee! (Apple did a 7-for-1 stock split in January 2014 and traded for around $100 a share in 2016, which is equivalent to $700 before the split.)

FIGURE 10-3. A tale of two stocks, part 2

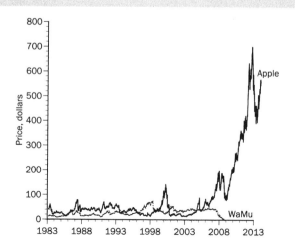

The stock market can be like riding a roller coaster, sometimes ex-hilarating, other times terrifying. Some investors find these roller-coaster rides so gut wrenching that they avoid stocks altogether. I know a woman who keeps her money in a safe in her kitchen. She doesn't want to worry about the stock market crashing, and she doesn't feel that money is real unless she can hold it in her hands. Personally, paper money doesn't seem all that real to me.

For other investors, uncertainty is the main attraction. Investing is a game—much like poker—that blends skill and luck, and it can be played against professionals with the results reported in the daily newspaper and on the internet. It is a game worth playing, and it is a game worth winning.

MUTUAL FUNDS

Many investors buy stocks through mutual funds. Mutual funds issue shares, like other corporations, but instead of using the share-holders' money to build factories and office buildings, they buy stocks and bonds. There are thousands of mutual funds catering to the specialized and varied tastes of investors. There is a fund for baptized Lutherans, one for airline pilots, and another for cemetery owners. One fund buys only aviation stocks; another buys stock in gold-mining companies. One fund invests in Australian securities; one in Ohio businesses. Others do not invest in alcohol, tobacco, gambling, or munitions stocks. The Vice Fund does the opposite, specializing in sinful industries.

Many people are drawn to mutual funds by their advertised ex-pertise, reasoning that just as they pay a doctor for medical services and a lawyer for legal assistance, so they should pay a professional for investment management. They choose a fund with an outstand-ing record and if this fund's subsequent performance is disappoint-ing, they switch to another fund that has been more successful.

Management fees depend on the number of assets managed, and

the top-performing funds are swamped by investors looking to share in the success. This investor chase for successful funds encourages funds to trade feverishly, looking for the quick profits that will lure more investors (and management fees).

Like his mentor, Benjamin Graham, Warren Buffett has been critical of the hyperkinetic activity of institutional investors who speculate about short-term price fluctuations instead of focusing on long-term investment values. In a Berkshire annual report, Buffett wrote that "the term 'institutional investor' is becoming one of those self-contradictions called an oxymoron, comparable to 'jumbo shrimp,' 'lady mud wrestler' and 'inexpensive lawyer.'" I would add that "value investor" is not an oxymoron, and that value investors should be leery of hyperactive mutual funds.

LOAD CHARGES AND OTHER FEES

Mutual funds can be bought through fund salespeople, insurance agents, stockbrokers, or directly from the fund itself. No matter which route is used, the fund may levy a sales charge, called a *load fee*. For a "full load" fund, the load is generally between 5 percent and 8.5 percent, split between the salesperson and the fund itself. Funds that sell directly to investors are generally "low loads," with a fee of 3 percent or less, all of which goes to the fund. Funds that don't charge load fees are called no-loads.

In addition, SEC Rule 12b-1 allows mutual funds to charge an annual fee—often, one percent or more—to cover marketing expenses (including sales commissions). To discourage early redemptions, funds with substantial 12b-1 fees may impose early redemption fees to ensure that investors either pay several years of 12b-1 fees or a substantial redemption fee. David Swensen, Yale's extraordinary portfolio manager, has said, "Shame on the SEC for allowing 12b-1 fees, shame on the directors for approving them, and shame on the mutual funds for assessing them."

How do they get away with it? It's our fault. The Security and Exchange Commission requires mutual funds to show all of their charges in a standard table in the prospectus, including estimates of how these fees affect a $1,000 investment over periods of one to ten years. Unfortunately, the table is not mandatory reading. A former director of the SEC's investment management division estimated that fewer than 10 percent of mutual fund investors ever open the prospectus.

Many mutual fund salespeople capitalize on short-term froth in the stock market by focusing their sales pitch on recently successful funds, giving the misleading impression that future investors are assured of a similarly spectacular performance. We fall for their babble because our dreams of easy riches make us gullible. Mutual fund families play this game, too, promoting funds that have had recent successes and not mentioning disappointments. Many in the industry suspect that some fund families have hundreds of disparate funds and keep creating new funds to ensure that they will have successes that can be promoted heavily.

Mutual funds have considerable latitude in reporting past results and some of them play sneaky games. For example, if two funds merge, the manager can choose which of the two performance records to attribute to the combined fund. For instance, if Fund A has earned 10 percent a year and Fund B has lost 10 percent, the manager can merge B into A and continue to report the fund's return as 10 percent a year. John Bogle, founder of the Vanguard Group, strongly criticized this practice, observing sarcastically that "we are able to get rid of our poor performing funds by merging them into sister funds with lustrous records, and the record of the 'turkey' simply vanishes into thin air." In 1993 Lipper Analytical Services reported that the annual return for diversified U.S. stock funds that stayed in business for the entire twenty-year period from 1973 to 1992 was 11.8 percent, compared to 11.4 percent for the S&P 500. However, 40 percent of the funds in business in the 1970s had disappeared by 1992. When the performance of these vanished funds is taken into account, the annual return for all diversified stock funds over this period dropped by more than a percentage point, to 10.5 percent.

While advertisements may be misleading and salespeople deceptive, the Securities and Exchange Commission requires a more complete and accurate disclosure in a mutual fund's prospectus. One of the best ways to see through the hype is to read it carefully. Not nearly enough people do.

DO MUTUAL FUNDS BEAT THE MARKET?

Study after study has found that, *before* expenses, mutual funds do as well, on average, as monkeys throwing darts. After expenses, two out of three funds do worse than the market. Professionally managed mutual funds charge an unconscionable amount for this inferior performance. As David Swensen wrote, "Overwhelmingly, mutual funds extract enormous sums from investors in exchange for providing a shocking disservice."

No problem. Even if two-thirds of the funds do worse than the market, just invest in the one-third that beat the market. Right? As one market observer put it, "The problem of picking a mutual fund seems to be simplicity itself: The investor should select whichever fund will give him the largest percentage return, year after year." Sure enough, investors pour money into recently successful mutual funds, paying big load fees in the belief that past performance ensures future success.

Unfortunately, funds with above-average records in the past are no more likely to do well in the future than are funds with below-average records. This is why the president of Morningstar, an independent mutual fund rating service, once said that rating mutual funds on their annual performance was "the dumbest thing imaginable." Nonetheless, they started doing just that the next year. There is always a market for dumb things.

INDEX FUNDS

Mutual funds are not the only professionally managed portfolios whose performance has been disappointing. Money managers as a whole underperform the market after management fees and other expenses, and there is little consistency in their performance— knowing which managers have done well in the past is little help in predicting which will do well in the future. As this evidence accumu- lated in the late 1960s, many realized that if most professionals do worse than the market indexes, the way to beat most investment professionals is to buy the indexes and keep costs down. Instead of trying to pick stocks that might beat a market index, an index fund buys the stocks in the index.

In 1971 Wells Fargo Investment Advisors started an index fund for pension funds and other institutional investors and soon grew to become one of the largest single investors in the stock market; its annual management fees are as low as 0.05 percent. John Bogle wrote his senior thesis at Princeton on the failure of mutual funds to beat the S&P 500 and concluded that the way to beat most mutual funds was to buy the stocks in the S&P 500. Bogle founded Van- guard in 1975 and, a year later, introduced the first index fund open to small investors. Vanguard now has more than 200 funds managing more than $2 trillion in assets. Its index funds routinely beat two- thirds of the managed funds.

Many reputable firms offer index funds that essentially own all the stocks in a stock market index. One of the most popular is the Vanguard 500 Index Fund, which contains the 500 stocks in the S&P 500. Because Vanguard does not pay people to pick stocks, the expenses are tiny—about 0.16 percent annually, or $16 on a $10,000 investment. That's less than the cost of making one trade a year; for example, selling Amazon to buy Google.

For an even broader portfolio, the iShares Core S&P Total U.S. Stock Market ETF covers 90 percent of all U.S. stocks, with an ex- pense ratio of 0.03 percent, and the Vanguard Total World Stock holds more than 98 percent of all the stocks traded anywhere in the world, with annual expenses of 0.17 percent.

Index portfolios do not beat the market. They are the market. But they won't do worse than the market, either, and that is comforting for some investors.

Many wise, seasoned, and admired investors—including Dave Swensen and Burton Malkiel—recommend investing in index funds. Even Warren Buffett, one of the gods of value investors, wrote in his 2013 Letter to Berkshire Shareholders that he wants the money he leaves to his heirs to be invested in an index fund:

> My advice to the trustee couldn't be more simple: Put 10% of the cash in short-term government bonds and 90% in a very low-cost S&P 500 index fund. (I suggest Vanguard's.) I believe the trust's long-term results from this policy will be superior to those attained by most investors—whether pension funds, institutions or individuals—who employ high-fee managers.

Oddly enough, Buffett did not recommend investing in his own company, Berkshire.

John Bogle's core argument is correct:

> In the stock market, some investors do better and some worse, but their aggregate returns equal the market's returns, minus the costs of investing. After all, they are the market. So if a fund matches the market's gross return and does so at a cost much lower than the average fund, it will always beat the average fund over time.

Bogle is comparing index funds to other mutual funds, but the same argument applies to all investing. If some investors index the market, the average return (before expenses) for all other investors must equal the index. If the index investors have lower fees and other expenses, they will, on average, do better than investors who do not index.

A reasonable response to the evidence that stock prices are hard to predict and that human emotions can lead us astray is to be passive. Instead of trying to pick the best stocks or the best time to buy stocks, buy all stocks and hold them all the time. Indexing is easy and cheap, and can shelter us from our emotions run amok.

Suppose, however, that the performance of those who do not index is not utterly and completely random. Suppose that there is a strategy—value investing—that is successful but not widely followed, perhaps because it is hard to control desire and emotion, two of Plato's three pillars of human behavior. If so, while the average investor gets an average result, those who have the discipline to be value investors do better than other investors. If so, they must do better than the average investor and may do better than indexing.

There is truth and wisdom in the advice that ordinary investors should park their money in an index fund. Unchecked human emotions can lead us to trade too much, to trust hot tips, to chase trends, to be caught up in speculative bubbles and fearful panics. Indexing protects us from ourselves. Investors who cannot control their desires and emotions should put their savings in a low-cost index fund (I love Vanguard, too) and leave it alone. They will sleep better and do better than they would being led around by desire and emotion.

Yes, indexing protects us from human foibles and follies that can lead us into making bad investment decisions. On the other hand, if we recognize these human imperfections and are not seduced by them, we may be able to take advantage of the fact that human errors and animal spirits create potentially profitable opportunities. That is the essence of value investing. Wishful thinking, fads, trend chasing, fear, greed, and other human emotions can cause Mr. Market's prices to surge above or collapse below intrinsic values, allowing value investors to buy stocks cheaply and sell stocks profitably.

Those investors who can be true value investors, putting aside wishful thinking, greed, fear, and other destructive human tendencies, can do better than indexing.

11

KISS

*It seems that perfection is reached not when there is nothing left
to add, but when there is nothing left to take away.*
—Antoine de Saint-Exupéry

Oddly enough, my experience as a value investor has taught me to keep it simple, stupid (KISS). I have always been a full-time professor—teaching, doing research, writing books, spending time with my spouse, raising six kids. I don't spend eight hours a day studying stocks or following the stock market. Most days, I don't even look at stock prices.

Keynes was a master investor, as well as a master economist, and he reportedly made his investment decisions while eating breakfast in bed, though his approach was the exact opposite of value investing. In the wonderful Chapter 12 of his treatise *The General Theory of Employment, Interest, and Money*, which revolutionized economics, Keynes argued that it is easier to anticipate changes in investor psychology than it is to estimate the intrinsic value of stocks. He likened buying and selling stocks to childhood games:

> It is, so to speak, a game of Snap, of Old Maid, of Musical Chairs—a pastime in which he is victor who says Snap neither too soon nor too late, who passes the Old Maid to his neighbour before the game is over, who secures a chair for himself when the music stops. These games can be

played with zest and enjoyment, though all the players know that it is the Old Maid which is circulating, or that when the music stops some of the players will find themselves unseated.

Keynes explained how the key to winning such games is to understand and anticipate one's opponents:

> Professional investment may be likened to those newspaper competitions in which the competitors have to pick out the six prettiest faces from a hundred photographs, the prize being awarded to the competitor whose choice most nearly corresponds to the average preferences of the competitors as a whole; so that each competitor has to pick, not those faces which he himself finds prettiest, but those which he thinks likeliest to catch the fancy of the other competitors, all of whom are looking at the problem from the same point of view. It is not a case of choosing those which, to the best of one's judgment, are really the prettiest, nor even those which average opinion genuinely thinks the prettiest. We have reached the third degree where we devote our intelligences to anticipating what average opinion expects the average opinion to be. And there are some, I believe, who practise the fourth, fifth and higher degrees.

This may have been easy for Keynes, but not for me! I share Keynes's enthusiasm for investing in one's spare time, but I am more comfortable buying stocks that are attractively priced than I am trying to guess which stocks are going in or out of favor. I play games with my children, but not with my investments.

When I have money to invest, I look at well-managed companies (as gauged, for example, by *Fortune*'s annual list of the most admired companies) that have large dividends and/or earnings relative to their stock price. I am wary of stocks whose prices have increased dramatically and tempted by stocks whose prices have fallen, figuring that I am more likely to find bargains among stocks the market hates than among stocks the market loves.

I buy what I like using an inexpensive online broker and forget about it. I don't waste time checking stock prices every day (or worse, every hour or minute). I do notice (how can one not notice?) if there is a stock market crash. I do notice if bubbly things are happening (like the *Wall Street Journal* article about Bill's Barbershop). That's about it.

Here are a few other KISS rules of thumb.

DISCOUNT BROKERS

Stocks can be bought and sold using full-service brokers such as Morgan Stanley, UBS, Merrill Lynch, Edward Jones, and Raymond James that compile mountains of data, prepare in-depth analyses, and make buy/sell recommendations. Investors have individual account executives (please don't call them "brokers") who give advice based on the firm's research. Many investors appreciate the individual attention and comfort of having someone help them make decisions, but they pay for it with high fees. In addition, account executives have a fundamental conflict of interest since the more their customers trade, the more revenue is generated for the brokerage firm.

Discount brokerage firms, in contrast, do little more than answer the phone, give current prices, and record trades. Cheapest of all are trades made over the internet without the assistance of account executives or telephone operators. Commissions are lower because the firm does not do research or offer advice and doesn't need as many employees to deal with customers. Many discount brokers give investors free internet access to enough information to make sensible investment decisions.

If you are going to buy and sell stocks yourself, choose a firm that offers low-cost online trading, such as Ameritrade, Charles Schwab, eTrade, Fidelity, Merrill Edge, or Vanguard, and that gives you free access to useful research. If you have a large portfolio, you might want to go with more than one broker, because the Securities Investor Protection Corporation (SIPC) only insures brokerage accounts up to $500,000 if a broker goes bust.

BUYING ON MARGIN

Buying stock with money borrowed from a brokerage firm is called *buying on margin*, where the margin is the money the stockholder puts up. If you buy 200 shares of ZYX stock for $50 a share (a total cost of $10,000), a brokerage firm with a 60 percent margin requirement will require you to put up at least $6,000 (and loan you the remainder). The brokerage firm charges you interest on this loan, but, as with any leveraged investment, you come out ahead if the rate of return on your stock exceeds the interest rate on your loan.

If your equity—the market value of your stock minus your current loan balance—falls below a specified maintenance margin, you will get a margin call from your broker requesting additional funds. The Fed requires a 25 percent maintenance margin, but many brokers use a more conservative 30 to 40 percent.

I've never bought stock on margin.

SHORT SALES

If you think a stock's price is heading downward, you can sell shares you don't own by selling stock that your broker borrows from another investor. This is called a *short sale*, and it must be covered at some point by buying stock to replace the borrowed stock. Short sellers try to follow the age-old advice to buy low and sell high, but they sell first and buy later.

Short sellers do not receive the proceeds from the short sale; the brokerage firm holds on to it and earns some interest for itself. Not only that, brokers require short sellers to put up margin, perhaps 50 percent, and then charge interest on the remaining fraction. Short sellers pay in-and-out commissions, lose the interest they could be earning on their margin, pay interest on the rest, and pay dividends on the underlying stock—seemingly expensive penalties for being a pessimist.

I've never sold stock short.

CHURNING IS DANGEROUS TO YOUR WEALTH

When first starting out, brokers try to build a client base by making cold calls to people who have been identified as potential customers, often as a result of advertisements offering free, no-obligation financial reports. Those who respond to the ad receive follow-up phone calls from brokers hoping to find customers. These cold calls are called "dialing for dollars" because the only way a broker can make money is by clients making trades.

Brokers have a persuasive incentive to recommend active portfolio management ("account upgrading" is the euphemism, churning the goal)—sell Wells Fargo to buy Chase; then sell Chase to buy Bank of America; then sell Bank of America to buy Wells Fargo; and on and on. Brokers are like sharks—they need movement to survive.

Most brokers are conscientious professionals who know that excessive expenses and dismal performance will alienate customers. As with any profession, however, some brokers are unscrupulous and, like vicious sharks, churn their clients' accounts mercilessly.

A front-page story in the *Los Angeles Times* that detailed some stockbroker abuses was subtitled "Beware, Unwary." In one case, a seventy-year-old retired radio actress saw her $550,000 nest egg shrink to $67,000 while thousands of pointless trades generated $310,000 in commissions. When she asked her broker about the blizzard of trade confirmation slips mailed to her, she says he told her to "throw them away." This is like this old joke: "How do you make a small fortune in the stock market? Start with a large fortune."

Most broker-client relationships are not horror stories, but the nightmares do warn that broker and customer objectives do not always coincide.

I avoid brokers by using online brokerage firms.

TRADING COSTS

Brokerage fees are either a percentage or a flat fee, or a combination of the two. For small trades, the commission can be staggering; for example, most brokerage firms have a minimum commission of, say, $9.99 even if you just buy one share of a $5 stock. As a percentage of the cost, brokerage fees drop for larger trades, but these savings may be offset by the effect of the transaction on the market price since it may take a significant price increase to find a seller and a substantial decrease to find a buyer. If you sell one stock to buy another, you have to pay two transaction costs. At, say, one percent round-trip, active trading becomes pretty expensive. Trading once a year, the stock you buy has to have a 2 percent higher annual return than the stock you sell to cover the cost of the trade. This differential rises to 24 percentage points if you trade every month. Please don't trade every month and, God forbid, don't day-trade.

DEFERRING GAINS AND
HARVESTING LOSSES

It is generally a bad idea to jump in and out of stocks—sell Apple to buy Google; then sell Google to buy Amazon; then sell Amazon to buy Apple; and on and on. One problem is the endless brokerage costs. Another is the taxes that must be paid on capital gains. If you own stocks, bonds, or other assets that have increased in value, these capital gains are taxable, but you don't pay the tax until you realize the gain by selling the asset. If, for instance, you buy 1,000 shares of stock for $20 a share and it rises to $30, you do not have to pay a tax on the $10,000 capital gain unless you sell. All realized capital gains are taxable, and up to $3,000 ($1,500 if married, filing separately) of realized losses can be used to reduce taxable income. Another wrinkle is that the capital gains tax rate is lower on long-term holdings (more than a year). The exact tax depends on multiple comparisons of short-term and long-term gains and losses, but we don't need to go into those details here.

DEFERRING GAINS

The lower tax rate on long-term gains provides an obvious incentive to defer the realization of gains, at least until they become lightly taxed long-term gains. Even after a year, there are persistent benefits from postponing taxes in order to continue earning dividends and capital gains on the deferred taxes.

In our example, suppose that you realize your $10,000 gain by selling. If it is a short-term capital gain and you are in a 28 percent tax bracket, you must pay the government $2,800, leaving only $17,200 to put back in the market. If you don't sell, you can continue earning dividends and capital gains on the full $20,000. In essence, the Internal Revenue Service (IRS) has loaned you your $2,800 tax liability, and the only "interest" you pay on this loan is taxes on the extra dividends and capital gains. Even better, there is no capital gains tax at all if the stock is held until your death, since your heirs do not pay taxes on capital gains that occurred before they receive their inheritance. No bank will loan you money at such favorable terms.

Table 11-1 shows some illustrative calculations for a portfolio of ten stocks that is initially worth $100,000. Every year for thirty years, the portfolio earns 5 percent dividends and 5 percent capital gains, a total return of 10 percent. The buy-and-hold strategy is to never sell, so the only taxes paid are 15 percent taxes on the dividends. The "annual trader" strategy is to turn the portfolio over every year, holding each year's portfolio just long enough to qualify for a long-term capital gains tax of 15 percent. The "active trader" strategy is to turn the portfolio over four times a year, with the capital gains taxed at a 28 percent rate.

One set of calculations assumes a $10 commission on each transaction; the other calculations assume no trading commissions in order to focus on the benefits of postponing capital gains taxes.

Turnover deflates performance dramatically, which illustrates the old saying, "The broker made money, the IRS made money, and two out of three ain't bad!" In the short run, the advantage of a buy-and-hold strategy is due mostly to the avoidance of brokerage fees; in the long run, the postponement of capital gains taxes becomes more important.

TABLE 11-1. Wealth for buy-and-hold vs. portfolio turnover

	10 Years	20 Years	30 Years
Buy and Hold	$242,222	$586,717	$1,421,161
Annual Trader, no cost	$226,098	$511,205	$1,155,825
Active Trader, no cost	$223,171	$501,529	$1,130,040
Annual Trader, $10/trade	$212,913	$453,318	$965,171
Active Trader, $10/trade	$201,406	$417,311	$877,001

HARVESTING LOSSES

One persuasive reason for selling a stock is to realize capital losses and get a tax credit. You can't make money by losing money; but once a loss has occurred, it can be profitable to realize the loss so that the tax credit can be invested. Suppose that the value of the

1,000 shares you bought for $20,000 falls to $15,000. If you realize your $5,000 loss by selling, you can deduct $3,000 from your current taxable income and carry forward $2,000 to be deducted from future income. In a 28 percent bracket, your $3,000 loss reduces your taxes by $840, which you can invest. Instead of having $15,000 invested, you will have $15,840 earning dividends and (you hope) capital gains.

A strategy of deferring gains and harvesting losses is very simple and appealing, effectively $100 bills from the IRS.

Every fall, I look at my portfolio to see if any prices are substantially lower than the prices I paid and, if so, I consider reaping the tax benefits from realizing capital losses.

TRACKING YOUR PERFORMANCE

Sixteen women in Beardstown, Illinois (population 5,766), got together in 1983 to form an investment club that they called the Beardstown Business and Professional Women's Investment Club. It was an irresistible story. They were grandmotherly (age 70) and got together to trade recipes, gossip, and stock tips. They reported an annual return of 23.4 percent for their first ten years, 10 percentage points better than the 14.9 percent annual return on the S&P 500.

They appeared on television and wrote a charming book called *Beardstown Ladies' Common-Sense Investment Guide* that included recipes for cooking food and picking stocks. It was a bestseller, so they wrote four more books, repackaging their recipes and common-sense advice.

It turns out they calculated their 23.4 percent return by comparing the size of their portfolio in 1994 to its initial value in 1983, not accounting for the monthly dues that had been put into the portfolio along the way. A large part of the reason that their portfolio was growing was that they kept putting in more money.

Professional accountants were brought in to straighten things out and they concluded that the actual annual rate of return on their stocks was only 9.1 percent, 5 percentage points *below* the S&P 500.

Being America, this revelation led to a class-action lawsuit against the book's publisher that was settled with the lawyers getting cash and the wronged customers being allowed to swap their Beardstown books for other books, such as *116 Ways to Spoil Your Dog.*

I sympathize with the Beardstown ladies because it takes a lot of work to do a correct accounting that includes all the money going into and out of a portfolio. Money going in from regular and irregular savings, money going out to pay for cars, colleges, and vacations. Portfolios being split during divorces and enlarged during marriages. Taxes being paid on realized capital gains and being saved on realized capital losses. Before writing this book, I considered digging through my records and figuring out how well I had done. I had a general idea that I had done well, but maybe I was being fooled by selective recall. I spent about an hour combing through old brokerage statements before I decided it wasn't worth the many more hours that would be required. For example, every year that I had realized capital gains or losses, I would have to redo my state and federal tax returns, taking the alternative minimum tax into account, in order to determine how much I paid or saved in taxes because of my gains and losses.

Then I remembered that I had started a self-directed retirement plan back in 1987. I found the initial documents and saw that I had put in $26,334. (The odd number reflected the rules for establishing such plans.) I never put another penny into this plan and I never took a penny out, so whatever this plan was currently worth was an accurate tabulation of how well the portfolio had done. The current market value was $1,812,639, which works out to be a 15.4 percent annual rate of return. The return on the S&P 500 over this period was 10.3 percent. If I had bought an S&P 500 index fund, with no expenses, my $26,334 would have grown to $481,726. The extra 5 percentage points over almost thirty years compounded to a portfolio nearly four times as large!

I hadn't bought any winning lottery tickets. I made a few contrarian investments, and I got out of the market during the dot-com bubble and got back in after the bubble popped. Mostly, I just bought first-rate companies at attractive prices relative to their dividends and/or earnings: Apple, Coca-Cola, GE, IBM, Johnson & Johnson, Unilever, Procter & Gamble, Costco, JP Morgan, Wells Fargo, and some closed-end funds (more on that later in Chapter 14).

My investment strategy has been similar in my other accounts, so I imagine that the results have been comparable; in fact, many of the stocks are the same. My returns in my nonretirement accounts may even be somewhat higher because they benefited from tax-harvesting losses on occasional clunkers.

TIMING THE MARKET

Wall Street is having a sale.
—Anonymous

If the alternative is indexing, then the question of timing stock purchases and sales is mostly a question of whether being out of the market is better than being in the market. Add in the presumption that stocks, on average, do better than Treasury bonds, and we should be pretty confident that stocks are overpriced before exiting the stock market.

Jumping in and out of the market weekly, daily, or even more frequently is undoubtedly a mistake. Short-term movements in stock prices are just too hard to predict. However, there are bubbly times when stocks are clearly overpriced and the prudent course is to wait out the bubble, and there are panicky times when the prudent course is to buy stocks at bargain prices.

Some signs of a bubble are anecdotal. When barbershop patrons think stocks can't fail. When people take out second mortgages to buy stocks. When investors measure a company's success by how much money it spends.

In 2000, I went to Bill's Barbershop in Dennis, Massachusetts, and heard people talking about stocks that were sure to double or triple in weeks, if not days.

In 2000, a relative told me that he was taking out a second mortgage to buy Qualcomm because it had great patents; when I asked him about Qualcomm's dividends and earnings, he didn't know and didn't care. I didn't really know or care, either. What was interesting to me was that he was going all in on a company with a great story, and he didn't know or care about anything beyond the great story. He evidently believed that no price is too high to pay for a stock with a great story.

In 2000, a friend told me that he had started a dot-com company, sold it for millions, and promptly started another—which he planned to sell as soon as possible. He had no interest in running companies—it was boring paying people to make things that customers wanted. His plan was to get rich fast by creating companies that investors wanted. Start it. Sell it. Move on. I asked him about his new company's profits and he said profits didn't matter. What mattered was his burn rate—how fast he could spend the money given him by venture capitalists. I thought he was joking. He wasn't.

In 2000, a friend who was a VP at a dot-com company told me about hits, the number of files downloaded from servers, including web pages, images, and JavaScript. Investors evidently thought it was good if a company had lots of hits. Perhaps they were confusing file requests with web page visits, or maybe they were looking for something to justify their stock purchases. Either way, her company obliged by cluttering their web pages with images in order to pump up their hit numbers. Investors paid real money for garbage.

In 2000, the anecdotal signs of a bubble were unmistakable, though I also remembered Keynes's admonition that "the market can remain irrational longer than you can remain solvent." It is risky to short the market—with short sales, options, or futures—but it is prudent to wait for sanity to return.

Part I of this book identified several value-investing tools. Let's apply the JBW equation, Shiller model, and Bogle model to three scenarios: March 2000 (when I warned of a bubble), December 2008 (when I urged investors to buy stocks), and August 2016 (the most recently available data). All the data were taken from Robert

Shiller's Online Data website, a wonderful source of useful facts and figures for value investors who want to assess the S&P 500.

THE JBW EQUATION

One investing benchmark is implied by the John Burr Williams (JBW) equation:

$$R = \frac{D}{P} + g$$

where R is the total annual return, D is the annual dividend, P is the current stock price, and g is the annual rate of growth of dividends.

We can apply this equation to the overall stock market by calculating the dividend yield for the S&P 500 and making an assumption about the long-run growth of dividends and perhaps the long-run growth of the economy. This total return estimate—the dividend yield plus the dividend growth rate—can be compared to the interest rate on long-term Treasury bonds plus whatever risk premium seems appropriate.

Table 12-1 compares the JBW valuations for the S&P 500 in March 2000, December 2008, and August 2016. In March 2000, the S&P 500 dividend yield was 1.16 percent. Adding in a 5 percent long-run growth rate for dividends, the predicted total return is 6.16 percent:

$$R = 1.16\% + 5\% = 6.16\%$$

This was *lower* than the 6.26 percent return on ten-year Treasury bonds, indicating that stocks were not an attractive long-term investment. Earning less than Treasury bonds with a lot more risk is not appealing.

In December 2008, in contrast, the S&P 500 dividend yield was 3.23 percent, and a 5 percent long-run growth rate gives an 8.23 predicted total return.

$$R = 3.23\% + 5\% = 8.23\%$$

This was 5.81 percentage points *above* the 2.42 percent return on ten-year Treasury bonds, indicating that stocks were an attractive long-term investment for all but the extremely risk-averse. Making 5.81 percent more per year, multiplied by the miracle of compound interest, is irresistible. If these return projections turned out to be correct, $100,000 in Treasury bonds would grow to $127,000 in ten years, while $100,000 in stocks would grow to $221,000.

As for the most recent data available at the time of this writing, August 2016, the S&P 500 dividend yield was 2.13 percent, and a 5 percent long-run growth rate gives a 7.13 predicted total return.

$$R = 2.13\% + 5\% = 7.13\%$$

That's 5.32 percentage points above the 1.81 percent return on ten-year Treasury bonds, again indicating that stocks are an attractive long-term investment.

TABLE 12-1. Three different valuations using the JBW equation

	Dividend Yield, %	Total Return, %	10-Year Treasury Rate, %	Total Return Minus Treasury Rate, %
March 2000	1.16	6.16	6.26	−0.10
December 2008	3.23	8.23	2.42	5.81
August 2016	2.13	7.13	1.81	5.32

SHILLER'S CYCLICALLY ADJUSTED EARNINGS YIELD

Robert Shiller calculates a cyclically adjusted P/E ratio (CAPE) by dividing the inflation-adjusted value of the S&P 500 by cyclically adjusted earnings (the average value of the inflation-adjusted earnings over the preceding ten years). For a value-investing benchmark, I noted previously (in Chapter 7) that we can calculate the cyclically adjusted earnings yield (CAEP) by taking the inverse of CAPE. The earnings yield is a rough estimate of the real rate of return on stocks, so we can compare this number to the real interest rate on ten-year Treasury bonds and see whether stocks or bonds look more attractive.

Table 12-2 shows the calculations, using an assumed 2.5 percent rate of inflation, the average over this period. In March 2000, the earnings yield (CAEP) was 2.31 percent, which was 1.45 percentage points lower than the real Treasury rate, indicating that stocks were an unappealing investment. In December 2008 and (to a lesser extent) in August 2016, the earnings yield was well above the Treasury rate, indicating that stocks were an attractive investment.

TABLE 12-2. Three different valuations using CAEP, the inverse of Shiller's CAPE

	Schiller's CAPE	CAEP, %	10-Year Treasury Rate, %	Real 10-Year Treasury Rate, %	CAEP Minus Real Rate, %
March 2000	43.22	2.31	6.26	3.76	−1.45
December 2008	15.37	6.51	2.42	−0.08	6.59
August 2016	26.2	3.82	1.81	−0.69	4.51

BOGLE'S TEN-YEAR HORIZON

John Bogle's model for estimating stock returns over a ten-year horizon is

$$\text{stock return} = \text{dividend yield} + \text{annual growth of earnings} + \text{annual change in P/E}$$

I can use the Bogle equation to assess the attractiveness of stocks in March 2000 and in August 2016, but there is a complication for December 2008. Earnings had fallen by more than 80 percent from a year earlier because of the severe economic recession. Stock prices only fell 40 percent because investors anticipated that the recession would be temporary. The price-earnings ratio consequently tripled, from 18 to 59—not because stock prices had risen, but because stock prices had not fallen as much as earnings. To use the Bogle equation, I would need to forecast a surge in earnings as the recession ended and a drop in the P/E ratio as earnings surged. It is doable, but more complex than the other calculations in this book, so I will not use the Bogle equation for December 2008.

Table 12-3 shows the Bogle calculations for March 2000, using the 1.3 percent dividend yield for the S&P 500 and assuming a 5 percent annual growth in earnings. The price-earnings ratio was 28.3 in March 2000, and I considered four different scenarios for the price-earnings ratio ten years ahead, in 2010. Unless investors expected a substantial increase in the price-earnings ratio for the S&P 500, stocks were not an attractive investment.

TABLE 12-3. Four scenarios, March 2000

	P/E in 2020	P/E Growth, %	Total Return, %	10-Year Treasury Rate, %	Total Return Minus 10-Year Treasury Rate, %
Pessimistic	10	−9.88	−3.72	6.26	−10.12
Historical	15	−6.15	0.01	6.26	−6.39
Optimistic	35	2.15	8.31	6.26	1.91
Delirious	60	7.8	13.96	6.26	7.56

Table 12-4 shows similar calculations for August 2016 using Bogle's model, now with a 2.13 percent dividend yield and again assuming a 5 percent annual growth in earnings. The S&P 500 price-earnings ratio was 24, and I considered four different scenarios for the price-earnings ratio in 2026. Unless the price-earnings ratio were to drop substantially, stocks look like a good investment.

TABLE 12-4. Four scenarios, August 2016				
	P/E in 2026	P/E Growth, %	Total Return, %	10-Year Treasury Rate, %	Total Return Minus 10-Year Treasury Rate, %
Historical	15	-4.59	2.54	1.81	0.73
Small Drop	20	-1.81	5.32	1.81	3.51
Unchanged	24	0	7.13	1.81	5.32
Optimistic	30	2.26	9.39	1.81	7.58

These three models come to the same conclusion. Stocks were too expensive for value investors in March 2000, so it was a good time to be out of the market (and I said so at the time). Stocks were cheap in December 2008, so it was a great time to be in the market (and I said so at the time). Stocks were inexpensive in August 2016, so it was a good time to be in the market (and I am saying so at this time). I don't know what will happen to stock prices over the next few months or years, but ten years from now, in 2026, I expect value investors who were fully invested in August 2016 to be pleased with the results.

PICKING STOCKS

It is a difference of opinion that makes horse races.
—Mark Twain

The value-investing philosophy is simple: Look for great companies whose stocks are inexpensive relative to their dividends and earnings. It is pretty much the same philosophy held by John Burr Williams, Benjamin Graham, Warren Buffett, and other value investors—great companies at a fair price. Buffett has two advantages over us ordinary value investors. First, his reputation gives him sweetheart deals. Companies that want a public-relations stamp of approval sell stock to Buffett at bargain prices that aren't available to the rest of us. Second, his insurance companies give him enormous leverage. When people buy insurance, their premiums plus whatever the company earns by investing the premiums are used to pay off claims for car insurance, home insurance, life insurance, and so on. Insurance companies set their premiums based on an assumption that they will earn modest returns—for example, Treasury rates—when they invest the premiums. Buffett's insurance companies set premiums comparable to those set by other insurance companies, but then invest the premiums in stocks that, on average, do a lot better than Treasury bonds. In essence, Buffett borrows money from policyholders at Treasury rates (currently around 2 percent) and invests the premiums in stocks giving double-digit returns. You and I can't borrow money at Treasury rates. But we can still be value investors.

The starting point is to identify great companies, then to decide whether their stocks are attractively priced. Let's apply the JBW, Shiller, and Bogle valuation measures to the three top companies in *Fortune*'s 2016 list of most admired stocks: Apple, Google, and Amazon.

APPLE

When I was a graduate student during the years 1969–1971, Yale's computer center was a brick building that had been home to an insurance company. There was a behemoth of a computer inside an air-conditioned and dust-controlled room. The rest of the building was row after row of keypunch machines that were used to prepare IBM punch cards. Students and professors sat at the keypunch machines, which were much like typewriters, and typed in data and software code, with each keystroke punching a hole in a card. Each card represented one line of instructions, so a complete program might fill several cardboard boxes, each holding 2,000 cards.

Computer users handed their boxes of cards to machine operators through a set of sliding glass windows, and the operators fed the cards into the giant computer. Users then waited for their output, which might take hours. If there were errors, users sifted through their cards looking for a mistake, corrected it, resubmitted their cards, and waited for the next round of output.

The never-ending click-clacking of the keypunch machines was awful, as were the long waits and treasure hunts for errors, but it was state of the art at the time. It was also stressful, and sometimes the stress got out of hand. One of my fellow PhD students, "Jack," had worked for nearly a year trying to debug the program he needed to finish his thesis. One day, when he handed his two boxes of punch cards through the window to the machine operator, the operator turned to load the cards into the card feeder, but tripped and spilled thousands of cards on the floor. Jack jumped through window and tried to choke the operator. Two other people pulled Jack away and explained that it was a prank. They had distracted Jack and swapped his boxes for two boxes of surplus cards, which the operator proceeded to drop and scatter. Jack was relieved, but not amused.

When I came to Pomona College in 1981, the college was using dumb terminals (keyboards and display monitors) scattered around campus and connected to the college's IBM mainframe. Dumb terminals were a big step up from punch cards, since the results came back quickly and the terminals were quiet!

However, the entire system was under the control of the computer center. The computer center decided what programs to put on the mainframe and they selected a relatively small number of programs that were easy for them to maintain. Users had few options.

Then came the personal computer revolution, so called because—unlike a dumb terminal—a personal computer has a built-in CPU and does not need to be connected to a mainframe. Users can choose the software they want, including software they have written themselves.

Pomona College's computer center resisted the revolution because it was easier for them to maintain a small set of programs on a mainframe. As a user, it was clear to me that the personal computer revolution might be delayed, but it would not be stopped. My wife and I gave our first son an Apple II for his ninth birthday. When he opened the box, I took the instructions and he took the computer. He had it up and running before I finished reading the instructions.

Legendary mutual fund manager Peter Lynch said that some of his biggest winners came from going to a mall with his daughters, giving them some money, and seeing where they spent it. He argued, "If you like the store, chances are you'll love the stock." His shopping strategy might be justified by the argument that new stores fly under Wall Street's radar. However, in lesser hands, his philosophy can lead investors to make the classic mistake of buying a stock because the company is great, not because the stock is cheap.

This was one of my (few) Peter Lynch moments. I knew that users wanted personal computers, not dumb terminals, and I saw firsthand how easy the Apple II was to use. Apple stock didn't pay dividends and its earnings were dodgy, but I bought some stock anyway. I also bought my son Apple stock for his high school graduation present. In retrospect, I was lucky. Commodore, Kaypro, Tandy, and dozens of other PC makers did not survive. Apple was sometimes near-death.

Apple has evolved into a mature company that derives most of its revenue from its iPhones, which, like the Macintosh and Apple II, were revolutionary. Apple still makes computers, of course, and has a solid Apple-ecosystem that is used by millions of Apple fans. Apple is now a money machine that can be assessed by value investors.

Let's value Apple today (August 2016) using the same three valuation methods we used to value the S&P 500 in Chapter 12: the JBW equation, Shiller's cyclically adjusted price-earnings ratio (CAPE), and the Bogle model.

The John Burr Williams (JBW) equation is

$$R = \frac{D}{P} + g$$

where R is the total annual return, D is the annual dividend, P is the current stock price, and g is the annual rate of growth of dividends.

For Apple stock in August 2016, the annual dividend was $2.28 per share and the stock price was around $100, giving a dividend yield of 2.28 percent:

$$\frac{D}{P} = \frac{\$2.28}{\$100.00} = 0.0228 \text{ (2.28 percent)}$$

In my assessment of the S&P 500, I assumed a 5 percent growth rate of dividends, roughly the long-run growth rate of dividends and the U.S. economy. Using that 5 percent growth rate here implies a 7.28 percent total return, which (as Table 13-1 shows) is 5.47 percentage points above the ten-year Treasury rate.

At the time, Apple's 2.28 percent dividend yield was slightly higher than that for the S&P 500, making it a slightly more attractive stock if we use the same 5 percent dividend growth rate for Apple and the S&P 500. This seems extremely conservative. Apple's dividends had increased by 10 percent a year since Apple instituted a dividend in 2012 and Apple's earnings per share had increased at a 55 percent annual rate over the past ten years and at a 41 percent annual rate over the previous five years.

Many feared that Apple was no longer a premier growth stock, that it was now just a mature money machine. It certainly gets harder to maintain a crazy growth rate as a company gets larger; but, even so, it was hard to imagine that Apple would grow more slowly than the average company in the S&P 500 over the next ten years. Plus, there is nothing inherently bad about being a mature money machine. In fact, it may be a safer investment than a young start-up with nothing more than hoped-for profits in the future.

Apple had been No. 1 in the annual Forbes ratings of the most admired companies for nine years running, 2008 through 2016. A sudden collapse seemed unlikely.

Apple's earnings certainly wouldn't grow by 40 or 50 percent forever, nor would its dividends grow by 10 percent forever, but a 5 percent growth rate for dividends was surely conservative.

TABLE 13-1. Using the JBW equation to value Apple stock, August 2016

	Dividend Yield, %	Total Return, %	10-Year Treasury Rate, %	Total Return Minus Treasury Rate, %
Apple	2.28	7.28	1.81	5.47
S&P 500	2.13	7.13	1.81	5.32

I also made a more complicated calculation of the present value of Apple's dividends, assuming that Apple's dividends grow at 10 percent a year for twenty years, then drop to a 5 percent growth rate, roughly the projected long-run growth rate of the economy.

We can calculate the present value of these projected dividends for any assumed required return. This is the intrinsic value of Apple stock. It turns out that if we discount the projected dividends by a 9.54 percent required return, the intrinsic value is $100.

Here are the implications:

1. Investors who would be happy with a 9.54 percent annual rate of return should be happy owning Apple stock.

2. If dividends grow more than assumed in these calculations, the return is even larger.

3. If dividends grow less than anticipated, the return is smaller; for example, if Apple's dividend growth rate drops to 5 percent after ten years, the return is 8.41 percent; if it falls to 5 percent immediately, the return is 7.28 percent.

This all makes sense. A 2.28 percent dividend yield gives a 7.28 percent return if dividends grow by 5 percent a year forever and a 12.28 percent return if dividends grow by 10 percent a year forever. If the dividend growth rate is 10 percent for a while and then drops to 5 percent, the return will be between 7.28 percent and 12.28 percent, and the return will be higher the longer the 10 percent growth rate is maintained.

Are these calculations dependent on the heroic assumption that Apple will be around forever? Not really. The heavy discounting of distant dividends makes them essentially meaningless.

Figure 13-1 shows the cumulative intrinsic value of Apple's dividends, using a 9.54 percent required return. For example, the cumulative value over a twenty-year horizon is the present value of the first twenty years of dividends. As shown, almost all of Apple's intrinsic value comes from the first 100 years. If Apple were to disappear 100 years from now, it would have essentially no effect on Apple's current intrinsic value.

(Nonetheless, it is good to use a model that assumes an infinite horizon, because it keeps us from guessing about what the price of Apple stock will be tomorrow or a year from now. The infinite-horizon model makes no assumptions about the future price of Apple stock.)

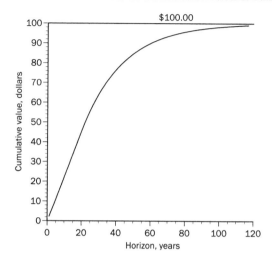

FIGURE 13-1. Cumulative intrinsic value of Apple

Now let's try Shiller's model. The cyclically adjusted P/E ratio (CAPE) can be misleading for individual companies that have been growing very rapidly. Figure 13-2 shows that Apple's earnings per share (in 2016 dollars) increased from $0.38 per share in 2006 to $9.22 per share in 2015, a 43 percent annual rate of increase. Because of Apple's rapid growth, the $3.73 average over this ten-year period greatly understates Apple's current and projected future earnings.

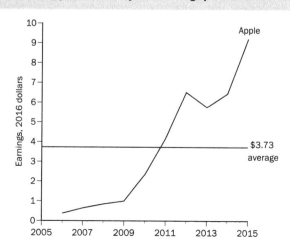

FIGURE 13-2. Apple inflation-adjusted earnings per share

Figure 13-3 shows the S&P 500's inflation-adjusted earnings. Here, the fluctuations around the average are more important than the growth in earnings over time, and it makes sense to calculate a ten-year average in order to smooth out these fluctuations and give a more accurate representation of earnings than would be provided by any single year. For Apple, in contrast, the growth over time is more important than the year-to-year fluctuations, and the ten-year average is a misleading representation of Apple's earnings.

FIGURE 13-3. S&P 500 inflation-adjusted earnings per share

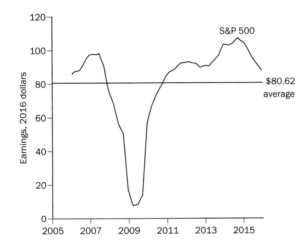

Nonetheless, I calculated the cyclically adjusted earnings yield (CAEP) by dividing Apple's average inflation-adjusted earnings by the inflation-adjusted price of Apple stock ($100):

$$\text{CAEP} = \frac{\$3.73}{\$100} = 0.0373 \ (3.73\%)$$

Since the earnings yield is a rough estimate of the real rate of return on stocks, I compared CAEP to the real interest rate on ten-year Treasury bonds.

Table 13-2 shows the calculations, using an assumed 2.5 percent rate of inflation, the average over the past several years. Apple was slightly less attractive than the overall S&P 500, but there was still a 4.42 percentage-point difference between the Apple's cyclically adjusted earnings yield and the real return on ten-year Treasury bonds. Taking into account the conservative $3.73 number for Apple's earnings, Apple becomes more attractive.

TABLE 13-2. Using Shiller's CAPE to value Apple stock.

	Shiller's CAPE	CAEP, %	10-Year Treasury Rate, %	Real 10-Year Treasury Rate, %	CAEP Minus Real Rate, %
Apple	26.8	3.73	1.81	−0.69	4.42
S&P 500	26.2	3.82	1.81	−0.69	4.51

This, too, makes sense. With Apple stock at $100 a share, a cyclically adjusted earnings figure of $3.73 gives an earnings yield of 3.73 percent, which is an estimate of the real return on Apple stock.

Cyclically adjusted earnings are intended to adjust for the ups and downs in business cycles. Movements in Apple's earnings during the years 2006 through 2015 were not due to a business cycle, but to Apple's growth. Its 2015 earnings of $9.22 don't really need be adjusted much for the business cycle, so it is reasonable to use an earnings figure that is closer to $9.22 than $3.73, which gives a projected real return substantially higher than the already attractive 3.73 percent.

One way to adjust a growth company's earnings for the business cycle is to fit a line to the earnings data, as in Figure 13-4. The fitted line smooths out the year-to-year fluctuations, as intended, but allows for growth. By this reckoning, Apple's 2015 cyclically adjusted earnings were $8.18, giving a CAEP of 8.18 percent, more than double the value using the ten-year average earnings of $3.73:

$$CAEP = \frac{\$8.18}{\$100} = 0.0818 \ (8.18\%)$$

This projected real return of 8.18 percent is 8.87 percent higher than the projected real return on ten-year Treasury bonds.

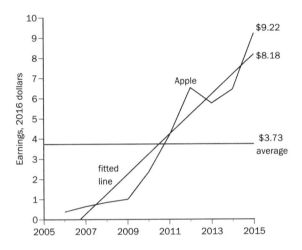

FIGURE 13-4. A regression line fit to Apple's earnings.

Let's now look at John Bogle's model for estimating stock returns over a ten-year horizon:

$$\begin{array}{ccccc} \text{stock} \\ \text{return} \end{array} = \begin{array}{c} \text{dividend} \\ \text{yield} \end{array} + \begin{array}{c} \text{annual growth} \\ \text{of earnings} \end{array} + \begin{array}{c} \text{annual change} \\ \text{in P/E} \end{array}$$

Apple's price-earnings ratio was 12 in August 2016, half that of the S&P 500. Table 13-3 shows the returns predicted by the Bogle model for the assumption that the price-earnings ratios in 2026 are still 12 for Apple and 24 for the S&P 500, and that both earnings grow at 5 percent annually. If the price-earnings ratio is constant and earnings are projected to grow at the same rate as dividends, Bogle's model and the JBW equation give the same total return values. Table

13-3 also shows the total returns if Apple's earnings grow at 10 per-cent annually for the next ten years, and if Apple and the S&P 500 both have a P/E of 20 in 2026. Since Apple's P/E would be going up and the S&P 500 P/E would be going down, this enhances Apple's return and diminishes the S&P 500 return.

TABLE 13-3. Using Bogle's equation to value Apple stock, August 2016.

	Earnings Growth, %	P/E in 2026	P/E Growth, %	Total Return, %	10-Year Treasury Rate, %	Total Return Minus 10-Year Treasury Rate, %
Apple	5	12	0	7.28	1.81	5.47
Apple	10	12	0	12.28	1.81	10.47
S&P 500	5	24	0	7.13	1.81	5.32
Apple	5	20	5.24	12.52	1.81	10.71
Apple	10	20	5.24	17.52	1.81	15.71
S&P 500	5	20	-1.81	5.32	1.81	3.51

As with the JBW and Shiller metrics, the Bogle model's implications make sense. In 2016, Apple had a dividend yield of 2.28 percent. If its dividends and earnings were to grow at 5 percent a year for ten years, and its P/E stays at 12, it will give investors a 7.28 percent return over this ten-year horizon. If Apple's earnings and dividends grow by more than 5 percent a year over the next ten years and/or its P/E is higher than 12 in 2026, the rate of return on Apple stock will be higher than 7.28 percent—perhaps much higher.

Table 13-4 summarizes the calculations for these three models. I concluded that the S&P 500 was an attractive investment and that Apple was even more so. In August 2016, I held an imprudently large fraction of my portfolio in Apple stock.

TABLE 13-4. Valuations of Apple and the S&P 500, August 2016.

	Total Return Minus Treasury Rate, %
DIVIDEND-DISCOUNT MODELS	
Apple, JBW with 5% dividend growth	5.47
Apple, dividend discount with 10% growth for 10 years, 5% afterward	6.60
Apple, dividend discount with 10% growth for 20 years, 5% afterward	7.73
S&P 500, JBW with 5% dividend growth	5.32
SHILLER MODEL	
Apple, with CAEP = 3.73%	4.42
Apple, with CAEP = 8.18%	8.87
S&P 500, with CAEP = 3.82%	4.51
BOGLE MODEL	
Apple, with 5% earnings growth and P/E = 12 in 2026	5.47
Apple, with 10% earnings growth and P/E = 12 in 2026	10.47
S&P 500, with 5% earnings growth and P/E = 24 in 2026	5.32
Apple, with 5% earnings growth and P/E = 20 in 2026	10.71
Apple, with 10% earnings growth and P/E = 20 in 2026	15.71
S&P 500, with 5% earnings growth and P/E = 20 in 2026	3.51

GOOGLE

In January 1994, just as the World Wide Web (WWW) was starting to get traction, two Stanford graduate students, Jerry Yang and David Filo, started a website. "Jerry and David's Guide to the World Wide Web" was a list of what they considered interesting web pages. A year later, they incorporated the company with the sexy name Yahoo. By now, they had a catalog of 10,000 sites and 100,000 Yahoo users a day, fueled by the fact that the popular Netscape browser had a Directory button that sent people to Yahoo.com.

As the Web took off, Yahoo hired hundreds of people to search for sites to add to its exponentially growing directory. They added graphics, news stories, and advertisements. By 1996, Yahoo had more than 10 million visitors a day. Yahoo thought of itself as a media company, sort of like *Fortune* magazine, where people came to be informed and entertained and advertisers paid for a chance to catch readers' wandering eyes. Yahoo hired its own writers to create unique content. As Yahoo added more content, such as sports and finance pages, it attracted targeted advertising—directed at people who are interested in sports or finance. Yahoo started Yahoo Mail, Yahoo Shopping, and other bolt-ons.

Then came Google in 1998 with its revolutionary search algorithm. Yahoo couldn't manually keep up with the growth of the Web, so it used Google's search engine for four years while it developed a competing algorithm. Meanwhile, Google established itself as the go-to search site and maintained a 90 percent worldwide share of the search market in 2016.

Larry Page graduated from the University of Michigan; Sergey Brin was born in Moscow and graduated from the University of Maryland. Both dropped out of Stanford's PhD program in computer science to start Google. Their initial insight was that a web page's importance could be gauged by the number of links to the page, so they created a powerful web crawler that could roam the Web counting links. This search algorithm, called PageRank, has morphed into other, more sophisticated algorithms, allowing Google to stay ahead of the pack of other search engines.

Google's ad revenue has generated an enormous cash flow, which it invests in other projects, including Google Chrome (which has displaced Microsoft's Internet Explorer as the most used browser); Google Docs, Google Sheets, and Google Slides (which threaten Microsoft Office), and of course, Google cars.

In 2015, I was invited to Science Foo Camp ("Sci Foo") organized by O'Reilly Media, Digital Science, and Google. ("Foo" stands for Friends of O'Reilly.) Sci Foo brings together about 250 invited academic, business, and government "thought leaders" for a weekend of conversation about science and technology. It is all-expenses-paid and held at the Googleplex, Google's corporate headquarters in Mountain View, California. I had never been to the Googleplex and free was hard to resist, so I said yes, even though I wasn't sure why they invited me. I had just written a book titled *Standard Deviations: Flawed Assumptions, Tortured Data, and Other Ways to Lie with Statistics*, which advised caution and skepticism when analyzing big data—Google's forte.

While I was at Sci Foo, I facilitated a session on regression to the mean and gave a five-minute lightning talk on the perils of mining big data for gold. Afterward, I wrote a blog that (roughly) replicated my talk. Here is an excerpt:

Big Data, Big Computers, Big Trouble

Many years ago, James Tobin, a Nobel laureate in economics, wryly observed that the bad old days when researchers had to do calculations by hand were actually a blessing. In today's language, it was a feature, not a flaw. The calculations were so hard that people thought hard before they calculated. Today, with terabytes of data and lightning-fast computers, it is too easy to calculate first, think later.

Over and over, we are told that government, business, finance, medicine, law, and our daily lives are being revolutionized by a newfound ability to sift through reams of data and discover the truth. We can make wise decisions because powerful computers have scrutinized the data and seen the light.

Maybe. Or maybe not.

Two endemic problems are nicely summarized by the Texas Sharpshooter Fallacy. In one version, a self-proclaimed marksman completely covers a wall with targets, and then fires his gun. Inevitably, he hits a target, which he proudly displays without mentioning all the missed targets. Because he was certain to hit a target, the fact that he did so proves nothing at all. In research, this corresponds to testing hundreds of theories and reporting the most statistically significant result, without mentioning all the failed tests. This, too, proves nothing because one is certain to find a statistically persuasive result if one does enough tests.

In the second version of the sharpshooter fallacy, the hapless cowboy shoots a bullet at a blank wall. He then draws a bull's-eye around the bullet hole, which again proves nothing at all because there will always be a hole to draw a circle around. The research equivalent is to ransack data for a pattern and, after one is found, think up a theory.

A concise summary is the cynical comment of Ronald Coase, another economics Nobel laureate: "If you torture the data long enough, it will confess."

Do serious researchers really torture data? Far too often. It's how well-respected people came up with the now-discredited ideas that coffee causes pancreatic cancer and people can be healed by positive energy from self-proclaimed healers living thousands of miles away.

An example of the first sharpshooter fallacy is a study provocatively titled "The Hound of the Baskervilles Effect," referring to Sir Arthur Conan Doyle's story in which Charles Baskerville dies of a heart attack while he is being pursued down a dark alley by a vicious dog:

> The dog, incited by its master, sprang over the wicket-gate and pursued the unfortunate baronet, who fled screaming down the yew alley. In that gloomy tunnel it must indeed have been a dreadful sight to see that huge black creature, with its flaming jaws and blazing eyes, bounding after its victim. He fell dead at the end of the alley from heart disease and terror.

The study's author argued that Japanese and Chinese Americans are similarly susceptible to heart attacks on the fourth day of every month because in Japanese, Mandarin, and Cantonese, the pronunciation of four and death are very similar.

Four is an unlucky number for many Asian Americans, but are they really so superstitious and fearful that the fourth day of the month—which, after all, happens every month—is as terrifying as being chased down a dark alley by a ferocious dog?

The Baskervilles study (isn't the BS acronym tempting?) examined California data for Japanese and Chinese Americans who died of coronary disease. Of those deaths that occurred on the third, fourth, and fifth days of the month, 33.9 percent were on day 4, which does not differ substantially or statistically from the expected 33.3 percent. So, how did the Baskervilles study come to the opposite conclusion? There are dozens of categories of heart disease and they only reported results for the five categories in which more than one-third of the deaths occurred on day 4. Unsurprisingly, attempts by other researchers to replicate their conclusion failed.

An example of the second sharpshooter fallacy is an investment strategy based on the gold-silver ratio (GSR), which is the ratio of the price of an ounce of gold to the price of an ounce of silver. . . . [I discuss the GSR in Chapter 4 of this book.]

Modern computers can ransack large databases looking for much more subtle and complex patterns. But the problem is the same. If there is no underlying reason for the discovered pattern, there is no reason for deviations from the pattern to self-correct.

These two sharpshooter fallacies are examples of data mining. Thirty years ago, calling someone a "data miner" was an insult comparable to being accused of plagiarism. Today, people advertise themselves as data miners. This is a flaw, not a feature. Big data and big computers make it easy to calculate before thinking, but it is better to think hard before calculating.

There I was in the Googleplex, the temple of big data, preaching skepticism about mining big data. Dozens of people told me afterward how much they enjoyed my sermon. Several worked at Google, including one guy who told me that my skepticism about big data was precisely why I was invited.

I was blown away. Too many companies undermine themselves by never questioning their business models. Google paid for me to come to the Googleplex and ask hard questions. When I got home, I bought Google stock.

Let's value Google today (August 2016) using the same valuation methods we used to value Apple. The dividend-discount model and John Burr Williams (JBW) equation cannot be used for stocks that do not pay dividends, and Google does not pay dividends, so I turned instead to the Shiller and Bogle models.

As I noted in valuing Apple, Shiller's cyclically adjusted P/E ratio (CAPE) can be misleading for companies that have been growing very rapidly. Google's earnings had been increasing at an annual rate of 33 percent over the past ten years and 14 percent over the past five years, and Figure 13-5 shows that Google's $14.25 average earnings per share during the years 2006 through 2015 surely understates Google's current and projected future earnings. (Google's earnings were $22.84 in 2015 and predicted to be $28.00 in 2016.)

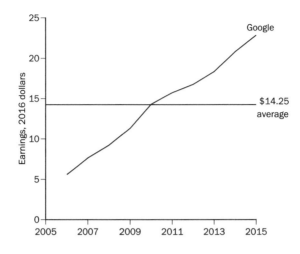

FIGURE 13-5. Google inflation-adjusted earnings per share.

Nonetheless, I calculated Google's cyclically adjusted earnings yield (CAEP) by dividing its average inflation-adjusted earnings by its inflation adjusted stock price.

$$\text{CAEP} = \frac{\$14.25}{\$780} = 0.0183 \ (1.83\%)$$

Since this 1.83 percent earnings yield is a rough estimate of a stock's real rate of return, I compared Google's CAEP to the real interest rate on ten-year Treasury bonds.

Table 13-5 shows the calculations, using an assumed 2.5 percent rate of inflation. Google was less attractive than the overall S&P 500 by this metric, but there was still a 2.50 percentage-point difference between the Google's cyclically adjusted earnings yield and the real return on ten-year Treasury bonds.

TABLE 13-5. Using Shiller's CAPE to value Google stock.

	Shiller's CAPE	CAEP, %	10-Year Treasury Rate, %	Real 10-Year Treasury Rate, %	CAEP Minus Real Rate, %
Google	54.7	1.83	1.81	-0.69	2.52
S&P 500	26.2	3.82	1.81	-0.69	4.51

Taking into account the fact that $14.25 is a conservative number for Google's earnings, its stock becomes more attractive. A line fit to Google's earnings is so close to actual earnings as to be barely distinguishable. This fitted line implies 2015 cyclically adjusted earnings of $22.73, which increases Google's CAEP and projected real return to 2.91 percent, which is 3.60 percent above the projected real return on ten-year Treasury bonds.

$$CAEP = \frac{\$22.73}{\$780} = 0.0291 \ (2.91\%)$$

Now, let's use John Bogle's model for estimating Google stock returns over a ten-year horizon:

$$\frac{stock}{return} = \frac{dividend}{yield} + \frac{annual\ growth}{of\ earnings} + \frac{annual\ change}{in\ P/E}$$

Google's price-earnings ratio was 28 in August 2016, somewhat above the S&P 500 P/E of 24. Table 13-6 shows the returns predicted by the Bogle model for the assumption that Google and S&P 500 earnings grow by 5 percent a year and that the price-earnings ratios in ten years (2026) are still 28 for Google and 24 for the S&P 500. Table 13-6 also shows the total returns if Google's earnings grow by 10 percent a year for the next ten years, and if Google and the S&P 500 both have a P/E of 20 in 2026. Since both P/Es would be going down, this reduces the ten-year annual return on both.

TABLE 13-6. Using Bogle's equation to value Google stock, August 2016.					
	Earnings Growth, %	P/E in 2026	P/E Growth %	Total Return, %	10-Year Treasury Rate, %	Total Return minus 10-year Treasury Rate, %
Google	5	28	0.00	5.00	1.81	3.19
Google	10	28	0.00	10.00	1.81	8.19
S&P 500	5	24	0.00	7.13	1.81	5.32
Google	5	20	-3.31	1.69	1.81	-0.12
Google	10	20	-3.31	6.69	1.81	4.88
S&P 500	5	20	-1.81	5.32	1.81	3.51

One of the appealing features of the Bogle model is that the calculations can be done in your head or on the back of an envelope. Google does not pay dividends, so the return is solely from the price appreciation over the next ten years. (If Google did pay dividends, we would simply add the dividend yield to the annual price appreciation.)

Google's projected price appreciation is due to the projected annual rate of increase in its earnings and the change (if any) in its price-earnings ratio. If the P/E is unchanged, then Google's annual price appreciation will be 5 percent, if its earnings grow by 5 percent, and 10 percent if its earnings grow by 10 percent. If Google's P/E goes up or down by, say, one percent a year, the projected return goes down or up by the same amount.

Table 13-7 summarizes my calculations for the Shiller and Bogle models. I concluded that the case for Google was not as compelling as the case for Apple, but I thought Google was more attractive than the overall S&P 500 because:

1. I expected Google's earnings to increase by at least 10 percent annually over the next ten years.

2. I thought it was unlikely that Google's P/E in 2026 would be less than that for the S&P 500.

I had a substantial holding of Google stock in August 2016, though not nearly as large as my Apple holdings.

TABLE 13-7. Valuations of Google and the S&P 500, August 2016.

	Total Return Minus Treasury Rate, %
SHILLER MODEL	
Google, with CAEP = 1.83%	2.52
Google, with CAEP = 2.91%	3.60
S&P 500, with CAEP = 3.82%	4.51
BOGLE MODEL	
Google, with 5% earnings growth and P/E = 28 in 2026	3.19
Google, with 10% earnings growth and P/E = 28 in 2026	8.19
S&P 500, with 5% earnings growth and P/E = 24 in 2026	5.32
Google, with 5% earnings growth and P/E = 20 in 2026	−0.12
Google, with 10% earnings growth and P/E = 20 in 2026	4.88
S&P 500, with 5% earnings growth and P/E = 20 in 2026	3.51

AMAZON

I was on sabbatical during the 2015–2016 academic year. As part of my transition back to teaching, I decided to get a new briefcase. My current briefcase had lasted thirty years and its beaten-down charm had morphed into beaten-down raggedy. My wife and children made faces, so I searched Amazon, found a briefcase I liked, and ordered it. With Amazon Prime, the shipping was fast and free.

When I opened the box, my wife and our four children made faces again. I shipped the briefcase back at Amazon's expense and my wife picked out a briefcase she liked. The shipping was fast and free, and so was the return when I found out that it was too small. It took three more tries before we found a briefcase that everyone liked. Yes, the time needed to reach a decision is proportional to the square of the number of people involved.

How can Amazon afford free shipping both ways? It can't. Amazon Prime costs $99 a year and includes free two-day shipping (same-day delivery in some places), free streaming of movies, television shows, music, and ebooks. Most returns are free, too.

Amazon sells more than $100 billion of stuff annually to 250 million active users, including more than 50 million Amazon Prime members, but it barely makes a profit. Some years, it loses money. It lost $241 million in 2014, but bounced back with a $596 million profit in 2015. Even the $596 million profit was only a razor-thin 0.55 percent on its 2015 revenue of $107 billion.

Amazon was founded by Jeff Bezos, whose mom was a teenager when he was born and whose stepfather was a Cuban refugee. He got bachelor of science degrees from Princeton in electrical engineering and computer science. Bright and tireless, he worked on Wall Street and then set out to conquer the retail world with Amazon. And conquer it he has.

Scalable technology is technology that allows a business to grow with very little incremental cost. If your business model is making necklaces by hand, the cost of making the thousandth necklace is about the same as the cost of making the first one. If your business model is making a downloadable app, the cost of getting the app to the thousandth customer is much less than the cost of creating the app for the first customer. If your business model is a web page that sells advice, the cost of selling advice to the thousandth customer is much less than the cost of setting up the page to sell advice to the first customer.

Scalability can create a winner-take-all market. If the cost of creating the product is huge and the cost of selling additional products is trivial, the initial cost creates an effective barrier to entry and the small cost of selling additional products allows an established firm with lots of customers to undercut the prices of new entrants. This is the rationale for the commonplace rule in Silicon Valley: "Growth first, revenue later." Big companies scare away competitors and undercut those who dare to compete. Once a company is established as the biggest, cheapest, and best known, it can collect monopolistic profits.

Amazon's strategy has been growth first. However, Amazon is no longer a start-up. It is a dominant company that should be ready to reap the rewards of a monopoly, yet every success seems to fund ever more ambitious projects: phones, tablets, one-hour delivery service, movies, cloud computing. Amazon is a terrific company, but where are the profits?

Amazon does not pay dividends, so, as with Google, I can't use the dividend-discount model and John Burr Williams (JBW) equation. Instead, I used the Shiller and Bogle models.

Figure 13-6 shows that, unlike Apple and Google, Amazon's earnings have not been growing rapidly. Indeed, the biggest investor complaint about Amazon is that it keeps spending money in order to get bigger and do more things—which leaves shareholders wishing that Amazon would use its market domination to earn some profits. Amazon's earnings have fallen by 4 percent a year over the past ten years and by 26 percent a year over the past five years.

FIGURE 13-6. Amazon inflation-adjusted earnings per share.

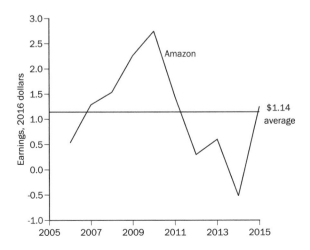

As with Apple and Google, I calculated Amazon's cyclically adjusted earnings yield (CAEP) and compared it to the real interest rate on ten-year Treasury bonds. Table 13-8 shows the calculations, using an assumed 2.5 percent rate of inflation. Amazon's cyclically adjusted price-earnings ratio is a mind-boggling 664.5, and its CAEP is a minuscule 0.15 percent (yep, fifteen-hundreds of one percent). By this measure, Amazon is not only less attractive than the S&P 500, its projected return is less than that on ten-year Treasury bonds.

TABLE 13-8. Using Shiller's CAPE to value Amazon stock.

	Shiller's CAPE	CAEP (%)	10-Year Treasury Rate, %	Real 10-Year Treasury Rate, %	CAEP Minus Real Rate, %
Amazon	664.5	0.15	1.81	−0.69	−0.54
S&P 500	26.2	3.82	1.81	−0.69	4.51

John Bogle's model for estimating stock returns over a ten-year horizon is

$$\frac{\text{stock}}{\text{return}} = \frac{\text{dividend}}{\text{yield}} + \frac{\text{annual growth}}{\text{of earnings}} + \frac{\text{annual change}}{\text{in P/E}}$$

Amazon's price-earnings ratio was a dizzying 600 in August 2016. I'm acrophobic when it comes to stocks, and a P/E of 600 terrifies me, as it should all value investors. Table 13-9 shows the returns predicted by the Bogle model for the assumption that the price-earnings ratios in 2026 are still 600 for Amazon and 24 for the S&P 500, and that both earnings grow at 5 percent annually. Table 13-9 also shows the total returns if Amazon's earnings grow by 10 percent a year for the next ten years, and if Amazon and the S&P 500 both have a P/E of 20 in 2026.

TABLE 13-9. Using Bogle's equation to value Amazon stock, August 2016.

	Earnings Growth, %	P/E in 2026	P/E Growth, %	Total Return, %	10-Year Treasury Rate, %	Total Return Minus 10-Year Treasury Rate, %
Amazon	5	600	0	5	1.81	3.19
Amazon	10	600	0	10	1.81	8.19
S&P 500	5	24	0	7.13	1.81	5.32
Amazon	5	20	–28.83	–23.83	1.81	–22.02
Amazon	10	20	–28.83	–18.83	1.81	–17.02
S&P 500	5	20	–1.81	5.32	1.81	3.51

Table 13-10 summarizes the calculations for the Shiller and Bogle models. I concluded that Amazon was too risky for my tastes. Its P/E cannot defy gravity forever. Perhaps Amazon's earnings will soar, which, by itself, will reduce the price-earnings ratio. But an increase in earnings with no dividends and the stock price unchanged doesn't give investors anything. Or maybe Amazon's P/E will fall because Amazon's stock price collapses, which is even worse for investors.

I love Amazon, but I don't like the stock. Its earnings may explode, but it is too perilous an investment for me.

TABLE 13-10. Valuations of Amazon and the S&P 500, August 2016.

	Total Return Minus Treasury Rate, %
SHILLER MODEL	
Amazon, with CAEP = 0.15%	–0.54
S&P 500, with CAEP = 3.82%	4.51
BOGLE MODEL	
Amazon, with 5% earnings growth and P/E = 600 in 2026	3.19
Amazon, with 10% earnings growth and P/E = 600 in 2026	8.19
S&P 500, with 5% earnings growth and P/E = 24 in 2026	5.32
Amazon, with 5% earnings growth and P/E = 20 in 2026	22.02
Amazon, with 10% earnings growth and P/E = 20 in 2026	–17.02
S&P 500, with 5% earnings growth and P/E = 20 in 2026	3.51

CLOSED-END FUNDS

Good intelligence is nine-tenths of any battle.
—NAPOLEON

Chapter 10 discussed mutual funds and the appeal of index funds. Some mutual funds may be even more attractive than index funds. To see this, we need to make an important distinction between open-end and closed-end funds.

Open-end funds increase or reduce the number of shares outstanding as more money is invested in the fund or withdrawn from the fund. Suppose that a mutual fund with the optimistic name BeatTheMarket has 10 million shares outstanding and owns a portfolio of stocks worth $100 million. Its net asset value (NAV) per share is calculated by dividing the market value of its portfolio by the number of shares the fund has issued.

$$\text{NAV} = \frac{\$100 \text{ million}}{10 \text{ million}} = \$10$$

If BeatTheMarket is an open-end fund, it will issue new shares or redeem existing shares at a price equal to the fund's net asset value of $10 a share. If investors buy a million shares at $10 apiece, the number of shares will go up to 11 million and the fund's assets will increase to $110 million, leaving its NAV at $10/share:

$$NAV = \frac{\$110 \text{ million}}{11 \text{ million}} = \$10$$

If, instead, investors were to redeem a million shares at $10 apiece, the number of shares would go down to 9 million and the fund's assets would fall to $90 million, again leaving its NAV at $10/share:

$$NAV = \frac{\$90 \text{ million}}{9 \text{ million}} = \$10$$

Fair's fair. Investors deal directly with the fund and their decisions to come or go are at a fair price, with no effect on the other shareholders.

CLOSED-END FUNDS

If BeatTheMarket is a closed-end fund, instead of an open-end fund, it issues a fixed number of shares—say, 10 million shares when it is created—and, once established, does not issue new shares or redeem old ones. Investors cannot buy new shares from the fund or sell their shares back to the fund. Instead, closed-end shares are traded on stock exchanges, where investors buy shares from existing shareholders or sell their shares to someone else—the same way that they buy or sell shares of GE and IBM.

IBM's stock price need not equal its book value; in fact, it is seldom, if ever, equal to its book value. IBM's stock price is whatever is needed to maintain a balance between people wanting to buy IBM stock and people wanting to sell. It is the same with closed-end funds. The market price of a closed-end fund need not be, and seldom is, equal to its net asset value.

Closed-end funds typically trade at a discount from net asset value, though some trade at premiums. The discounts ebb and flow,

increasing when small investors leave the stock market and shrinking when they return. Before the Great Crash of 1929, the naive enthusiasm and greed of small investors gave the average closed-end
fund a 50 percent premium. One closed-end fund, the Goldman
Sachs Trading Corporation, sold for a 100 percent premium. (After
the crash, its price dropped 98 percent.)

Figure 14-1 shows that discounts of 20 to 30 percent were common in the 1970s, but then declined, perhaps because investors became more aware of the existence of closed-end fund discounts and
the advantages of buying funds at a discount.

FIGURE 14-1. Average closed-end fund premium (+) or discount (-) from net asset value

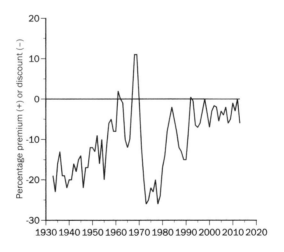

A DISCOUNT IS AN ADVANTAGE

A critic of closed-end funds wrote that "frequently, closed-end
shares representing $25 in assets will be selling for $20. Such profits
may be largely illusory, however, because when the time comes to
sell, the discount may persist." The closed-end advantage does not
depend on the disappearance of the discount. Even if the discount

never narrows, closed-end funds can be financially advantageous simply because investors earn dividends and capital gains on more stock than they paid for.

Suppose that BeatTheMarket is a closed-end fund with a NAV of $10 and a market price of $8, a 20 percent discount. Each share of BeatTheMarket implicitly owns stocks that would cost $10 if purchased directly. If BeatTheMarket can be bought for $8, investors pay $8 and receive dividends and capital gains on $10 worth of stock. If the annual dividends and capital gains are 10 percent of $10, investors receive $1 in dividends and capital gains on an $8 investment—a 12.5 percent return. Why pay $10 for stock that you can buy for $8?

Closed-end funds do have expenses, typically around one percent a year, a figure that is roughly consistent with a 10 percent discount. But these expenses do not explain why funds sell for 20 percent or 30 percent discounts. Nor do they explain why so many people invest in load funds, paying a premium over net asset value, when they could buy shares in a closed-end fund at a discount from net asset value. Closed-end funds may not beat the market, but they certainly beat open-end funds, especially those with load fees. Compared to open-end funds, closed-end funds are $100 bills on the sidewalk.

The explanation that most observers have settled on is that mutual funds are not bought, but sold, in the sense that people do not buy funds based on their own independent research but are instead sold funds by people who benefit from the sale, much like people are sold products by infomercials. Closed-end funds have no salespeople because they do not issue new shares. Large investors prefer to manage their own portfolios while small investors, the natural audience for mutual funds, are persuaded to buy open-end funds with load charges by salespeople who profit from the load.

I always have an eye out for closed-end funds selling for large discounts.

THE JAPAN FUND

If a closed-end fund sells at a discount from its net asset value, it is worth more dead than alive, in that its shareholders would benefit if the fund sold its portfolio and distributed the proceeds to its shareholders, either directly or by repurchasing the fund's stock.

Let's look again at BeatTheMarket, a closed-end fund with 10 million shares outstanding and holding stocks with an aggregate market value of $100 million, giving a net asset value of $10 a share. If the fund can repurchase one million of its shares in the open market for $8 a share (a 20 percent discount from NAV), this will cost $8 million, reducing its assets from $100 million to $92 million and reducing the number of outstanding shares from 10 million to 9 million. The net asset value increases from $10 to $10.22:

$$\text{NAV} = \frac{\$92 \text{ million}}{9 \text{ million}} = \$10.22$$

If the fund continues to sell at a 20 percent discount, the market price rises to $8.17.

The repurchase of shares at a discount always increases the net asset value of the remaining shares. Shareholders who sell do so voluntarily; those who stay enjoy an increase in the net asset value of their shares. Win-win. If a fund's repurchase plan narrows the discount, so much the better.

An even more shareholder-friendly plan would be for BeatThe-Market to liquidate its $100 million stock portfolio and give its shareholders $10 a share, 25 percent more than the market price of their BeatTheMarket stock.

Why don't closed-end funds routinely repurchase shares whenever a discount appears? The most convincing reason is that management fees depend on the size of a fund; so, while repurchases are good for shareholders, they are not good for management. A liquidation would be even worse for fund managers as it would cost them their jobs.

Sometimes this understandable reluctance is overcome by aggressive investors who gain control of the fund and liquidate its assets. In the 1930s, Claude Odell made millions of dollars by liquidating closed-end funds.

A more recent case involved T. Boone Pickens III, the youngest son of the famous corporate raider. In 1987 he announced that he and several partners had acquired a 5.5 percent stake in the Japan Fund, which was then selling at a 20 percent discount from net asset value. With $700 million in assets, this 20 percent discount implied a $140 million gap between the market value of the Japan Fund's shares and the liquidation value of its assets.

Fearful that Pickens would force a liquidation, the fund's managers recommended that shareholders approve a resolution converting the company into an open-end fund. This move would eliminate the discount, thereby increasing the value of the fund's shares and satisfying Pickens and other shareholders while preserving the managers' jobs. The resolution was overwhelmingly supported by those shareholders who voted, but not enough voted to give it the necessary approval by 51 percent of all outstanding shares. The fund's managers quickly resubmitted the resolution and lobbied even harder for shareholder approval. The second time around, it did pass, and Pickens and his partners had a $10 million profit for their efforts on behalf of all shareholders.

It is interesting that, even after the conversion resolution passed in May 1987, the fund's discount did not immediately go to zero but hovered around 5 percent. The open-end conversion would not happen until July and investors were evidently worried that the inflated Japanese stock market might crash. Either that, or $100 bills were lying on the sidewalk.

I was tempted to go for a 5 percent profit on a two-month investment, but I decided to pass. A friend of mine, a Stanford professor of economics, invested heavily in the Japan Fund, even taking out a home equity loan to buy shares. He figured that a 5 percent return over two months was a briefcase full of $100 bills. It would have been more prudent to hedge his position by selling Nikkei futures. If the Japanese stock market crashed, the profits on his futures would offset the drop in the fund's net asset value. Instead, he took an unhedged position.

There were some scary ups and downs over the next two months, but the Japan Fund's NAV when it went open-end was about the same as when he bought shares, and he made his 5 percent profit.

There was a very different situation in 1986. The Korea Fund, a closed-end fund that invests in Korean stocks, had 5 million shares outstanding with a net asset value of $18 and a market price of $32, a 78 percent *premium* over net asset value. At the time, it was difficult for Americans to invest directly in Korean stocks, and the Korea Fund was the only U.S. fund that the Korean government allowed to buy Korean stocks. Americans were willing to pay a 78 percent premium to do so through the Korea Fund. The idea that Korean companies were prospering was compelling. The idea that Korean investors did not know this and had wildly underestimated the value of Korean stocks was preposterous.

The Japan Fund, which sold at a discount, could help its shareholders by repurchasing shares. The Korea Fund, which sold at a premium, could help its shareholders by issuing new shares. It did. The Korea Fund sold 1.2 million new shares at $32, raising $38.4 million. This increased the fund's net asset value from $18 to $20.71. Existing shareholders happily saw the net asset value of their shares increase 15 percent because new shareholders happily overpaid.

On December 31, 2015, Korea Fund shares sold for $31.85—a 10.2 percent discount from net asset value. A $10,000 investment in the Korea Fund in 1986 would have grown to $63,000 compared to $171,000 for a dollar investment in the S&P 500. The Korean miracle was real, but buying Korea Fund stock at an unrealistic premium was a distinctly poor investment.

FIRST FINANCIAL FUND

There was a time when banking was a boring profession—basically assessing the credit worthiness of local loan applicants (many of whom the bankers knew personally) and keeping accurate records. It was said to be as easy as 1, 2, 3. Pay your depositors one percent, loan the money out at 2 percent, and be on the golf course by 3 p.m.

In the 1960s and early 1970s, savings and loan associations (S&Ls) paid their depositors 2 to 5 percent interest and loaned the money out in mortgages at 4 to 8 percent, enough to pay depositors, cover expenses, and make a profit, too.

Mortgage rates topped 8 percent in 1971 and hit an unprecedented 10 percent in 1978. Most observers thought that interest rates would soon fall to more normal levels. They were wrong. Interest rates went higher still, to 18 percent plus in 1981. Homeowners who had mortgages with single-digit interest rates were lucky. The S&Ls they had borrowed from were not so lucky.

S&Ls had to raise deposit rates to double-digit levels to hold on to their depositors, but were earning single-digit interest rates on mortgages written in the 1960s and 1970s. The net worth of S&Ls nationwide fell from $23 billion at the end of 1977 to a frightening −$44 billion at the end of 1981. Yes, that is a negative sign in front of the dollar sign. The S&L industry was bankrupt. Nearly a quarter of the S&Ls operating in the 1970s collapsed or merged in the early 1980s.

So widespread and severe was the damage that Edward Yardeni, a Yale classmate and chief economist at Prudential-Bache, a major brokerage firm, defied the conventional wisdom and predicted a drop in interest rates. His outside-the-box reasoning was that the Federal Reserve would lower interest rates to bail out banks and S&Ls. In February 1985, he wrote, "The Fed must lower interest rates to offset the erosion of the financial system's net worth. . . . Otherwise the financial system will collapse."

He was right. Interest rates tumbled downward.

Unfortunately, Congress intervened in a clumsy way by deregulating the industry, allowing S&Ls to move away from their traditional emphasis on home mortgages and make more business loans. Some states, including California and Texas, allowed state-chartered S&Ls to invest in almost anything, including restaurants, health clubs, and wind farms.

S&Ls that were bleeding money and technically bankrupt had a choice—moan and groan through their death pangs or throw the dice and hope for a lucky roll. Bankrupt S&Ls could gamble with taxpayer money. Their net worth was already negative and the top executives would soon be unemployed; nothing worse could happen to them. If they took a huge gamble and lost, it would just be more money that the government had to pay their insured depositors. But if the gamble paid off, it might save the bank, and their jobs. These technically bankrupt S&Ls were zombie banks—dead, but walking about because of the magic of government intervention. No surprise that many zombie banks rolled the dice.

Others took advantage of the newfound freedom. Instead of applying for a loan that might be rejected, real estate developers took over S&Ls and loaned themselves money. It was cheaper for developers to pay deposit interest rates than to pay loan rates, and easier to get your loan approved if you owned the bank. They sometimes even paid themselves large fees for finding such attractive borrowers—themselves! One developer acquired an $11 million savings bank in California and increased its assets to $1 billion in less than three years, using half the deposits to finance the developer's real estate deals. He was unapologetic: "Who would you rather lend to, yourself or a stranger?"

Interest rates fell after 1982, but losses in the banking industry continued. The problem was no longer an interest rate squeeze, but mounting loan defaults—caused too often by excessive risk-taking or outright fraud: depositor money squandered on desert land and lavish bonuses. By 1990, the S&L industry had a negative net worth of at least $200 billion. The government finally realized its mistake.

It began supervising S&Ls more closely and moving quickly to chop off the heads of zombie banks.

First Financial Fund (FF) was launched in May 1986, in the midst of the S&L crisis, with the objective of investing in midsize banks and S&Ls. What a terrible idea! First Financial's stock price quickly fell to a 20 percent discount from NAV. I saw this evidently dumb idea as an opportunity. If most investors think the banking industry is going under, bank stocks are probably cheap. Remember Warren Buffett's advice: "Be fearful when others are greedy and greedy when others are fearful."

As for the fundamentals, the First Financial's 2 percent dividend yield was okay, the price-earnings ratio of 6 was seductive, and the fact that the managers were repurchasing the fund's stock at a 20 percent discount showed me that they cared about shareholders. Still, it was mostly a contrarian strategy based on my suspicion that the stock market had probably overreacted to the banking crisis, making banks and S&L stocks bargains and making First Financial's 20 percent discount on these bargain prices a double bargain. I invested a large amount in First Financial in 1986 and 1987, at a 20 percent discount to NAV, and held on for the ride.

First Financial's annual return was 19.4 percent during its first twenty years, compared to 11.6 percent for the S&P 500. An investment of $10,000 in First Financial at its inception was worth $345,000 twenty years later, compared to $90,000 for a similar investment in the S&P 500. It was a good twenty years for the overall stock market, but it was a great twenty years for First Financial.

Unfortunately, First Financial's success attracted the interest of an outside group that gained control of First Financial in 2006. The outside group changed the fund's name to First Opportunity Fund in 2008, and the fund was delisted from the New York Stock Exchange in 2010 when its focus changed from investing in banks and S&Ls to investing in hedge funds. Figure 14-2 shows First Financial's cumulative return compared to the S&P 500 from its inception in 1986 until its delisting in 2010.

If bought at the beginning and held the entire time First Financial was in existence, a $10,000 investment in FF would have grown
to $191,000 compared to $87,000 from an investment in the S&P
500. An investor prescient enough to get out in 2006, when outside
investors gained control of First Financial, would have done even
better.

I got out in 2004, too early, but it is foolish to think that one can
buy at the bottom and sell at the top, except by accident. My simple
logic for selling was my concern about the outside group's inten-
tions. If it ain't broke, don't fix it. I could see the possible upside
from an outside group taking over a company that was doing badly
and shaking things up. But where was the upside from shaking
things up at a company that was doing wonderfully?

The intended lesson from this example is that value investors
should be alert for contrarian opportunities. Just as the dot-com
bubble was a time to sell, panics and crises are times to buy.

FIGURE 14-2. Cumulative return on First Financial (FF) and the S&P 500.

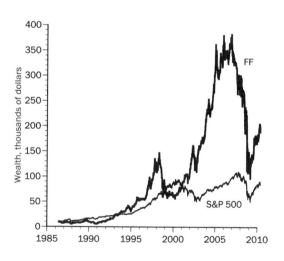

DUAL-PURPOSE FUNDS

Dual-purpose funds are closed-end funds with two shareholder classes: income and capital. The income shareholders receive all the dividends from the stocks in the fund's portfolio; the capital shareholders receive all the capital gains on the fund's termination date, typically ten to twenty years after the fund's inception.

On the termination date, the income-shareholders receive a specified redemption price (usually their initial investment), or the value of the fund's assets if this is less than the redemption price. The capital-shareholders get any excess of the fund's assets over this redemption price.

Consider a fund that starts by selling one million income shares for $10 and one million capital shares for $10, with a fifteen-year termination at a $10 redemption price for the income-shareholders. Each income share receives dividends on $20 worth of stock, plus $10 back in fifteen years. If the fund's stocks have a 5 percent dividend yield, the income-shareholders get a 10 percent dividend since they invested $10 and get dividends on $20.

The capital shares, meanwhile, have 2-to-1 leverage. If the value of the portfolio increases by 50 percent, from $20 to $30, the value of the capital shares increases by 100 percent, from $10 to $20. If the portfolio goes up 100 percent, the capital shares go up 200 percent.

Dual-purpose funds were created to meet the differing needs of investors, particularly when dividends and capital gains are taxed at different rates. Individuals and institutions in low tax brackets have a natural affinity for the generous dividends paid to the income shares. The capital shares hold special appeal to investors who pay lower taxes on capital gains than on dividends, and to investors who seek leverage.

No one can be made worse off by splitting the fund's shares into two classes, because investors can, if they want, buy equal amounts of both. If you own one percent of the income shares and one percent of the capital shares, you get one percent of the profits, no matter how they are divided, just as if the company were an ordinary closed-end fund. But there are two big differences. First, a dual-purpose fund gives investors flexibility in varying the proportion of dividend income to capital gains. Second, a dual-purpose fund's discount must go to zero on the termination date.

Figure 14-3 shows the seventeen-year history of the Gemini Fund, a very successful dual-purpose fund that was started in 1967 and terminated on December 31, 1984. In 1974 the capital shares sold at close to a 40 percent discount and the combined income and capital shares were at a 15 percent discount. For anyone who wanted to invest in stocks over the next ten years, this was an appealing way to do so. The capital shares had tremendous leverage with a huge discount that was guaranteed to vanish.

FIGURE 14-3. Gemini Fund's premium (+) or discount (-) from net asset value.

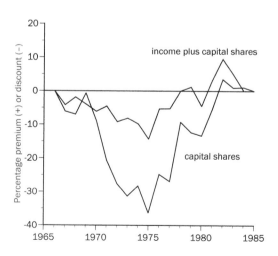

At the time, I was a low-paid assistant professor at Yale with not much money to invest. As it turned out, a $10,000 investment in the S&P 500 in January 1974 would have grown to $18,000 by 1985, a 5.6 percent annual rate of return. My $10,000 invested in Gemini Capital shares grew to $110,000, a 24.4 percent annual rate of return. Move over Warren Buffett!

SPECIAL OPPORTUNITIES

One of the funny things about the stock market is that every time one
person buys, another sells, and both think they are astute.
—William Feather

Every once in a while, Mr. Market offers special opportunities for buying or selling stocks. Remember, Mr. Market is not an all-wise impartial judge who tells us what things are really worth. Mr. Market spouts prices that are sometimes reasonable and sometimes foolish. Value investors who can distinguish the reasonable from the foolish can take advantage of Mr. Market's foolishness.

This is not easy. Yes, Mr. Market makes mistakes, but market prices that seem baffling to you and me may not be mistakes. It is easy to be lured by the promise of easy money. (I know from personal experience!) It takes willpower to step back and ask the pertinent questions:

1. Is this information from a reliable source? Ignore hot tips from auto mechanics about environmental companies.

2. Is it illegal insider information? Don't do time for doing a crime.

3. Why isn't it already embedded in the market price? Don't others know? Are others confused?

MASSIVELY CONFUSED INVESTORS

Stocks are identified by ticker symbols that were originally created to speed up the transmission of trading reports on ticker tape machines. Actively traded stocks were given single-letter ticker symbols; for example, the Atchison, Topeka, and Santa Fe Railway (A) and American Telephone and Telegraph (T). Today, New York Stock Exchange stocks have one to three letters plus additional characters that can be used to identify the type of security; for example, Citigroup (C), General Electric (GE), and Berkshire class A (BRK.A). Ticker symbols are usually abbreviations of a company's name, and companies sometimes become known by these abbreviations: GE, IBM, 3M.

Companies choose their ticker symbols, though exchanges can reject a choice that is offensive, misleading, or duplicates another company's symbol. In practice, the company's choice is almost always honored. One notable exception was Furr's/Bishop's Inc., which applied for the symbol FBI, but was rejected because this is the well-known acronym for the Federal Bureau of Investigation. In a perfectly efficient market, this shouldn't have mattered, but apparently the ticker-approvers thought it did.

The efficient market hypothesis says that investors cannot use public information to beat the market. A stock's ticker symbol is no secret and it would be surprising if a stock's performance were related to its ticker symbol. Surely, savvy investors focus on a company's profitability, not its ticker symbol!

Investors are not always savvy. After Charles Lindbergh's historic 1927 flight from New York to Paris, there was a surge in the price of airline stocks including Seaboard Air Line Railroad, even though Seaboard was a railroad whose name "Air Line" referred to its long stretches of straight track.

In his Harvard economics PhD thesis, Michael S. Rashes reported several instances where investors were confused about

ticker symbols. Two completely different firms, Massmutual Corporate Investors (traded on the NYSE with the ticker symbol
MCI) and MCI Communications (traded on the NASDAQ with
the ticker symbol MCIC), exhibited a strong correlation in their
prices, apparently because investors who wanted to invest in MCI
Communications mistakenly bought Massmutual stock. Rashes
wrote an article about this and other examples using the wonderful
title, "Massively Confused Investors Making Conspicuously Ignorant Choices."

Rashes also found that Transcontinental Realty Investors (TCI)
was mistaken for Tele-Communications Inc., causing TCI's price
to be affected by news about the possible takeover of Tele-
Communications by Bell Atlantic and later AT&T. Similarly, Castle
Convertible Fund, a mutual fund with the ticker symbol CVF,
briefly fell 32 percent after the *Financial Times* published a report of
impending losses for the Czech Value Fund, which it abbreviated
as CVF. A 1998 *Barron's* article was bullish on the Morgan Stanley
Asia Pacific Fund, but the ticker symbol was misprinted as APB,
rather than APF. The ticker symbol APB belongs to the Barings
Asia Pacific Fund, which opened up 30 percent the first trading day
after the *Barron's* article appeared.

In 1999, AppNet Systems filed for an initial public offering (IPO)
under the ticker symbol APPN, which was currently being used by
Appian Technology. In the two days following the filing (when it was
not yet possible to trade AppNet stock), 7.3 million shares of Appian
Technology stock were traded (compared to 200 shares the day before AppNet's IPO filing) and the price increased by 142,757 percent. During the initial public offering of Ticketmaster
Online-CitySearch using the ticker symbol TCMS, shares of Temco
Service Industries, whose ticker symbol was and had previously
been TCMS, rose from $28.875 to $65 before investors realized their
mistake and the price plunged to $25.50. When online retailer Ama-
zon had an IPO in 1997 using the ticker symbol AMZN, a company
called Amazon Natural Treasures, which had been using the ticker

symbol AMZN before Amazon went public (and switched to AZNT afterward), rose from $1 a share to $3 and then fell back to $1 after investors realized their mistake.

The Pokémon GO smartphone game burst on the scene in the summer of 2016. Users can find various Poké items superimposed on a map of their own actual geographic location and can capture wild Pokémon by throwing Poké Balls at them. Pokémon GO was an inexplicable success, quickly downloaded by more than 100 million people. Seemingly everywhere, kids were walking around with their faces glued to their smartphones. Some were hit by cars. Dozens of adults crashed their cars while playing and driving, including one person who slammed into a police car. (I won't make any jokes about the Darwin Awards for people who voluntarily improve the gene pool.)

Pokémon GO was developed by Niantic, a Google spin-off, using Google Maps. Nintendo had invested in Niantic, and Figure 15-1 shows that during a two-week period (July 5 to July 18), Nintendo's stock more than doubled, from $17.63 to $37.37, while daily trading volume surged from 26,000 shares to more than 13 million. Investors evidently had not spent much time investigating the extent of Nintendo's investment and the effect it might have on Nintendo's profits. On July 24, Nintendo issued a statement saying it had only a 13 percent interest in Niantic. Nintendo stock promptly plummeted 18 percent, the maximum allowed on the Tokyo stock exchange.

Commentators blamed the run-up and subsequent crash on "retail investors" who had not done their homework. I'm pretty sure that more than a few professional investors hadn't done their homework, either. If the much-maligned small investors had pushed Nintendo's stock price higher than the pros thought appropriate, the pros would have sold heavily, keeping the price from doubling.

FIGURE 15-1. Nintendo stock trading blindsided by Pokémon GO.

Yes, these are isolated examples of massively confused investors. They don't demonstrate that the stock market is completely nuts, but they do make one wonder about the assertion that Mr. Market never makes a mistake.

GOING AGAINST THE FLOW

Chapter 9 includes a discussion of a study I did (with two colleagues) of professional forecasts of corporate earnings. We found that the most optimistic predictions tended to be too optimistic and the most pessimistic predictions tended to be too pessimistic. One consequence was that, on average, stocks with pessimistic earnings forecasts outperformed stocks with optimistic forecasts.

In August 2015, I had $100,000 to invest and decided to test this strategy with real money. I had access to a pretty comprehensive database of real-time corporate-earnings forecasts made by professionals who are paid a lot of money to make these forecasts. I restricted my analysis to companies with forecasts from at least twenty-five analysts to ensure that the companies were prominent, highly visible, and closely scrutinized. Any systematic inaccuracies could not be explained away as careless guesses about unimportant companies. I used the median prediction to reduce the influence of outliers.

I had planned to divide the $100,000 evenly among the ten companies with the most pessimistic forecasts. All ten turned out to be in the energy sector. So, I bought a diversified portfolio of energy-related companies by investing $100,000 in Vanguard Energy Fund on August 19, 2015.

An all-energy portfolio, by itself, is not very diversified. True diversification would involve stocks from many sectors of the economy. Not to worry. I didn't own any energy stocks in the rest of my portfolio.

This was a challenging test of a contrarian strategy. It is not easy to invest in stocks that others loathe—especially stocks in an industry that others shun. My wife repeated the dire warnings she read about the energy sector and advised me not to throw away money on these stocks. This fortified my resolve. I remembered the advice to be greedy when others are fearful, and there was certainly a lot of fear about energy stocks. It was probably true that their earnings for the next few years would be dismal, but I also suspected that Mr. Market may have overreacted. I know that value investors look for good companies at bargain prices—not bad companies at bargain prices—but I also know that bargains can be found among bad companies.

The first few months were not pretty. Five months in, the S&P 500 was down 11 percent and my Vanguard Energy Fund was down 24 percent. This was another test of contrarian temperament. Let's take a moment for a pop quiz: When prices plunge, is a contrarian-investor's first reaction to:

a. Sell everything in order to contain the damage.

b. Buy more at even better prices.

The correct answer is (b), following the adage, "If you like a stock at $100, you will love it at $75." In this case, I didn't buy more, but I didn't bail out, either.

I was happy to see energy rebound. Figure 15-2 shows the one-year return, from August 19, 2015, to August 19, 2016, on the Vanguard Energy Fund and the S&P 500. The return on the S&P 500 was 5.0 percent; the return on the energy fund was 12.4 percent.

FIGURE 15-2. A contrarian investment

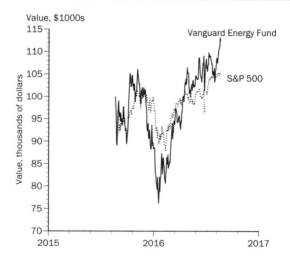

In practice, a strategy based on earnings forecasts is difficult for most people to implement because they don't have access to the database I used. However, there are some useful lessons.

As lesson one, this story is yet more tangible proof that contrarian strategies can pay off. Don't be afraid to invest in stocks that others hate; that's just another reason the stocks may be cheap. In fact, if a stock is inexpensive relative to its earnings and dividends, it is usually because other investors don't like something about the stock.

This principle is true not only of stocks, but also bonds, real estate, and other investments. For example, low-rated bonds with a substantial risk of default are called *junk bonds*. John Kenneth Galbraith, an illustrious Harvard professor, wrote that "anyone who buys a junk bond known as a junk bond deserves on the whole to lose." Why would any rational investor buy a junk bond when it is clearly labeled a junk bond? Because everything has a price. As long as a bond has some chance of paying some interest, somebody will pay some price for it. The price will be low and the potential yield high, but there will be a buyer. That is why junk bonds are also known euphemistically as *high-yield bonds*—they must offer high yields to persuade investors to hold them.

During the savings and loan crisis in the 1980s, some S&Ls bought junk because they were buying it with other people's money—their federally insured deposits. S&Ls were willing to borrow from their depositors at 5 to 10 percent interest to invest in junk bonds promising 15 to 20 percent returns because the profits, if any, would go to the S&L and the losses would be covered by federal deposit insurance. Heads, the S&L wins. Tails, the federal government loses.

As it turned out, up until the end of 1989, junk bonds were profitable for thrifts. A 1989 General Accounting Office report found that junk had not contributed to the S&L crisis up to that point and that junk bonds had, in fact, been one of the S&L industry's most profitable investments.

However, the years surveyed in this report had been recession free. Concerned about potential future defaults and recognizing the one-sided bets S&Ls were making with federally insured deposits, the 1989 Financial Institutions Reform, Recovery, and Enforcement Act (FIRREA) prohibited thrifts from buying additional junk bonds and gave them five years to sell their current holdings. As FIRREA neared completion, some thrifts made substantial last-minute junk purchases. One industry analyst said that these thrifts "realized this was their last window of opportunity, so they jumped in. It was a case of speeding up at the yellow light." During the last forty days before FIRREA was enacted, ten of these hot-rod thrifts bought a total of more than $1 billion in junk bonds, increasing their holdings by 19 percent.

In retrospect, their timing couldn't have been worse. With further purchases prohibited and sales mandated, FIRREA created an excess supply of junk. Coupled with Drexel-Burnham's bankruptcy, the junk bond market collapsed, as prices fell some 10 to 15 percent in the first three months after FIRREA's prohibition went into effect. The same industry analyst quoted previously continued the analogy: "After they got to the [yellow] light, the market went over the cliff."

This is yet again an example of how market prices need not equal the best estimate of the value of an investment. Junk bonds were not more likely to default after FIRREA passed. The intrinsic value of their anticipated cash flow was unchanged, yet market prices collapsed because thrift institutions could no longer hold junk. It is as if prohibiting pension funds from buying Coca-Cola stock somehow changed the intrinsic value of Coke stock.

Trust Company of the West (TCW) recognized that the drop in junk prices was not warranted. Wall Street was having a sale on junk bonds and TCW loaded up. It turned out to be a spectacular investment. After the junk collapse, junk bond prices nearly doubled over the next three years—which is yet another example of the first lesson to be learned from my energy investment: A contrarian strategy can be wise, not foolish.

A second lesson from my energy investment is: don't panic if Mr. Market doesn't like your investment. The tax benefits from harvesting losses is a good reason to sell stocks that have gone down in price. Selling because you fear prices may fall further is not a good reason. If anything, falling prices may be a persuasive reason to buy more.

The third lesson is a reminder that contrarian investors need to have the temperament to buy stocks that others hate and resolve not to panic if prices fall.

When AT&T acquired the Canadian telephone company Metronet (renamed AT&T Canada) in June 1999, foreigners were not allowed to own more than 33 percent of a Canadian company; so AT&T bought 31 percent of the shares and agreed to buy the remaining 69 percent by June 2003, either for itself or for resale to a Canadian company. AT&T agreed to a floor on the buyout price starting at $37.50 Canadian dollars in June 2000, with the floor rising by 17 percent a year to $60 in June 2003. To prevent an infinite stalling strategy, AT&T also agreed that if it had not purchased the remaining 69 percent by July 2003, it would sell AT&T Canada and pay whatever was needed to ensure that AT&T Canada shareholders got at least their preset floor.

At the time of the acquisition in June 1999, AT&T Canada stock was selling for $84.01. AT&T had big plans for making the company even more valuable, so the floor price did not seem like a big deal. However, AT&T Canada floundered, losing $325 million in 2000 and $456 million in 2001, and its stock price fell below the floor in May 2001. I saw a story about this unusual situation in October 2001. Since the floor was guaranteed to increase by 17 percent a year, it seemed like a guaranteed annual return of 17 percent.

I did a little research and found that some hedge funds had noticed this quirky situation, too, and their lawyers had concluded that about the only way AT&T could get out of the contract was to declare bankruptcy, which seemed unlikely since they had far more assets than the cost of fulfilling their AT&T Canada commitment. The only real uncertainty for American investors (like me) was that the buyout price was in Canadian dollars and I live my life using U.S. dollars. If the value of the U.S. dollar were to drop relative to the Canadian dollar, my annual return would be less than 17 percent. Of course, if the U.S. dollar were to appreciate, my annual return would be more than 17 percent. I figured that the U.S. dollar was as likely to appreciate as depreciate, so I was looking at an expected annual return of 17 percent. I also figured that AT&T knew that the cost of fulfilling this contract was rising by 17 percent a year, so it would buy the shares as soon as possible.

This was definitely not a value play. AT&T Canada was a mess. It was losing money and paid no dividends—not the honey that attracts value investors. Still, it seemed to be a unique opportunity. I bought shares in October 2001 at a price equal to the current floor price and, a year later, in October 2002, AT&T fulfilled its contractual obligation by purchasing the remaining 69 percent stake at the prevailing floor price. I had my 17 percent return.

LEHMAN BROTHERS

Henry, Emanuel, and Mayer Lehman, the sons of a Bavarian cattle merchant, immigrated to Montgomery, Alabama, in the 1840s. They started a dry-goods store in 1844 that evolved into a cotton-trading business and, eventually, the fourth-largest U.S. investment bank in 2002—named, appropriately enough, Lehman Brothers.

Between 2002 and 2007, Lehman invested heavily in mortgages made to so-called subprime borrowers who would not normally qualify for mortgages. At the time, many investment banks bundled mortgages into mortgage-backed securities. Traditionally, home buyers borrowed money from a local bank and paid off their mortgage over, say, thirty years. A mortgage-backed security is a collection of mortgages purchased from banks and resold to investors, with the monthly mortgage payments passed through to the owners of the mortgage-backed security.

In theory, mortgage-backed securities allow insurance companies, pension funds, and other investors to make home loans part of their portfolios. They also channel more money to mortgage lending because every time a bank makes a mortgage loan and sells it, the bank gets more money for more mortgage loans.

In practice, local banks are best able to evaluate the strength of the local real estate market and the creditworthiness of borrowers, and they have a clear incentive to do so when they are going to hold a mortgage for thirty years. If the borrower defaults, the bank is stuck with the bad loan. However, if the mortgage is sold to someone else, it is no longer the bank's problem; so the bank doesn't have as much incentive to scrutinize loans carefully. Banks made profits based on the number of mortgages they originated, not on the monthly mortgage payments.

This problem was exacerbated by the creation of national mortgage brokers who have little knowledge of local real estate markets and no personal knowledge of loan applicants. Their compensation is based on making mortgages, and making mortgages is what they did, including NINJA loans to applicants with No Income, No Job, and No Assets. At the first sign of trouble, the borrower disappears like a Ninja in the night. Too many mortgage loans were made (often at initially low teaser rates) to people who had no realistic chance of making the mortgage payments. Too many mortgage brokers got rich selling NINJA loans to unsuspecting investors.

Somehow, these mortgage-backed bundles of subprime loans were rated AAA, and naive investors bought them. The idea must have been that the odds were low that every NINJA loan would default. But if NINJA borrowers were counting on home prices rising and selling their homes before the teaser loan rates expired, most NINJA borrowers would be in trouble if home prices stopped rising.

Not only that, but investment banks created collateralized debt obligations (CDOs), which are bundles of mortgage-backed securities sliced into so-called tranches. Investors who bought the lowest ("junior") tranches received a disproportionate share of the interest and coupons from the underlying mortgages, but were the first to lose their income if borrowers defaulted. Investors who bought the highest ("senior") tranches received less interest and coupons, but were the last to be affected if borrowers defaulted.

As if that weren't complicated enough, investment banks created CDOs-squared, which are CDOs backed by the tranches of other CDOs. A junior CDO-squared consisted of junior tranches from several CDOs. In theory, this offered more diversification than a junior tranche from a single CDO. In practice, if falling home prices caused one junior CDO to crash, most would.

The legal documents were thousands of pages long, read by few, and understood by fewer. Many investors ignored the sound advice, "Don't invest in something you don't understand."

Lehman created a lot of CDOs and ended up holding a lot of the junior tranches. We don't know if this was because Lehman couldn't offload the junior tranches to other investors or if Lehman thought junior tranches were a profitable investment. Lehman was highly leveraged, borrowing billions of dollars to invest billions of dollars. When the profits on their investments were larger than the interest on the loans used to finance these investments, Lehman's employees and stock holders made a lot of money. Lehman's CEO, Richard Fuld, was paid $485 million between 2000 and 2007.

It is wise advice to expect the unexpected. Lehman expected the expected until the unexpected happened. Home prices stopped rising and started falling. Strapped borrowers couldn't make their mortgage payments and couldn't sell their homes for enough money to pay off their mortgages. Home builders stopped building and ripples from unemployed construction workers spread through the economy. Many borrowers lost their jobs and then their homes. Lehman started losing lots of money on its highly leveraged CDOs.

Lehman was also heavily involved with credit default swaps. In a credit default swap (CDS), one party pays a fee to pass the risk of a loan or bond default on to someone else. For example, a pension fund might own a bond issued by a corporation or foreign government and be concerned that the borrower may default. The pension fund buys a CDS from a third party, which agrees to buy the bond from the pension fund at face value if the borrower defaults.

The pension fund has purchased default insurance. In theory, the third party that sold the insurance is acting like all sensible insurance companies. It has assessed the chances of default and determined that the expected value of the cost is less than the fee. If it is a large, financially secure institution with a diversified portfolio of credit default swaps, it assumes that it will be little affected by an occasional default. It will be in a world of trouble, however, if some macroeconomic event, like a global recession, causes a wave of defaults—just like insurance companies operating in Chicago were bankrupted by the Great Chicago Fire of 1871.

A lot of institutions didn't use credit default swaps for insurance, but for speculation. A hedge fund might buy billions of dollars of credit default swaps on bonds it doesn't own, which is an unhedged bet that the borrowers will default. Lehman had, in fact, purchased $250 billion in CDS contracts on bonds it didn't own. Ironically, $400 billion in CDS contracts had been created by investors who wanted to bet for and against Lehman's bankruptcy.

The U.S. Treasury and Federal Reserve have often operated under the assumption that some companies are "too big to fail," meaning that because of the interconnected nature of the financial system, the failure of a large company will have ripple effects that cripple the economy. If a large bank fails, it won't be able to repay its loans from other banks. If these other banks can't collect their loans, they may go bankrupt, too, which means they can't repay their loans. Perhaps even worse, if companies are worried about a company failing, they won't lend them money or sell them anything for fear that they won't be repaid. For a bank, this might mean they can't buy stocks or bonds; for an industrial company, it might mean that they can't buy the raw materials they need to keep operating. It becomes a self-fulfilling prophecy in that, unable to borrow money or buy things, a company that is thought to be in danger of failing does fail. The larger the company, the larger the risk of a contagious collapse. Thus the federal government considers some companies to be too big to fail. If a too-big-to-fail company is endangered, the Treasury and Fed step in to lend it money to save the company (and the financial system).

The unintended consequence is that companies that consider themselves too big to fail are encouraged to take excessive risks, knowing that they will reap outsize gains if their gambles pay off and that they will be bailed out by the government if their gambles fail.

In March 2008, Bear Stearns was rocked by losses on its subprime mortgages, mortgage-backed securities, and CDOs. The Federal Reserve acted quickly to supply $29 billion to finance JPMorgan Chase's purchase of Bear Stearns, explaining that it wanted to avoid a "chaotic unwinding" of Bear Stearns investments.

Six months later, Lehman Brothers was hit by life-threatening losses from its subprime mortgage securities. Lehman's stock price collapsed and a Wall Street friend told me that Lehman stock was a great investment. Lehman Brothers' real estate alone was worth more than its stock was selling for and the government wouldn't let such a prominent bank fail. I invested a small amount ($20,000) because I thought my friend might be right, but I kept my investment small because I knew that, no matter how valuable its real estate, its mortgage-related losses might be even larger.

At the same time that the federal government was pushing Bank of America to acquire financially troubled Merrill Lynch, the Treasury and Fed stood aside and let Lehman fail (perhaps because of criticism of the Bear Stearns bailout, perhaps because Treasury Secretary Henry Paulson had been CEO of Goldman Sachs and this somehow influenced the decision to save one company and not the other).

Ironically, Lehman's failure confirmed the too-big-to-fail argument by precipitating a financial crisis and near meltdown of financial firms and markets worldwide. Paulson persuaded Congress to authorize a $700 billion bailout fund, of which $160 billion was used to prop up American International Group (AIG) and another $170 billion was used to stabilize the nine largest U.S. banks.

My friend was wrong, and we got burned. In retrospect, it was not a sure thing, one way or the other. It was a gamble because inves-tors didn't know the extent of Lehman's losses or whether the fed-eral government would bail out Lehman. I might have won my bet, but I didn't. Lehman was a hot tip that fizzled.

CROSSLAND SAVINGS

The U.S. banking system has a wild and scary history. The Bank of the United States was founded in 1791, with $2 million raised from the federal government and $8 million from private citizens. Mod-eled after the Bank of England, its eight branches stored private and government deposits and made loans to citizens and to the govern-ment. The Bank also issued bank notes (currency) that could be re-deemed for gold or silver. At the time, fewer than a hundred other banks were in operation, all smaller and located on the East Coast.

In 1810, on a narrow vote, Congress failed to renew the Bank's charter and it closed. In the succeeding ten years, state-chartered banks and bank notes of varying repute multiplied. One historian wrote that "corporations and tradesmen issued 'currency.' Even bar-bers and bartenders competed with banks in this respect . . . nearly every citizen regarded it as his constitutional right to issue money." One successful Midwestern banker related his start in the business: "Well, I didn't have much to do and so I rented an empty store and painted 'bank' on the window. The first day a man came in and de-posited $100, and a couple of days later, another man deposited an-other $250 and so along about the fourth day I got confidence enough in the bank to put in $1.00 myself."

In 1816 the Second Bank of the United States was chartered. It actively speculated, particularly in western land, and its Baltimore branch made so many bad loans that it went bankrupt in 1818. In 1819 a new head of the Second Bank reduced its speculative activi-ties by restricting new loans and forcing some borrowers to pay off old ones, putting a discernible crimp in commerce. The next president of the Second Bank, Nicholas Biddle, reinstituted the First Bank's policy of refusing to accept bank notes that were not redeemable in gold or silver.

Because of these unpopular policies, the fight to renew the Bank's charter in 1832 was bitter. (Biddle's brother, who was director of the St. Louis branch, was killed in a duel fought at a distance of five feet because of Biddle's nearsightedness.) The populist president Andrew Jackson removed government deposits from the Second Bank and vetoed a bill renewing its charter. Rechartered by the state of Pennsylvania, Biddle's bank failed in 1841 after excessive speculation and questionable loans to bank officers.

After the restraining power of the Second Bank of the United States was lifted, there was a surge of new banks and of unbacked bank money. Banks in the East were usually managed conservatively, with substantial reserves of gold and silver and a readiness to redeem their money with precious metal. Banks in other parts of the country were more loosely managed and were willing to lend unbacked paper to farmers and businessmen settling new territories. When the land was fertile and business good, the communities and their banks prospered; when crops and businesses failed, their banks failed with them.

Thousands of private banks were established by financiers, blacksmiths, trading-post owners, and other entrepreneurs. Banks were regulated by the states in which they operated, and regulations regarding precious-metal reserves were unevenly enforced. A Massachusetts bank with $500,000 in notes outstanding was found to have $86.48 in reserves. In Michigan, a common collection of reserves (including hidden lead, glass, and tenpenny nails) passed from bank to bank, ahead of the state examiners. Opening a bank and issuing bank notes seemed like a pretty easy way literally to make money. It was an occupation that attracted the most reputable and public-spirited people and the lowest and most down-and-out scoundrels. Many helped the country prosper, and many simply redistributed its wealth.

By the time of the Civil War, there were some 7,000 different types of bank currency in circulation, of which 5,000 were counterfeit issues. Because of widespread uncertainty about the financial condition of banks (and the authenticity of notes), bank notes traded at discounts from their face value. For example, a merchant might accept a $10 bank note in payment for $8 worth of merchandise. With the South and the Mississippi Valley not represented in Congress, the federal government levied a 1%, 2%, and then 10% annual tax on currency issued by state-chatered banks. State bank notes consequently declined, replaced by checking accounts. Nationally chartered banks issued national bank notes, which were more uniformly printed and backed by government bonds deposited with the Treasury.

Most countries have just a handful of banks, with hundreds of branches. By the 1980s, there were tens of thousands of banks in the United States, mostly mom-and-pop banks protected by anticompetitive laws. Banks were not allowed to pay interest on checking accounts and there were interest-rate ceilings on savings accounts. Banks were not allowed to cross state lines, and the number of branches within a state were limited. In Illinois, for example, banks could only have one branch, which kept the big banks in Chicago from poaching customers throughout rural Illinois.

Eventually, technological advances and political pressure from consumers and big banks led to a consolidation of the U.S. banking system, accelerated by the financial crises in the late 1970s and early 1980s.

In New York, for example, many small banks had been established decades ago to serve local neighborhoods or groups sharing a common ethnicity or occupation. One of these banks was Brevoort Savings Bank, founded in 1890 by Henry Lefferts Brevoort, whose family tree traced back to the first Dutch settlers in Brooklyn. The Brevoorts intended the Brevoort Savings Bank to provide safe deposits and fair loans to local families, who would no longer have to travel miles to get to a bank. Brevoort Savings Bank was the only bank in the Bedford neighborhood of Brooklyn, which had been settled by the Dutch in the 1600s. Brevoort was always well run, but it succumbed to the merger wave in the 1970s and 1980s, as small banks consolidated and, in essence, became branches of a larger entity.

The East Brooklyn Savings Bank, which had been chartered in 1860, changed its name to the Metropolitan Savings Bank (Brooklyn) in 1969 and acquired Brevoort Savings Bank in 1970, Fulton Savings Bank (Brooklyn) in 1977, Spring Valley Savings & Loan Association in 1980, Brooklyn Savings Bank in 1981, and Greenwich Savings Bank in 1981.

Most of these banks were more than 100 years old. Brevoort had been chartered in 1890, Fulton in 1870, Spring Valley in 1889, Brooklyn Savings in 1827, and Greenwich in 1833. The acquisition of the Greenwich Savings Bank included its majestic headquarters (now called the Haier Building and a New York City landmark), which has a domed ceiling with a 3,000-square-foot, 72-foot-high stained-glass skylight.

The Metropolitan Savings Bank changed its name to the Federal Metropolitan Savings Bank in 1983 and to Crossland Savings in 1985. Headquartered in Brooklyn, Crossland Savings was the largest savings bank in New York State in the 1980s. With $6.5 billion in deposits, Crossland moved away from traditional residential mortgage lending in the 1980s into commercial real estate loans. Commercial real estate is risky because of uncertainties about rental rates and occupancy rates. If rents turn out to be lower than predicted or expenses and vacancy rates turn out to be higher than expected, commercial borrowers may fall behind or even default on their loans. On the other hand, banks can generally charge higher rates on commercial real estate loans than on residential mortgages because the risks are greater. By the end of the 1980s, half of Crossland's loans were for commercial real estate, including acquisition and construction loans. Crossland lost $442 million in the first nine months of 1989, mostly due to delinquencies and defaults on its real estate loans. Rumors circulated that Crossland was on the verge of collapse and its stock price plummeted.

Was this an overreaction, or was Crossland going through its death throes? The manager of one of the nation's largest college endowments told me that he was investing in Crossland Savings because it had an irresistible stockpile of unused capital losses. He expected a profitable bank to buy Crossland in order to use these accumulated capital losses to reduce its taxable income. By his reckoning, the capital losses alone were worth much more than the market price of Crossland's stock, not to mention the real estate its 110 branches were sitting on. The $5 billion in deposits, mostly from hundreds of thousands of small depositors who didn't seem to mind being paid relatively low interest rates, was also a plus, though the hundreds of millions of dollars in delinquent loans were a big minus.

I hadn't been investing long and figured that this endowment manager knew more than I did, so I bought a few thousand dollars' worth of Crossland stock in 1990. Figure 15-3 shows what happened.

In an unexpected twist, Crossland was accused of tax fraud in 1991. Crossland was said to have set up six dummy companies in Delaware and shifted $152 million of its income to these Delaware companies in order to avoid paying New York state and city taxes on the income. This accusation was not the reason for Crossland's failure, but it suggested that something might be amiss in their operations and/or accounting.

The Federal Deposit Insurance Corporation (FDIC) took over Crossland in 1992 and pumped in $1.2 billion to keep it afloat. Three years later the FDIC sold Crossland to Republic Bank of New York for $529.6 million. My friend's hot tip was not so hot. (Note to self: Be skeptical of hot tips, even tips from highly reputable and successful investors.)

FIGURE 15-3. Crossland Savings' slalom

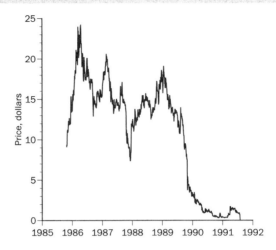

ROYAL DUTCH/SHELL

The Royal Dutch Petroleum Company (based in the Netherlands) and the Shell Transport and Trading Company (based in the United Kingdom) joined forces in 1907 to do battle with John D. Rockefeller's Standard Oil, the largest oil refiner in the world. Royal Dutch would focus on production, Shell on distribution. Together, they might survive.

The curious thing about their agreement was that Royal Dutch and Shell kept their existing shareholders and their stock continued to trade on various stock exchanges even though all revenue and expenses were consolidated by the mothership, named Royal Dutch Shell, which was owned 60 percent by Royal Dutch Petroleum and 40 percent by Shell. Whatever earnings Royal Dutch Shell reported, 60 percent were attributed to Royal Dutch Petroleum, 40 percent to Shell. Whatever dividends Royal Dutch Shell paid, 60 percent went to Royal Dutch Petroleum shareholders, 40 percent to Shell shareholders. If Royal Dutch Shell were ever to be sold, 60 percent of the proceeds would go to Royal Dutch Petroleum shareholders, 40 percent to Shell shareholders.

On intrinsic value grounds, whatever Shell Transport was worth, Royal Dutch Petroleum was worth 50 percent more. If the stock market valued these stocks correctly, the market value of Royal Dutch Petroleum stock should always be 50 percent higher than the market of Shell Transport stock. But it wasn't!

Figure 15-4 shows the ratio of the market value of Royal Dutch Petroleum stock to the market value of Shell Transport stock from March 13, 1957, when both stocks were traded on the New York Stock Exchange, until July 19, 2005, when the two companies merged fully and their stocks stopped being traded separately.

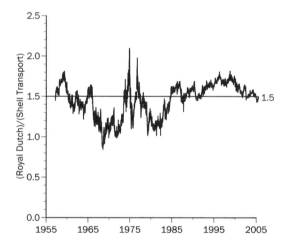

FIGURE 15-4 Royal Dutch Petroleum vs. Shell Transport

Royal Dutch Petroleum stock was seldom worth exactly 50 percent more than Shell stock. Sometimes it was 40 percent overpriced; sometimes it was 30 percent underpriced. Even if there had been a logical reason for Royal Dutch to be worth more or less than 50 percent of Shell (and there wasn't any that I could think of), there was certainly no reason why the excess or deficit should fluctuate wildly. Forty-six percent of the time, the mispricing was larger than

10 percent; 18 percent of the time, the mispricing was larger than 20 percent.

In theory, arbitragers could have profited handsomely from this mispricing, and their arbitrage trades should have eliminated the mispricing. When Royal Dutch traded at a premium to the 1.5 ratio, an arbitrager could have bought Shell stock and sold Royal Dutch stock short, betting on the premium disappearing, and these purchases of Shell and short sales of Royal Dutch should have helped the premium vanish.

This is exactly what one hedge fund, Long-Term Capital Management, did in 1997, when the premium was 8 to 10 percent. Long-Term bought $1.15 billion of Shell stock, sold $1.15 billion of Royal Dutch stock short, and waited for the market to correct. Long-Term was run by an all-star management team, including two finance professors who won Nobel prizes in 1997, and its Royal Dutch/Shell hedge was a smart bet based on persuasive logic, not just statistical patterns that may have been coincidental and meaningless. The ratio of the market values should go to 1.5 eventually and Long-Term would profit from its smart hedge.

However, as Keynes observed during the Great Depression:

> This long run is a misleading guide to current affairs. In the long run we are all dead. Economists set themselves too easy, too useless a task if in tempestuous seasons they can only tell us that when the storm is past the ocean is flat again.

Keynes was mocking the belief that, in the long run, the economy will be calm and everyone who wants a job will have a job. Keynes believed that the storm of an economic recession is more important than a hypothetical long run that no one will ever live to see. It is the same in finance. Trades that might be profitable in the long run can be disastrous in the short run.

Long-Term's net worth at the beginning of 1998 was nearly $5 billion. In August, an unforeseen storm hit. Russia defaulted on its debt and perceived measures of risk rose throughout financial markets. Long-Term had placed bets in many different markets, but an awful lot of them were bets that risk premiums would decline. After the Russian default, risk premiums rose everywhere, and Long-Term was in trouble—big trouble.

Long-Term argued that all it needed was time for financial markets to return to normal—for the storm to pass and the ocean to become flat again—but Long-Term didn't have time. Its tremendous leverage created enormous losses. Long-Term lost $550 million on August 21, 1998, and $2.1 billion for the entire month, which was nearly half its net worth.

Long-Term tried to raise more money so that it could wait out the storm, but frightened lenders didn't want to lend it more money. They wanted their money back.

Keynes was not only a master economist; he was also a legendary investor. Remember his observation: "Markets can remain irrational longer than you can remain solvent." Perhaps markets overreacted to the Russian default. Perhaps Long-Term's losses would have turned into profits eventually. But it couldn't stay solvent long enough to find out.

Long-Term Capital Management had to close its Royal Dutch/ Shell position, and unfortunately, the Royal Dutch premium, instead of declining, had gone above 20 percent and Long-Term lost $150 million.

On September 23, 1998, Warren Buffett faxed Long-Term a one-page letter offering to buy the firm for $250 million, roughly 5 percent of its value at the beginning of the year. The offer was take it or leave it and would expire at 12:30 p.m., about an hour after the fax had been sent. The deadline passed and the funeral preparations began.

The Federal Reserve Bank of New York feared that the domino effect of a Long-Term default would trigger a global financial crisis. The Federal Reserve and Long-Term's creditors took over the hedge fund and liquidated its assets. The creditors got their money back, Long-Term's founding partners lost $1.9 billion, and other investors got an expensive lesson in the power of leverage.

Notice in Figure 15-4 that premium did disappear eventually, when the companies merged in 2005, with the Royal Dutch shareholders getting 60 percent of the shares in the combined company and Shell shareholders getting 40 percent.

The Royal Dutch/Shell mispricing is compelling evidence that Mr. Market's prices are sometimes wacky. Whatever the "correct" value of Shell stock, Royal Dutch was worth exactly 50 percent more, yet Mr. Market quoted prices sometimes higher and other times lower. This example also demonstrates how arbitrage does not necessarily eliminate mispricings and how arbitrage can be risky, even if done correctly by the best and brightest investors. An academic study of a dozen comparable arbitrage situations found that in many cases the mispricing lasted for several years and worsened before it improved.

Personally, I learned of the Royal Dutch/Shell mispricing in the early 1990s, but I never took a hedged position—partly because of the risk and partly because of my (perhaps irrational) dislike of short sales. I also never invested in Royal Dutch Petroleum or Shell Transport—though, if I had, I would have picked the one that was cheaper.

The main lesson for value investors is simple. Some aficionados of the efficient market hypothesis believe that stock markets can be trusted to set the correct prices—and that investors should accept these prices as the best estimates of what a stock is really worth. Balderdash! It is hard to disprove their fanciful claim for most stocks because we don't know for certain what a stock is really worth. The Royal Dutch/Shell example is one case where we do know exactly what Royal Dutch stock was worth in comparison to Shell stock—and we know that market prices were wrong, by a substantial amount and for a long period of time.

The fact that Mr. Market's prices are sometimes silly and usually too volatile means that value investors can take advantage of Mr. Market's fickleness. However, value investors should still ask themselves if they know something Mr. Market doesn't know. Value investors should not buy Apple stock just because iPhone sales increased, since other investors surely know that, too. But value investors should not be intimidated by arguments—even from Nobel laureates—that market prices are the best estimates of what stocks are worth.

UNILEVER

Unilever was created in 1930 by the merger of the Dutch company Margarine Unie and the British company Lever Brothers—hence the name Unilever. The Dutch company made margarine and the British company made soap, and both products are made with palm oil, so it made sense to join forces and negotiate lower prices for imported palm oil. Today, Unilever is one of the world's largest consumer-goods companies, with more than 400 brands, including Axe/ Lynx fragrances, Dove toiletries, Hellmann's mayonnaise, and Lipton tea.

The 1930 merger maintained two separate companies that are treated as equals: Unilever NV, headquartered in Rotterdam, and Unilever PLC, headquartered in London. The two companies have the same CEO and board of directors. The shareholders have the same rights and are paid the same dividends.

Both companies have the same intrinsic value, yet the market prices of their stocks sometimes diverge.

Figure 15-5 shows the ratio of the price of Unilever PLC to Unilever NV back to 1960, when both stocks were traded on the New York Stock Exchange. Up until the 1980s, the mispricing was astounding. Eighty-seven percent of the time, the mispricing was larger than 10 percent; 53 percent of the time, the mispricing was larger than 20 percent. Figure 15-5 shows that the mispricing often lasted years and got worse before it got better, though the mispricing has been smaller in recent years.

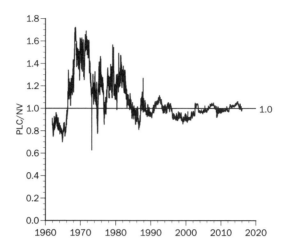

FIGURE 15-5. Unilever PLC vs. Unilever NV

(Even if there is some overlooked reason why one company is worth more than the other, the company's stock should consistently reflect this advantage. For example, if Unilever PLC was worth 5 percent more than Unilever NV, the ratio of their market values should always be 1.05, not sometimes 1.7 and other times 0.6.)

Like the Royal Dutch/Shell mispricing, this example is more indisputable evidence that markets do not invariably set "correct" prices, in any meaningful sense of the word. No matter what the intrinsic value of Unilever PLC, the intrinsic value of Unilever NV is identical. If the stock market sets different prices for these two stocks, at least one price does not equal intrinsic value. Most likely, neither price is equal to intrinsic value.

As with the Royal Dutch/Shell mispricing, I never tried to arbitrage the Unilever mispricing by buying one stock and shorting the other. I have invested in Unilever—always choosing whichever stock was cheaper at the time.

16

INVESTING IN YOUR HOME

Buy land, they're not making it anymore.

—MARK TWAIN

Bill grew up in Porterville, a small town in California's great Central Valley. He was valedictorian of his high school class of twelve students. Bette grew up in Indio, a small California desert town that was perhaps best known for its annual date festival, which features camel races and a surprising variety of foods made with dates—including date ice cream.

Bill and Bette married in 1942 and bought their first home in 1946: a 900-square-foot, two-bedroom home, 100 yards from a railroad track in a modest suburban community that was close to Bill's job in Southern California's aerospace industry. They paid $4,000 for this home with a $500 down payment and a $3,500 mortgage.

By 1954, they had four children, the oldest age nine, a three-year-old, a one-year-old, and a newborn. They needed a bigger home and Bill's growing salary allowed them to afford one. They bought a three-bedroom, two-bath tract home in La Habra, another quiet Southern California town. They sold their first home for $8,000 and paid $13,000 for their new home.

They raised their family in this home until their children were grown and Bill and Bette had grown tired of how crowded and congested Southern California had become—not at all like their childhoods in Porterville and Indio. In 1990, Bill retired and they sold their La Habra home and bought a condominium on Golf Course Road in Thatcher, Arizona. Bill taught at the local community college and played golf almost every day; Bette took photography classes at the community college and took pictures of Arizona's natural beauty.

Bill's pension from his aerospace employer, his Social Security payments, and the money they netted from selling their La Habra home and buying a home in Thatcher provided them with a secure, comfortable retirement.

Their lifetime of homeownership turned a $500 investment into a comfortable retirement nest egg. In addition, the rent they saved every year for decades paid for college for all four of their children. Their home was the best investment they ever made. I know because they were my parents.

THE INTRINSIC VALUE OF A HOME

The biggest investment that many people will ever make is the house they live in, yet they don't think of their home as an investment. Homes aren't like stocks. Homes are just where we happen to live, right? Nope. A home is an investment just like stocks.

Stocks pay dividends. What is the income from a home? A *New York Times* writer couldn't figure it out. He said that "houses have no underlying revenue stream (such as a stock's corporate earnings) on which to base an assumption of true value." He was completely and utterly wrong. Homes do have income. It's subtle, but it's absolutely crucial for understanding how a home can be valued the same way as stocks.

For a landlord, the income is obvious—the monthly rent check from the tenants. If you own your home, there is income, too, but it is harder to see because no one gives you a check each month. The income is the rent you *don't* have to pay. If you rent a home for $1,500 a month, this money goes out of your bank account and into your landlord's account. If you own your home, $1,500 doesn't leave your bank account. This $1,500 is not theoretical. It is real dollars that you can use for food, clothing, and entertainment. This $1,500 is income from your home.

Home buyers don't usually think this way. Some homeowners consider their home a "necessary expense," like food and clothing. They figure their home is worth what other homes are selling for (what are called *comps*). If a similar house sold for $400,000, that's what their home is worth. That's like saying that stocks are a necessary expense and a stock is worth what similar stocks sell for. Value investors know better.

A second, very different type of home buyer thinks real estate is a speculative road to riches. They buy homes to "flip" a short while later for a profit, the way stock traders count on a line of greater fools. They are too quick to assume that however fast home prices have gone up in the past, they will continue doing so in the future. They think they can buy a house for $400,000 and sell it a few months later for $450,000. Money for nothing. Value investors know better.

IF I BOUGHT IT, IT MUST BE WORTH WHAT I PAID

Some financial advisers view residential housing as a foolproof investment that does not require financial analysis. A former managing director at Salomon Brothers argued that "there is no bad time to buy." A prolific real estate author and professor was only slightly more restrained, stating that "90 to 95 percent of people [who buy a house] will say it is the best investment I ever made."

Humorist Will Rogers seconded Mark Twain's argument when he offered this tempting reason for optimism: "Don't wait to buy land. Buy land and wait, the good Lord ain't makin' any more of it." The same argument could be made about anything with a fixed supply, including many things that would not be taken seriously as invest-ments, including Lisa computers, Chrysler New Yorkers, and last year's clothing fashions. (If you don't know what a Lisa computer or Chrysler New Yorker is, that makes my point.)

George and Mary Parker learned this lesson another way. The Parkers live in Naples, Florida, a small city on the southeastern coast of Florida. The Naples beach has been voted the best beach in the United States, and the town itself boasts that it has more golf courses, millionaires, and CEOs per capita than any other city in the country. After the dot-com stock market crash, the Parkers sold their stocks and started investing in real estate by buying small Na-ples homes in older neighborhoods on the wrong side of the high-way—away from the beach.

Home prices in Naples more than doubled between 2001 and 2005 and, along the way, the Parkers made a lot of money flipping homes. They bought their first Naples property in 2001 for $180,000, with a $30,000 down payment and a $150,000 mortgage. They made some cosmetic repairs and sold it nine months later for $210,000. They used the profits to buy two similar homes, which they sold in less than a year. By 2005, they owned thirteen homes, all very much like the first home they bought in 2001. In fact, they bought one home in 2002, sold it in 2003, and bought it back again in 2005 for twice what they had paid in 2002. Sometimes they rented their homes to help make the mortgage payments; other times, they flipped a home before they had time to find a tenant.

The Naples housing market weakened in 2006 and the easy flip-ping ended. The Parkers' rental income didn't cover their mortgage payments and buyers weren't lining up to buy homes. The Parkers tried to sell one home through a real estate auction, but the highest bid was 30 percent less than the price they had paid. The Parkers re-fused to accept this bid or to consider the possibility that they had paid too much. George argued that the prices they paid were okay because appraisers valued the homes at close to their purchase prices.

Where did the appraisers' numbers come from? From comps, of course. The house they bought in 2002 and repurchased in 2005 was appraised at $220,000 in 2002 and at $450,000 in 2005 because that's what similar houses were selling for in 2002 and 2005. These appraisals didn't mean that the house was actually worth $220,000 in 2002 and $450,000 in 2005. A Beanie Baby wasn't worth $500 because some fool paid $500 for it. A dot-com stock wasn't worth $1,000 because some fool paid $1,000 for it. A Naples rental property wasn't worth $450,000 because the Parkers paid $450,000 for it. A home isn't worth $450,000 unless it generates enough income to justify the price. The Parkers' properties didn't.

THE HOME DIVIDEND

Peter Lynch, the legendary mutual fund manager, wrote:

> Because of leverage, if you buy a $100,000 house for 20 percent down and the value of the house increases by 5 percent a year, you are making a 25 percent return on your down payment.

This fixation with price appreciation is horribly misleading. It is very much like buying a stock because you think the price is going up. That's what speculators do, but not value investors—either in the stock market or the real estate market. Value investors think about the income from stock and real estate.

Some people recognize that because we have the option of buying or renting, we should compare monthly rent with monthly mortgage payments. For example, in its 2002 housing report, the Harvard Joint Center for Housing Studies estimated that the average renter paid $481 per month while the buyer of the median single-family home paid an $821 monthly mortgage payment. This is another of those apples-and-oranges comparisons that is only superficially relevant. The average rental property may be much smaller than the

median home, and in a different place, too. The three most important things in real estate are location, location, location. We need to
compare the cost of buying or renting the same property, not the
cost of renting a two-bedroom apartment in Detroit with the cost
of buying a four-bedroom home in Atlanta.

A 2005 article in *Fortune* magazine did a better job by using a real
example:

> [The Olsons] crunched a few numbers. This time they de-
> cided to rent—and they're saving a bundle. For $2,350 a
> month, they have a four-bedroom, 2,100-square-foot home.
> If they were to purchase that same home today for $700,000
> (the going rate for a similar home in the neighborhood), the
> monthly payment on a thirty-year, $630,000 mortgage at 6.1
> percent would run them more than $3,800.

However, this analysis is flawed too. The monthly mortgage payment depends on the down payment and the length of the mortgage. Suppose, for an extreme example, you pay cash for a house and
have no mortgage payments. Is buying therefore guaranteed to be
better than renting?

In addition, *Fortune* neglects the fact that the interest portion of
the mortgage payment is tax-deductible and omits property taxes,
insurance, and maintenance expenses. It also ignores the fact that
rents will probably increase over time, while mortgage payments are
constant and then end when the loan is repaid.

Just like stocks, think of a home as a money machine and estimate the cash coming out of the machine. The income that a home
generates is the rent a homeowner would otherwise have to pay a
landlord. There are expenses, too. Homeowners make mortgage
payments and pay property taxes, homeowner's insurance, and
maintenance expenses when a faucet drips and the walls need to be
repainted. A home's net income is the difference between the income and expenses. Because this net income is as real as the dividends from a stock portfolio, I call it the home dividend.

There are surely nonfinancial considerations that make renting and owning different. Renters might not like the pumpkin-orange walls the landlord picked out. Renters don't get any financial benefit from remodeling a kitchen or landscaping a yard. Renters might have less privacy than homeowners. These are all arguments for why owning is better than renting and, to the extent they matter, why home-dividend calculations underestimate the value of homeownership.

It is not true that you can't go wrong buying a home. The claim by the former Salomon Brothers director that "there is no bad time to buy" is embarrassingly silly. Everything has a price that is too low and a price that is too high. An apple is a bargain at a penny and too expensive at $100. The question for value investors is whether the home dividend makes the price a bargain or a mistake. It is the same question value investors ask about stocks.

A HOME IN FISHERS, INDIANA

Let's look at a very specific example. In the summer of 2005, a three-bedroom, three-bathroom, 1,917-square-foot house in Fishers, Indiana, was purchased for $135,000 with a 20 percent down payment ($27,000) and a thirty-year mortgage. Fishers is an attractive Indianapolis suburb. The median family income is over $100,000 and *Money* magazine ranked Fishers among the top 50 places to live in the United States in 2005, 2006, 2008, 2010, and 2012.

I estimated the home dividend by making a list of the financial benefits and expenses from homeownership—the cash going in and the cash going out. Table 16-1 shows the estimated values for the first year. The details are explained in the Appendix at the end of this chapter.

TABLE 16-1. After-tax home dividend for a home in Fishers, Indiana.

Rent savings	$15,000
Mortgage payment	–$7,522
Property tax	–$2,619
Tax savings	$2,447
Insurance	–$334
Utilities	0
Maintenance	–$1,350
Home dividend	**$5,622**

The biggest benefit is the rent saving; the biggest expense is the mortgage payment.

The bottom line is a first-year home dividend of $5,622. After one year, the homeowners will have $5,622 more in their bank account than they would have if they were renting. Just like a stock portfolio that pays a $5,622 dividend, this $5,622 is their home dividend.

Is $5,622 a good return on their investment? As with stocks, we should compare the dividend with the size of the investment. When you buy a home, your investment is the cash you put up for the down payment and closing costs. Here, the down payment is $27,000. We'll add $3,000 in closing costs to make it an even $30,000 investment. They invested $30,000, which they could otherwise have invested in stocks. The $5,622 first-year home dividend is a 19 percent after-tax rate of return on their investment! Where else could they invest $30,000 and get a $5,622 dividend the first year?

The home dividend will get bigger each year because rents will increase, but the mortgage payments won't (if it is a fixed-rate mortgage). Let's assume that rents, property taxes, insurance, and maintenance all grow by 3 percent a year. The home dividend will be $5,942 in the second year, $8,843 in the tenth year, $13,471 in the twentieth year, and $19,478 in the thirtieth year. Then the mortgage payments stop. The home dividend jumps to $27,744 in the thirty-first year and keeps on growing. What a great investment!

Just like stocks, we can calculate the present value of the home dividends and compare this intrinsic value to the $30,000 cost. Figure 16-1 shows the intrinsic values for after-tax required returns up to 30 percent. The breakeven return is 23.8 percent. This home is an attractive investment for any after-tax required return below 23.8 percent.

For an after-tax required return of, say, 10 percent, the present value of this $30,000 investment is $106,000. This is like buying a stock for $30 a share that is really worth $106. For an after-tax required return of 5 percent, it is like paying $30 for a stock worth $476. These are genuine $100 bills on the sidewalk.

FIGURE 16-1. Present value of the home dividend

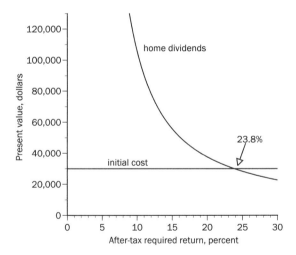

CASH IS KING

When I presented this example at a conference organized by the Brookings Institution, a prominent economics professor said that I was wrong because his sister lives in Indianapolis and home prices there only go up by 2 to 3 percent a year. He missed the point completely. Why is this home in the Fishers suburb such a great investment? Not because I assumed home prices will increase rapidly. I didn't make any assumptions at all about home prices! Just like the intrinsic value analysis of a stock, I assumed that the home buyer never sells. All the value comes from the income generated by the investment. A home is a money machine just like stocks.

Too many homeowners focus on comps and price appreciation when they should instead be thinking about their home dividend. When you buy a home to live in, you get home dividends equal to your rent savings and tax benefits minus your mortgage payments and other expenses. In the Fishers example, you would have to earn a 23.8 percent after-tax return on a $30,000 stock investment to do as well. Where are you going to find another investment that gives you such a wonderful return? Where are you going to find an investment that gives you as much pleasure as the home you live in?

We can also calculate the future value of your investment if you buy the Fishers home and invest the annual home dividend in a stock portfolio paying a modest 5 percent after-tax return each year. After thirty years, you will have $668,379 and be living in your home rent-free and mortgage-free. After fifty years, you will have $2,948,642.

I haven't said anything yet about how much home prices increase. Now I will. Table 16-2 shows your total after-tax wealth, invested home dividends plus the value of your home, if home prices increase by zero, 3 percent, or 5 percent a year over the next fifty years.

TABLE 16-2. Future wealth from Fishers home, investing the home dividend at 5 percent.

Price Increase	Home Dividend	Home Equity	Total
0%	$2,949,000	$135,000	$3,084,000
3%	$2,949,000	$591,000	$3,540,000
5%	$2,949,000	$1,548,000	$4,497,000

Even in the case of 5 percent annual price increases, most of the increase in your wealth comes from the home dividends.

Price appreciation can certainly be an added bonus, but it isn't the most persuasive reason for buying a home. Don't buy a home because you think the price will be 10 percent higher a year from now. Do buy a home because you plan to live in it for a while and believe that it is cheaper to pay off a mortgage than to pay a landlord.

THE LONG VIEW

Suppose that you live in one area for sixty years. And suppose that you change houses every ten or fifteen years. You marry and divorce. You have children and your children grow up. You change jobs and so on. For whatever reasons, you might own four or five different homes during these sixty or so years. Annual ups and downs in home prices aren't all that important. If you sell your home for a higher price than you paid for it, you will also pay a high price for your next home. If you sell your home when prices are low, you will also pay a low price for your next home. Over long horizons, the income you get from owning your home—your home dividend—will usually be much more important than zigs and zags in home prices.

Once you focus on years and years of home dividends, a home is not as unpredictable an investment as you might think. While buying a home might seem risky, not buying is risky, too. If you wait too long, you might get priced out of the market and have to pay rent for the rest of your life. Or think of it this way. You need a place to live—which you can pay for with rent or with mortgage payments. Which is riskier: making constant mortgage payments or making rent payments that can change every year?

Some people don't consider their home to be part of their wealth. They say, "Everyone has to live somewhere." Yes, everyone has to live somewhere. But you can choose to be a renter or an owner. A home is a place to live, but homeownership is an investment.

Others say, "But I will never sell my home and live in the street, so my home isn't really valuable like stocks." You don't have to sell your stocks for them to be profitable investments. Their value comes from the cash they generate. The same is true of your home. Remember Warren Buffett's advice: "I never attempt to make money on the stock market. I buy on the assumption that they could close the market the next day and not reopen it for five years." Think about your home in the same way. Don't try to predict home prices next week, next year, or five years from now. If it helps, assume that the real estate market closes after you buy your home.

Now you can focus on what really matters—the home dividend. If your mortgage payments (and other expenses) are less than what you would pay in rent, your home is paying you a monthly home dividend. When your mortgage is paid off, you will be living in a home with some relatively low expenses (such as property taxes and maintenance) and saving thousands of dollars in rent. All the money you don't pay to a landlord is money that you can spend on food, clothing, entertainment, whatever you want. Yes, your home is valuable, like stocks, even if you never sell your home.

RENTAL PROPERTIES

Once you understand that the investment value of a home depends on the home dividend, you also know how to value rental properties. Buy a rental property for the income, not because you think the price will increase rapidly.

We've seen that the income from a home comes from the rent savings. If the rent savings are large enough to make a home a profitable investment, then it would seem that buying the home and renting it to someone else will also be a profitable investment. This general idea is correct, but a few details complicate matters.

One detail is that when you buy a home and live in it, you save rent every single month. But if you buy a home and rent it out, you only collect rent if you have tenants. If there is a gap between when one tenant moves out and the next tenant moves in, you lose rent while the home is vacant. You also lose rent if tenants refuse to pay and it takes a while to evict them.

Your maintenance expenses might also increase. If you live in your own home and have a leaky faucet, you can just slip in a new washer. If you are a landlord and the property is not close by, you might have to pay a plumber $75 to slip in a washer. Also, people who own the house they live in are more likely to take good care of it. People living in a stranger's home are more likely to be careless or destructive. So your maintenance expenses are likely to be larger if you rent a home to someone else than if you live in it yourself. Finally, the tax rules are different for owner-occupied homes than for rental properties.

ADVERSE SELECTION

Adverse selection occurs when high-risk people take advantage of deals intended for low-risk people. For example, if life insurance companies cannot distinguish those in poor health from those in good health, it must offer the same premium to both. Those in poor health are more likely to buy such policies and file claims, and this reduces the insurance company's profits.

In the real estate market, an adverse-selection problem arises if people choose to rent because they believe they are likely to lose their job, are not handy around the home, are accident prone, or have unruly children and pets. I am not saying that these are universal traits, only that these characteristics might be more prevalent among renters. If they are, landlords might find themselves with tenants who are unemployed klutzes with destructive children and pets.

MORAL HAZARD

There is a moral hazard problem when a person behaves differently if someone else is paying the bills. For example, a person might be less concerned about the cost of medical tests if the insurance company pays for the tests.

In extreme cases, unscrupulous people crash insured automobiles and burn down insured buildings. There's even a joke that goes like this: Two friends meet each other unexpectedly at a European resort. The first person explains that he bought a warehouse and it burned down; he is using the insurance proceeds to pay for his vacation. The second person responds that he bought a building that was destroyed by a flood and that he, too, is spending the insurance money on a vacation. "Gee," the first person asks, "how do you start a flood?"

Deliberately causing damage to collect insurance is illegal. But it is not illegal to be less careful. In the real estate market, it seems self-evident that most people will take better care of a home if they own it than if they rent it. Some friends of mine learned this lesson the hard way. They rented out their Vermont home while they spent a year in Scotland with relatives. Their tenants piled mattresses in the front yard so that their children could jump off the roof, roasted marshmallows around a campfire on the living room floor, and ripped a bathroom sink out of the wall and took it with them when they moved out. Would these tenants have done any of these things to their own home?

That story is real. The next is a joke (I hope). Jack lives in New Hampshire and his heating bills have skyrocketed. Seeing all the trees around him, he realizes that he can heat his home by burning logs. One day, he calls his friend Mack to come over and bring an ax and a chain saw. Jack found an old oil drum at the town dump and wants to put it in the basement. The drum won't fit through the cellar door, so Jack uses the ax to cut some posts and widen the opening. Once the drum is in the basement, the plan is to burn logs in the drum and let the heat rise to warm the house. The next problem is how to get the heat from the basement into the house. No problem. Jack also found an old heating grate at the dump. He walks into the living room, traces an outline of the grate on the wooden floor, and then uses the chain saw to cut a slightly smaller hole that the grate can rest on. He nails the grate in place with two-by-fours. Problem solved. No one will fall through the hole in the floor and the heat from the burning logs will warm the house nicely. Mack admires Jack's ingenuity, but asks what the insurance company will think of this heating system.

Jack replies, "Insurance? That's the owner's problem!"

LONG-DISTANCE LANDLORDS

My wife and I live in Southern California, where home prices make homes in many other parts of the country look like irresistible investments. As in the Fishers example, home prices are so low relative to the home dividend that buying a home to live in has a double-digit after-tax return.

This wasn't a temporary aberration. We looked at decades of data and found homes to be attractively priced for many years in many parts of the heartland. In the Indianapolis area, homes were a good investment twenty-five years ago and have become an even better investment over time. Rising rents and falling mortgage rates have increased home dividends greatly, while home prices have risen by a leisurely 2.2 percent a year. The average Indianapolis home that we looked at in 2005 cost $14,000 a year to rent but could be bought for only $146,000. People who are going to live in Indianapolis for many years can almost surely look forward to a very rewarding return from buying a home there.

When my wife and I saw these stacks of $100 bills, we looked into becoming long-distance landlords, buying single-family homes in Indianapolis, Atlanta, Dallas, and many other parts of the country and renting them to local residents. But the closer we looked, the less attractive this idea appeared. We would have to research the neighborhoods and fly out to look at the homes before buying them. We would have to pay someone to screen prospective tenants and keep an eye on the houses. We would have to pay someone to do home repairs. (It doesn't make sense to fly to Indianapolis to replace a washer!) Property management companies will take care of most of the details, but their fees are typically 5 to 10 percent of the rent. We would also need to deal with vacancies, unpaid rent, and damage to the property. The costs just kept piling up.

In addition, the income kept shrinking. If you own your own home, you get lots of tax breaks that landlords do not get. Most important, a landlord's rent is taxable income, but homeowners don't pay taxes on the rent they save by living in their own homes. Expenses are also handled differently, and the proverbial bottom line is that the prospective after-tax income is generally much lower when buying a home to rent than when buying the same home to live in.

FISHERS, INDIANA, AGAIN

Let's look again at the three-bedroom, three-bath house in Fishers, Indiana. Table 16-1 showed that the homeowners' estimated first-year home dividend was $5,622. Let's see what the home dividend would be if this home had been rented to someone else for $15,000 a year.

Table 16-3 shows the income and expenses. The details are explained in this chapter's Appendix. The home dividend is much smaller for a landlord than for someone who buys the house to live in.

TABLE 16-3. Home dividend, owner-occupied or rented.

	Owner-Occupied	Landlord
Rent	$15,000	$15,000
Mortgage payment	–$7,522	–$7,522
Property tax	–$2,619	–$3,564
Income tax benefit	$2,447	0
Insurance	–$334	–$612
Utilities	0	0
Maintenance	–$1,350	–$1,350
Home dividend	$5,622	**$1,952**

The biggest factors that cut into the home dividend are:

1. Many states, including Indiana, levy higher property taxes on rental properties than on owner-occupied homes.

2. Landlords do not receive a tax saving from mortgage interest and property taxes because these must be used (together with depreciation and other expenses) to avoid paying taxes on the rental income. Owner occupiers do not have to give up their tax saving because their rent savings are not considered taxable income. They can consequently use mortgage interest and property taxes to reduce the taxes they pay on their other income.

The landlord numbers in Table 16-3 might be too optimistic. I initially assumed that the maintenance expenses are $1,350, regardless of whether the buyer lives in the home or rents it out. I used the same maintenance expense for each case because I wanted to focus on how the home dividend is affected by the different tax rules for owner-occupied homes and rental properties.

In practice, the maintenance costs are probably going to be higher if the home is rented. Table 16-4 shows that if the maintenance expenses are doubled, from $1,350 to $2,700, the home dividend falls from $1,952 to $602. The home dividend is almost gone!

TABLE 16-4. A rental home with higher maintenance expenses.

Rental income	$15,000
Mortgage payment	–$7,522
Property tax	–$3,564
Taxes	0
Insurance	–$612
Utilities	0
Maintenance	–$2,700
Home dividend	$602

If we allow for slightly higher maintenance expenses and/or months when the home is vacant, the home dividend can turn negative. This home might still be attractive as a rental property because we are only looking at the first-year home dividend, and the home dividend is likely to improve over time as rents increase and mortgage payments do not. The point is simply that the home dividend can be a lot lower for a rental property than for an owner-occupied home.

There are two lessons. First, just like the home you live in, the investment value of a rental property depends on the home dividend. Second, a home can look a lot more financially attractive if you are buying a home to live in than if you are buying the home so that you can rent it to someone else.

APPENDIX TO CHAPTER 16

FIRST-YEAR HOME DIVIDEND IN FISHERS

T able 16-5 shows the components of the first-year home dividend for the home in Fishers, Indiana, both as an owner-
occupied home or rental property.

TABLE 16-5. Home dividend, owner-occupied or rented.

	Owner-Occupied	Landlord
Rent	$15,000	$15,000
Mortgage payment	–$7,522	–$7,522
Property tax	–$2,619	–$3,564
Income tax benefit	$2,447	0
Insurance	–$334	–$612
Utilities	0	0
Maintenance	–$1,350	–$1,350
Home dividend	**$5,622**	**$1,952**

Here is where these numbers came from.

Rent. It cost $1,250 a month ($15,000 a year) to rent a comparable
house. This is the rent savings for a homeowner, the rental income
for a landlord.

Mortgage payment. In the summer of 2005, the interest rate on a
thirty-year, fixed-rate mortgage was 5.7 percent, and the mortgage
payments were $626.83 a month, or $7,522 a year.

Property tax. In Indiana, property-tax rates are set each year to raise enough revenue to pay for government spending. I estimated that the tax rate on this home would be 2.7 percent. Indiana residents are eligible for a $3,000 homeowner exemption if they have a mortgage. They are also eligible for a homeowner exemption of $35,000 or half the value of the house, whichever is less, if the home is the owner's primary residence. The 2.7 percent tax is levied on the difference between the assessed value and homeowner exemptions: 0.027 ($135,000 − $3,000 − $35,000) = $2,619. Rental properties and vacation homes are not eligible for the larger exemption. So, a landlord pays a property tax of 0.027 ($135,000 − $3,000) = $3,564.

Tax savings. Of the $7,522 in mortgage payments made the first year, $6,120 is interest on the loan and $1,402 is a partial repayment of the amount borrowed. Homeowners can include the $6,120 in interest and the $2,619 in property taxes as itemized deductions on their federal income tax return. In a 28 percent federal income tax bracket, this saves 0.28 ($6,120 + $2,619) = $2,447 in federal income taxes.

Indiana residents do not deduct mortgage interest from their state taxable income, but they are allowed to deduct up to $2,500 of either property taxes or rent from taxable income. Here, the homeowners would be able to deduct $2,500 either way, so there is no net gain or loss in their state income taxes from owning a home instead of renting. (As explained at the end of this appendix, there is no state or federal tax liability or benefit for landlords.)

Insurance. The annual cost of homeowner's insurance is $508; if the owners were renting, they would pay $174 for renter's insurance. The difference is $508 − $174 = $334. For a landlord, the cost of rental-property insurance is $612.

Utilities. I assumed that the homeowners would incur the same expenses for their telephone, electricity, gas, and other utilities if they were renting. So, there is no difference here between buying and renting, and there is no cost for the landlord.

Maintenance. I estimated the homeowner's annual maintenance expenses to be one percent of the value of the house: 0.01 ($135,000) = $1,350. The expense is probably higher if the owner rents the home out instead of living in it. Nonetheless, I initially assumed that the maintenance expense is the same for both so that we can focus on how the home dividend is affected by the fact that the tax laws are different if the owner lives in the home or rents it out.

Adding up all the entries, the bottom line is a home dividend of $5,622 for a homeowner and $1,952 for a landlord.

A LANDLORD'S TAXES

If you live in your own home, you do not pay taxes on the implicit income—your rent savings. If you rent the home to someone else, you may have to pay taxes on the rental income minus expenses. So we need to list the tax-deductible expenses and calculate the taxes (if any) that need to be paid. These calculations are shown in Table 16-6.

TABLE 16-6. First-year taxable income for a rental home.

Rental income	$15,000
Interest portion of mortgage payment	–$6,120
Property tax	–$3,564
Insurance	–$612
Utilities	0
Maintenance	–$1,350
Depreciation	–$3,682
Taxable income	–$328

The interest portion of mortgage payments is tax-deductible. Of the $7,522 in mortgage payments made the first year, $6,120 is interest. The other expenses are the same as in Table 16-5. In addition, a landlord is allowed to claim a depreciation expense for the structure (but not for the land) because the structure will eventually wear out, but the land presumably won't. I assume the value of the structure is equal to 75 percent of the total value: 0.75 ($135,000) = $101,250. I depreciate the structure straight line over 27.5 years, which means that the structure is assumed to last 27.5 years and to lose 3.636 percent of its initial value each year: 100/27.5 = 0.03636. The annual depreciation expense is consequently 0.03636 ($101,250) = $3,682.

Adding up all the entries, there is a loss for tax purposes. People who are not real estate professionals typically cannot deduct rental losses against other income because the rental property would then be a tax shelter rather than a real business. (There is a "small investor" exception because the law is intended to curtail the use of rental properties as tax shelters by wealthy persons.) Notice that the landlord's home dividend in Table 16-5 is positive even though there is a loss for tax purposes. This is one reason why the government is concerned about the use of rental properties as tax shelters.

AFTERWORD

SUMMING IT UP

Overheard a seductive stock tip? Saw a story about a cool product or a hot stock? Quick payoffs are fool's gold. To make money in the market, you need to think about stocks differently, not as get-rich-quick schemes, but as Money Machines.

Investing in the stock market doesn't have to be reckless speculation—gambling on guesses about zigs and zags in stock prices. You can become a value investor by forming your own opinions about what stocks are really worth, and taking advantage of the market's fickle nature. Where others see risks, you can see opportunities.

Value investing is the secret to the success of Benjamin Graham, Warren Buffett, and other legendary investors. It can be your secret, too.

MONEY MACHINES

It's all about the cash. Resist the temptation to base your investment decisions on guesses about Mr. Market's prices. Don't buy stocks foolishly at inflated prices, hoping to sell to even bigger fools at still higher prices.

Instead, think of investments as money machines and think about what you would be willing to pay for the cash they generate over an indefinite horizon. If you are right about the cash, you will be happy with the investment, no matter what Mr. Market says.

EASY MONEY?

Get-rich-quick schemes are inherently suspect. If they worked, the promoter would be using the scheme instead of peddling it. Be skeptical of hot tips. They are usually false or, if true, already reflected in the price.

The efficient market hypothesis says that market prices take into account all relevant information so that no investor can take advantage of other people's ignorance. There is wisdom in the observation that it will never be clear that a stock's price is about to surge or collapse—for if it were obvious, there would not be a balance between buyers and sellers.

Stock prices reflect investor expectations and will not rise or fall when things that are expected to happen do happen. Stock prices will change if the unexpected happens. However, by definition, it is impossible to predict the unexpected. Therefore, the argument goes, it is impossible to predict changes in stock prices. Value investors do not try to predict blips and dips in stock prices, but we all should remember that what everyone knows isn't worth knowing. The true benchmark for gauging your investment ideas is not how today differs from yesterday or how tomorrow will differ from today, but how tomorrow will differ from what others expect.

MR. MARKET IS NOT ALWAYS RIGHT

Some efficient-market enthusiasts argue that the fact that changes in stock prices are difficult to predict proves that the stock market always sets the correct prices, the prices that God herself would set. However, stock prices may be difficult to predict because of unpredictable, sometimes irrational, revisions in investor expectations— as if God determined stock prices by flipping a coin. If so, market prices are hard to predict, but are not good estimates of intrinsic value.

Stock prices are sometimes wacky. During speculative booms and financial crises, the stock market leaves suitcases full of $100 bills on the sidewalk. Still, when you think you have found an easy way to make money, ask yourself if other investors have overlooked a $100 bill on the sidewalk or if you have overlooked a logical explanation.

If a stock's price goes down after you buy it, think about whether there is a good reason for this dip or if it is just noise. If there is a good reason, consider harvesting the tax benefits by selling the stock. If the price drop is noise, this is an opportunity to buy more shares at an even better price.

PROCESSING INFORMATION

Possessing information is knowing something that others do not know. Processing information is thinking more clearly about things that are well known. This distinction is important because even if stock prices take into account sales, profits, interest rates, and other relevant facts, prices may be distorted by common human errors in processing information. The stock market is only semi-efficient. Three examples are confusing a great company with a great stock, hot tips, and chasing trends.

Some investors are more skilled than lucky. However, the pervasive unpredictability of stock prices makes it hard to separate the truly talented from the lucky and the liars. The stock market is not all luck, but it is more luck than nervous investors want to hear or successful investors want to admit.

It is tempting to think that, as in any profession, good training, hard work, and a skilled mind will yield superior results. It is tempting to think that you are one of the gifted. You are not alone! Very few investors think they are below average, even though half are. After all, who would sell one stock and buy another if they thought they would be wrong more often than right? Being human, we count every profitable decision as a confirmation of our wisdom. We blame every mistake on bad luck or the irrationality of other investors.

This overconfidence is why so many investors jump in and out of stocks, believing they know more than investors on the other side of their trades. It is why so many investors hold so few stocks, believing that their picks are destined to succeed. It is why so many investors won't sell their losers, despite the tax benefits, believing that other investors will eventually agree that these are great stocks.

PATTERNS

In any set of data, even randomly generated data, it is possible to find patterns if one looks long enough. Ransacking data for patterns demonstrates little more than persistence: "If you torture the data long enough, it will confess."

It is not surprising that investors and computers can discover rules that explain the past remarkably well, but are unsuccessful in predicting the future. If there is no underlying reason for the discovered pattern, there is no reason for the pattern to persist. Value investors do not try to predict stock prices, so they do not waste time looking for patterns and they are not tempted by patterns they happen to notice.

HIGH HOPES

In a Ponzi scheme, money from new investors is paid to earlier ones. The insurmountable problem is that the number of new investors needed to keep a Ponzi scheme going multiplies too rapidly to be sustained. Ponzi schemes are an example of the useful principle that investments that sound too good to be true probably aren't true.

Speculative bubbles are like Ponzi schemes in that they are fueled by wishful thinking that cannot continue indefinitely. Prices climb higher and higher, beyond reason, in that nothing justifies the rising prices except the hope that prices will keep going up. Then the bubble pops, buyers vanish, and prices collapse.

Some people do not think that bubbles are possible. Since markets always set the correct prices, whatever prices markets set must be correct. It is hard to take this circular argument seriously. A bubble exists when rising prices cannot be justified by an asset's intrinsic value. This is clearly true of collectibles like Beanie Babies that have no intrinsic value. It is also true of stocks that do not generate enough cash to justify their market prices, but are instead being bought so that they can be sold.

Value investors resist bubbles because they are not counting on selling their stocks at higher prices. Value investors are sellers, not buyers, during speculative bubbles (and buyers during panics).

INTRINSIC VALUE

A stock's intrinsic value is the present value of its dividends if the stock were held forever. Even though we don't live forever, let alone hold stocks forever, this perspective forces us to think about the cash that companies generate instead of guessing whether the market price tomorrow will be higher or lower than today's price.

The two main economic drivers of the stock market are the profits that companies generate and the interest rates used to discount these profits. Remember that if you are trying to predict which direction stock prices are headed based on predictions about the economy and interest rates, what matters is how your predictions differ from the predictions already embedded in stock prices. For example, it is not enough to predict that profits will increase; you need to predict whether profits will increase by more or less than the market expects. Value investors do not play this game because they are not trying to predict stock prices.

Companies that do not pay dividends can be valued using the

Shiller, Bogle, and economic value added (EVA) models, though I am leery about investing in firms that do not pay dividends.

STOCK STRATEGIES

Instead of trying to predict short-term zigs and zags in stock prices, value investors evaluate individual stocks and the market as a whole by looking for good companies that have low stock prices relative to their dividends, earnings, and assets.

Such comparisons are often implicitly a contrarian strategy, doing the opposite of what the herd is doing. Stock prices are most likely to be low relative to dividends, earnings, and assets when most investors are gloomy and are most likely to be high when most investors are ebullient. Thus value investors tend to buy in the midst of gloom and sell in the midst of euphoria, effectively following Warren Buffett's advice: "Be fearful when others are greedy and greedy when others are fearful."

One appealing metric is the John Burr Williams (JBW) equation based on the dividend yield and an assumption about the long-run growth of dividends, perhaps the economy's long-run growth rate. This total return estimate—the dividend yield plus the dividend growth rate—can be compared to the current interest rate on Treasury bonds plus whatever risk premium satisfies you.

Another appealing metric is a comparison of Robert Shiller's cyclically adjusted earnings yield to the inflation-adjusted ten-year Treasury rate. Another is the Bogle model for estimating stock returns over a ten-year horizon:

$$\frac{\text{stock}}{\text{return}} = \frac{\text{dividend}}{\text{yield}} + \frac{\text{annual growth}}{\text{of earnings}} + \frac{\text{annual change}}{\text{in P/E}}$$

These models can be applied to the market as a whole (as gauged by the S&P 500, for example) or to individual stocks. There is no guarantee it will work in the future, but the top-10 companies on

Fortune's annual list of the most-admired companies have beaten the S&P 500 soundly. An appealing value strategy is to focus on the most-admired companies and use the JBW, Bogle, and Shiller models to assess whether these stocks are attractively priced.

DODGY STRATEGIES

It is risky to extrapolate a few years of a company's earnings several decades into the future. In addition, growth per se is not valuable. A company that reduces its dividends in order to expand the company always increases the firm's growth (as long as profits are positive) but doesn't increase the value of its stock unless the profit is larger than the shareholders' required return. Firms can also create an illusion of growth by acquiring companies with relatively low price-earnings ratios.

The Law of the Conservation of Investment Value says that the value of a firm depends on the cash it generates, regardless of how that cash is packaged or labeled. Nothing is gained or lost by combining two income streams or by splitting income in two and calling one part one thing and the rest something else. This principle helps us understand why mergers, stock splits, stock dividends, cash dividends, share repurchases, and stock sales do not directly help or hurt shareholders.

Don't worship earnings per share. There are lots of ways that companies can increase earnings per share without benefiting shareholders: investing in marginally profitable ventures; acquiring companies with low price-earnings ratios; doing a reverse stock split. Value investors don't drink the Kool-Aid because they compare a stock's intrinsic value to its market price.

FOIBLES AND FOLLIES

Anchoring is a general human tendency to rely on a reference point; for example, judging the value of something by the price that was paid for it. A stock isn't worth $50 because you bought it for $50. A house isn't worth $400,000 because you paid $400,000 for it. Just because mortgage rates were 6 percent in the past doesn't mean they will be 6 percent in the future.

The price you paid for a stock is a sunk cost that you cannot go back and change. Yet many investors are reluctant to sell losers, despite the tax benefit, because selling for a loss is an admission that they made a mistake buying the stock in the first place. Think about whether a stock is cheap or expensive at its current price, not whether the price is higher or lower than the price you paid. Don't make foolish wagers trying to recoup your losses. Get over them and move on.

A company whose earnings are up dramatically this year (or over the past few years) is more likely to have experienced good luck than bad luck and, most likely, will regress toward the mean in the future, disappointing overly optimistic investors. Don't be among them.

The most optimistic earnings predictions are likely to be overly optimistic, which is why the stocks of companies with the most optimistic earnings forecasts usually do worse than stocks with relatively pessimistic forecasts. Similarly, because of regression, stocks that are deleted from the Dow Jones Industrial Average generally outperform the stocks that replace them.

The bottom line is simple and sweet: Mr. Market's mistakes create opportunities for sensible value investors. Form your own opinion about what stocks are really worth and, remember, stocks are money machines.

REFERENCES

Allen, F. L. 1931. *Only Yesterday: An Informal History of the 1920s.* New York: Harper & Brothers.

Alter, A. L., and D. M. Oppenheimer, 2006. "Predicting Short-Term Stock Fluctuations by Using Processing Fluency." *Proceedings of the National Academy of Sciences* 103: 9369–9372.

American Association of Individual Investors. 1983. "Computerized Investing." December 1983/January 1984.

Anderson, John, and Gary Smith. 2006. "A Great Company Can Be a Great Investment." *Financial Analysts Journal* 62 (4): 86–93.

Andrew, John. 1985. "Some of Wall Street's Favorite Stock Theories Failed to Foresee Market's Slight Rise in 1984." *Wall Street Journal*, January 2.

Arbel, Avner, and Bikki Jaggi. 1982. "Market Information Assimilation Related to Extreme Daily Price Jumps." *Financial Analysts Journal* (November/December): 60–66.

Arbel, A., S. Carvell, and P. Strebel. 1983. "Giraffes, Institutions, and Neglected Firms." *Financial Analysts Journal* 39 (3): 57–63.

Arbel, A., and P. Strebel. 1982. "The Neglected and Small Firm Effects." *Financial Review* 17 (4): 201–208.

———. 1983. "Pay Attention to Neglected Firms." *Journal of Portfolio Management* 9 (2): 37–42.

Arkes, H. R., and C. Blumer. 1985. "The Psychology of Sunk Costs." *Organizational Behavior and Human Decision Processes* 35(1): 124–140.

Associated Press. 1995. "Republic Bank Will Acquire CrossLand Savings for $530 Million," September 25.

Aurora, Anita, Lauren Capp, and Gary Smith. 2008. "The Real Dogs of the Dow." *Journal of Wealth Management* 10 (4): 64–72.

Avery, Sue. 1983. "Market Investors Will Be High on Redskins Today." *Los Angeles Times*, January 30.

———. 1983. "Morning Briefing: Wall Street 'Skinish on Big Game." *Los Angeles Times*, January 30.

Ball, R., and P. Brown. 1968. "An Empirical Evaluation of Accounting Income Numbers." *Journal of Accounting Research* (Autumn): 159–178.

Banz, R. 1981. "The Relationship Between Return and Market Value of Common Stocks." *Journal of Financial Economics* 9: 3–18.

Barber, B. M., Y.-T. Lee, Y.-J. Liu, and T. Odean. 2011. "Do Day Traders Rationally Learn About Their Ability?" University of California Davis. Working paper series.

Barberis, N. C., and R. Thaler. 2003. "A Survey of Behavioral Finance." In *Handbook of the Economics of Finance*, edited by G. Constantinides, M. Harris, R. and Stulz, 1054–1123. Amsterdam: Elsevier.

Barron's. 1979. "Private Fiefdom?—McGraw-Hill Stockholders Are Getting a Raw Deal," February 5.

———. 1980. "More 'Scorched Earth'—Who Is Standing Up for Shareholder Rights?" May 5.

———. 1980. "Corporation or Fiefdom?—Conflicts Between Shareholders, Management Mount," July 7.

———. 1981. "One Shareholder, One Vote?—Scholars Challenge Some Widespread Myths About Corporations," August 24.

———. 1982. "What Price Stewardship?—Management Keeps Putting Its Interest Ahead of Shareholders," February 15.

Bary, Andrew. 1999. "The Road Back: Fund Manager Nick Adams, Once a Whiz in Finance Stocks, Shakes Off a Bad Year." *Barron's*, June 14.

Basu, S. 1977. "Investment Performance of Common Stocks in Relation to Their Price-Earnings Ratios: A Test of the Efficient Market Hypothesis." *Journal of Finance* 32: 663–682.

Bates, James. 1988. "Reality Wears Loser's Jersey in Super Bowl Stock Theory." *Los Angeles Times*, September 18.

Baum, Gabrielle, and Gary Smith. 2015. "Great Companies: Looking for Success Secrets in All the Wrong Places." *Journal of Investing* 24 (3): 61–72.

Begg, I. M., A. Anas, and S. Farinacci. 1992. "Dissociation of Processes in Belief: Source Recollection, Statement Familiarity, and the Illusion of Truth." *Journal of Experimental Psychology: General* 121: 446–458.

Bernstein, Peter L. 1975. "A Green Light for Stocks." *New York Times*, February 2.

————. 1988. *Against the Gods: The Remarkable Story of Risk.* New York: John Wiley & Sons, 175–176.

Bigus, A. W. 1973. "Whatever Happened to Mutual Funds?" *Esquire*, December, 48–54.

Bing, Alexander, III, and Michael F. Wilcox. 1983. "Market Commentary," L. F. Rothschild, Unterberg, and Towbin, November 4.

Bishop, Jerry E. 1987. "Stock Market Experiment Suggests Inevitability of Booms and Busts." *Wall Street Journal*, November 17.

Bishop, R. 2003. "Lindbergh's Influence on Aviation." *Tar Heel Junior Historian* 43: 1.

Blodget, Henry. 2008. "Why Wall Street Always Blows It." *The Atlantic*, December.

Blume, Marshall E., and Robert F. Stambaugh. 1983. "Biases in Computed Returns: An Application to the Size Effect." *Journal of Financial Economics* 12 (3): 387–404.

Bogle, John C. 1991. "Investing in the 1990s." *Journal of Portfolio Management* (Spring): 5–14.

————. 1995. *Bogle on Mutual Funds.* Burr Ridge, IL: Irwin.

————. 2005. *The Battle for the Soul of Capitalism.* New Haven, CT: Yale University Press.

Bohmfalk, J. F., Jr. 1960. "The Growth Stock Philosophy." *Financial Analysts Journal* 16 (6): 122.

Branch, B. 1977. "A Tax Loss Trading Rule." *Journal of Business* 50: 198–207.

Brannigan, Martha. 1986. "Too Good to Be True." *Wall Street Journal*, December 1.

————. 1996. "Pied Piper." *Financial Analysts Journal* (May/June): 56–64.

Brauchli, Marcus W., and Myoshi Kanabayashi. 1990. "Land Prices in Japan Are Getting So Steep the Nation Is Jittery." *Wall Street Journal*, March 23.

Brealey, Richard A., and Stewart C. Myers. 1988. *Principles of Corporate Finance*, 3rd ed. New York: McGraw-Hill, 380.

Brimelow, Peter. 1985. "Rating the Advisers." *Barron's*, July 15, 6–7.

Brooks, John. 1973. *The Go-Go Years.* New York: Ballantine.

Brown, Ken. 2001. "Anti-AT&T Investors May Look to Canada for Likely 28% Gain." *Wall Street Journal*, November

Brunson, D. 2003. *Super System: A Course in Power Poker*, 3rd ed. New York: Cardoza.

Buffett, Warren. 1979. "You Pay a Very High Price in the Stock Market for a Cheery Consensus." *Forbes*, August 6, 25–26.

Buffett, Warren E. 1984. "The Superinvestors of Graham-and-Doddsville." *Hermes: The Columbia Business School Magazine*, 4–15.

———. 1997. Berkshire Hathaway 1996 Chairman's Letter.

———. 2013. Annual Letter to Berkshire Shareholders, February 28.

BusinessWeek. 1974. "Charles Ponzi's Legacy." June 29, 61.

———. 1979. "Tenuous Play in Synthetic Fuels," July 23.

———. 1986. "The Man of Steel," October 20, 52.

———. 1987. "How to Double Your Shares Without Spending a Dime," March 9, 122.

Cappiello, Frank. 1986. "A Sure Path to Market Success—Find Companies That Have a 'Niche.'" *Hume MoneyLetter*, November 5, 1–2.

Carswell, John. 1960. *The South Sea Bubble*. London: Cresset Press, 142.

Cendrowski, Scott. 2012. "It's All About the Dividends." *Fortune*, April 9.

Chan, K., 1988. "On the Contrarian Investment Strategy." *Journal of Business* 61 (2): 147–163.

Chase, C. David. 1987. *Mugged on Wall Street*. New York: Simon & Schuster.

Chincarini, Ludwig. 2012. *The Crisis of Crowding: Quant Copycats, Ugly Models, and the New Crash Normal*. New York: Bloomberg Press.

Clements, Jonathan. 1993. "In Fund Results, 2 + 2 Can Equal 3 or 5." *Wall Street Journal*, April 5.

Clotfelter, C. T., and P. J. Cook. 1993. "The "Gambler's Fallacy" in Lottery Play." *Management Science* 39 (12): 1521–1523.

Cole, Kevin, Jean Helwege, and David Laster. 1995. "Stock Market Valuation Indicators: Is This Time Different?" *Financial Analysts Journal* 52 (3): 56–64.

Collins, J. 2001. *Good to Great*. New York: HarperCollins.

Consumers Digest. 1982. *Get Rich Investment Guide*, vol. 3, no. 4. Chicago: Consumers Digest, 63.

Cooper, Michael J., Orlin Dimitrov, and P. Raghavendra Rau. 2001. "A Rose.com by Any Other Name." *Journal of Finance* 56 (6): 2371–2388.

Coval, J. D., and T. Shumway. 2005. "Do Behavioral Biases Affect Prices?" *Journal of Finance* 60 (1): 1–34.

Cowles, Virginia. 1960. *The Great Swindle*. New York: Harper, 143.

Crane, Burton. 1959. *The Sophisticated Investor*. New York: Simon & Schuster.

Cross, Frank. 1978. "The Behavior of Stock Prices on Fridays and Mondays." *Financial Economics* (June/September): 95

Crum, R. L., D. J. Laughhunn, and J. W. Payne. 1981. "Risk-Seeking Behavior and Its Implications for Financial Models." *Financial Management* 10 (5): 20–27.

Cutts, Robert. 1990. "Power from the Ground Up: Japan's Land Bubble." *Harvard Business Review* (May/June): 164–172.

Darvas, Nicholas. 1960. *How I Made Two Million Dollars in the Stock Market*. New York: American Research Council.

Davis, L. J. 1987. "The Next Panic." *Harper's Magazine*, May, 44.

De Jong, A., L. Rosenthal, and M. A. van Dijk. 2009. "The Risk and Return of Arbitrage in Dual-Listed Companies." *Review of Finance* 13: 495–520.

DeBondt, W. F. M., and R. Thaler. 1985. "Does the Stock Market Overreact?" *Journal of Finance* 40: 793–805.

———. 1987. "Further Evidence on Investor Overreaction and Stock Market Seasonality." *Journal of Finance* 42: 557–580.

DeChow, P., and R. Sloan. 1997. "Returns to Contrarian Investment Strategies: Tests of Naive Expectations Hypotheses." *Journal of Financial Economics* 43: 3–27.

Dennis, Debra K., and John J. McConnell. 1986. "Corporate Mergers and Security Returns." *Journal of Financial Economics* (June): 143–187.

D'Mello, R., S. P. Ferris, and C. Y. Hwang. 2003. "The Tax-Loss Selling Hypothesis, Market Liquidity, and Price Pressure Around the Turn-of-the-Year." *Journal of Financial Markets* 6: 73–98.

Dodosh, Mark N. 1980. "Splitting 5 for 1, American Telnet Makes 43 3/4-Cent Stock 'Affordable.'" *Wall Street Journal*, August 14.

Donnelly, Barbara. 1990. "Formula May Determine If Buying a Home or Renting Is Way to Go." *Wall Street Journal*, January 23.

Dorfman, Dan. 1973. "Heard on the Street." *Wall Street Journal*, February 2, 29.

Dorfman, James. 1987. "An Appraisal: Enormous Volume Could Be a Good Sign, Some Say." *Wall Street Journal*, October 19.

Dorfman, John R. 1988. "Obscure Investment Letter Tops Performance Survey." *Wall Street Journal*, June 7.

Dorfman, John R., and Bradley A. Stertz. 1991. "Toyota and Honda May Be

Broadly Admired but the Stocks Are Widely Viewed as Lemons." *Wall Street Journal*, January 14.

Dorsey-Palmateer, Reid, and Gary Smith. 2004. "Bowlers' Hot Hands." *American Statistician* 58 (1): 38–45.

———. 2007. "Shrunken Interest Rate Forecasts Are Better Forecasts." *Applied Financial Economics* 17 (6): 425–430.

Downes, John, and Jordan Elliot Goodman. 1986. *Barron's Finance and Investment Handbook*. Woodbury, NY: Barron's, 476.

Dreman, David. 1982. "The Madness of Crowds." *Forbes*, September 27, 201.

———. 1982. *The New Contrarian Investment Strategy*. New York: Random House.

Dreman, David, and M. A. Berry. 1995. "Analysts Forecasting Errors and Their Implications for Security Analysis." *Financial Analysts Journal* 51: 30–40.

Dunn, Donald H. 1975. *Ponzi: The Boston Swindler*. New York: McGraw-Hill.

Dunn, Patricia C., and Rolf D. Theisen. 1983. "How Consistently Do Active Managers Win?" *Journal of Portfolio Management* (Summer): 47–50.

Dyl, E. 1977. "Capital Gains Taxation and Year-End Stock Market Behavior." *Journal of Finance* 32: 165–175.

Easterwood, J. C., and S. R. Nutt. 1999. "Inefficiency in Analysts' Earnings Forecasts: Systematic Misreaction or Systematic Optimism?" *Journal of Finance* 54: 1777–1797.

Economist, The. 1981. "They Say That Misery Is Just a Guy Called Joe," September 26, 83.

Edwards, Robert D., and John Magee. 1948. *Technical Analysis of Stock Trends*. Springfield, MA: Stock Trend Service.

Einhorn, Steven G., and Patricia Shangquan. 1984. "Using the Dividend Discount Model for Asset Allocation." *Financial Analysts Journal* (July/August).

Elia, Charles J. 1974. "Heard on the Street." *Wall Street Journal*, April 10, 35.

———. 1974. "Heard on the Street." *Wall Street Journal*, December 4, 43.

Ewing, Terzah. 1999. "Stock Snafu Hits Traders on Internet." *Wall Street Journal*, April 1, C1.

Fama, Eugene F. 1965. "The Behavior of Stock Market Prices." *Journal of Business* (January): 34–105.

———. 1991. "Efficient Capital Markets: II." *Journal of Finance* 46: 1575–1617.

Fama, E., and M. Blume. 1966. "Filter Rules and Stock Market Trading." *Journal of Business* 39: 226–241.

Fama, E., and K. R. French. 1992. "The Cross-Section of Expected Stock Returns." *Journal of Finance* 47: 427–465.

———. 1993. "Common Risk Factors in the Returns on Bonds and Stocks." *Journal of Financial Economics* 33: 3–53.

———. 2000. "Forecasting Profitability and Earnings." *Journal of Business* 73: 161–175.

Fess, Simeon D. 1930. Quoted in *New York World*, October 15.

Fidelity Investments. 1987. *Investment Vision*, November–December, 9.

Financial World. 1980. "The Superstar Analysts," November.

Fischhoff, B. 1982. "For Those Condemned to Study the Past: Heuristics and Biases in Hindsight." In *Judgment under Uncertainty: Heuristics and Biases*, edited by D. Kahneman, P. Slovic, A. Tversky, 332–351. Cambridge: Cambridge University Press.

Fisher, Kenneth L. 1987. *The Wall Street Waltz*. Chicago: Contemporary Books, 48.

Fisher, Lawrence. 1998. "Initial Offering of Ticketmaster Rises Four Times Opening Price." *New York Times*, December 4.

Fisher, Philip A. 1958. *Common Stocks and Uncommon Profits*. Hoboken, NJ: John Wiley & Sons.

Flanigan, James. 1986. "Stock Market Clock May Soon Strike Midnight." *Los Angeles Times*, March 14.

———. 1989. "Wall Street's Disaster Was All Too Real." *Los Angeles Times*, January 22.

Forbes. August 27, 1984; September 16, 1985; and September 8, 1986.

Freeland, Chrystia. 2009. "Lunch with the FT: David Swensen." *Financial Times*, October 12.

Friedman, Jack P. 1990. *Encyclopedia of Investments*, 2nd ed. Boston: Warren, Gorham & Lamont, 759.

Friend, Irwin, Marshall Blume, and Jean Crockett. 1971. *Mutual Funds and Other Institutional Investors: A New Perspective, Twentieth Century Fund Study*. New York: McGraw-Hill.

Galbraith, John Kenneth. 1986. "A Classic Case of 'Euphoric Insanity.'" *New York Times*, November 23.

Garber, Peter M. 1986. "The Tulipmania Legend," Brown University.

Gardner, D., and T. Gardner. 1996. *The Motley Fool Investment Guide: How the Fools Beat Wall Street's Wise Men and How You Can Too.* New York: Simon & Schuster.

———. 2000. "Farewell, Foolish Four," *Motley Fool,* December 11. Retrieved August 28, 2013, from http://www.fool.com/ddow/2000/ddow00121.htm.

Garvey, R., A. Murphy, and F. Wu. 2007. "Do Losses Linger? Evidence from Proprietary Stock Traders." *Journal of Portfolio Management* 33 (4): 75–83.

Genesove David, and Christopher Mayer. 2001. "Loss Aversion and Seller Behavior: Evidence from the Housing Market." *Quarterly Journal of Economics* 116 (4): 1233–1260.

Gibbons, Michael R., and Patrick Hess. 1981. "Day of the Week Effects and Asset Returns." *Journal of Business* 54 (4): 579–596.

Gilovich, T., R. Vallone, and A. Tversky. 1985. "The Hot Hand in Basketball: On the Misperception of Random Sequences." *Cognitive Psychology* 17 (3): 295–314.

Givoly, D., and A. Ovadia. 1983. "Year-end induced sales and stock market seasonality." *Journal of Finance* 38: 171–185.

Glassman, James K. 1996. "Open Your Mind to Closed-End Funds." *Washington Post*, April 7.

Glassman, James K., and Kevin A. Hassett. 1999. "Dow 36,000." *Atlantic Monthly*, September, 37–58.

———.2000. *Dow 36,000: The New Strategy for Profiting from the Coming Rise in the Stock Market.* New York: Three Rivers Press.

Gold, Max, Jeff Levere, and Gary Smith. 2013. "Tax-Loss Selling and the Year-End Behavior of Dow Jones Stocks." *Accounting and Finance Research* 2 (1): 40-46.

Goldman, Sachs, & Co. 1987. "Portfolio Strategy," September.

———. 1988. "Portfolio Strategy," September, 22.

Gongloff, Mark. 2006. "Where Are They Now: The Beardstown Ladies, Once Icons of an Emerging Investor Class, They're Still Together—Buying and Holding." *Wall Street Journal*, May 1.

Goolsbee, Austan. 2006. Interview by Kai Ryssdal, American Public Media, May 5.

Graham, Benjamin. 1954. *The Intelligent Investor*. New York: Harper.

Graham, Benjamin, and David L. Dodd. 1934. *Security Analysis*. New York: McGraw-Hill.

Granville, Joseph. 1980. Quoted in "Joseph Granville's weekly market letter," *The Economist*, September 27, 105–106.

Gropper, Diane Hal. 1985. "How John Neff Does It." *Institutional Investor*, May, 88.

Hamilton, Walter. 1998. "Returns Come Back to Haunt 'Ladies.'" *Los Angeles Times*, March 18.

Hampton Numismatics. 1986. Mail advertisement, August.

Hasher, L., D. Goldstein, and T. Toppino. 1977. "Frequency and the Conference of Referential Validity." *Journal of Verbal Learning and Verbal Behavior* 16: 107–112.

Haug, Espen Gaarder. 2007. *Derivatives: Models on Models*. New York: Wiley & Sons.

Haugen, R., and J. Lakonishok. 1988. *The Incredible January Effect*. Homewood, IL: Dow Jones-Irwin.

Hawkins, Eugene H., Stanley C. Chamberlin, and Wayne E. David. 1984. "Earnings Expectations and Security Prices." *Financial Analysts Journal* (September/October): 24–38.

Hazard, C. C. 1972. *Confessions of a Wall Street Insider*. Chicago: Playboy Paperback.

Head, Alex, Gary Smith, and Julia Wilson. 2009. "Would a Stock by Any Other Ticker Smell as Sweet?" *Quarterly Review of Economics and Finance* 49 (2): 551–561.

Herman Tom, and Mathew Winkler. 1987. "Economic Expansion Will Keep Going for at Least Another Year and Interest Rates Won't Change Much, Say Analysts in Survey." *Wall Street Journal*, July 6.

Herskovitz, Jon. 2004. "Love Is in the Air: Southwest Passengers Find Love in an Empty Seat." Reuters, July 7. Retrieved April 28, 2005, from http://msnbc.msn.com/id/5444145.

Higgins, E. T. 1996. "Knowledge Activation: Accessibility, Applicability, and Salience." In *Social Psychology: Handbook of Basic Principles*, edited by E. T. Higgins and A. Kruglanski, 133–168. New York: Guilford.

Hiltzik, Michael A. 1985. "Churning: Trading in Stock Abuse." *Los Angeles Times*, June 19.

Hirshleifer, D. 2001. "Investor Psychology and Asset Pricing." *Journal of Finance* 56 (4): 1533–1597.

Hirshleifer, D., and T. Shumway. 2003. "Good Day Sunshine: Stock Returns and the Weather." *Journal of Finance* 58(3): 1009–1032.

Hogarty, T. 1970. "Profits from Mergers: The Evidence of Fifty Years." *St. John's Law Review* (Spring): 389.

Holland, Bart K. 2002. *What Are the Chances?* Baltimore: Johns Hopkins University Press.

Hotelling, Harold. 1933. Review of "The Triumph of Mediocrity in Business, by Horace Secrist." *Journal of the American Statistical Association* 28: 463–465. Secrist and Hotelling debated this further in the *Journal of the American Statistical Association* 29 (1934): 196–199.

Hulbert, Mark. 2005. "Gambling on Granville." *MarketWatch*, March 16.

Hume & Associates. 1986. *The Superinvestor Files: The GSR Trade*. Atlanta, GA: Hume Publishing, 19.

Icahn, Carl. 1986. Quoted in "The Man of Steel," *Newsweek*, October 20, 54.

Ip, Greg. 1997. "The New Math: Are Some High P/E Stocks 'Bargains'?" *Wall Street Journal*, December.

Isen, A. M., B. Means, R. Patrick, and G. P. Nowicki. 1982. "Some Factors Influencing Decision-Making Strategy and Risk Taking." In *Affect and Cognition*, edited by M. S. Clark, S. Fiske, 243–261. Hillsdale, NJ: Lawrence Erlbaum Associates.

Jaffe, J., D. Keim, and R. Westerfield. 1989. "Earning Yields, Market Values, and Stock Returns." *Journal of Finance* 44: 135–148.

Jaideep Bedi, et al. 2003. "The Characteristics and Trading Behavior of Dual-Listed Companies." Reserve Bank of Australia, June.

Jegadeesh, N., and S. Titman. 1993. "Returns to Buying Winners and Selling Losers: Implications for Stock Market Efficiency." *Journal of Finance* 48: 65–91.

Jennings, Bob. 1987. Mail advertisement from Confidential Report, Boca Raton, Florida, July.

Jensen, Michael C. 1968. "The Performance of Mutual Funds in the Period 1945–64." *Journal of Finance* (May): 389–416.

Jensen, M. C. 1978. "Some Anomalous Evidence Regarding Market Efficiency." *Journal of Financial Economics* 6: 95–101.

Jensen, Michael C. 1984. "Takeovers: Folklore and Science." *Harvard Business Review* (November/December): 109–121.

Jensen, M., and G. Benington. 1970. "Random Walks and Technical Theories: Some Additional Evidence." *Journal of Finance* 25: 469–482.

Joint Center for Housing Studies of Harvard University. 2002. "The State of the Nation's Housing."

Jorion, P., and W. Goetzmann. 1999. "Global Stock Markets in the Twentieth Century." *Journal of Finance* 54: 953–980.

Joy, O. Maurice, and Charles P. Jones. 1979. "Earnings Reports and Market Efficiencies: An Analysis of Contrary Evidence." *Journal of Financial Research* 2 (1) : 51–64.

Kahneman, D., and A. Tversky. 1973. "On the Psychology of Prediction." *Psychological Review* 80: 237–251.

———. 1979. "Prospect Theory: An Analysis of Decision under Risk." *Econometrica* 47 (2): 263–292.

Kaplan, Gilbert, and Chris Welles. 1969. *The Money Managers*. New York: Random House.

Keim, Donald. 1980. "Size-Related Anomalies and Stock Return Seasonality: Further Empirical Evidence." Graduate School of Business, University of Chicago.

Keynes, John Maynard. 1924. "Alfred Marshall, 1842–1924," *Economic Journal* 34. Reprinted with slight changes in Pigou, A. C., ed. 1925. *Memorials of Alfred Marshall*. London: Macmillan, and in Keynes, J. M. 1933. *Essays in Biography*, London: Macmillan.

———. 1936. *The General Theory of Employment, Interest, and Money*. New York: Macmillan, chap. 12.

Kidder, Peabody & Co. 1987. "Current Recommendation Update: International Business Machines."

———. 1987. "Portfolio Consulting Service," May 20.

Kindleberger, Charles P. 1978. *Manias, Panics, and Crashes*. New York: Basic Books.

Kinsley, Michael. 1986. "Let's Hear It for a Drop in Home Values." *Wall Street Journal*, June 5.

Kirby, Robert. 1988. Quoted in Randall Smith, "A Few Institutions Dominated Big Market Sell-Off, Report Says," *Wall Street Journal*, January 11.

Kratz, Ellen Florian. 2005. "Fear of Falling." *Fortune*, December 26, 84.

Krefetz, Gerald. 1984. *How to Read and Profit from Financial News*. New York: Ticknor & Fields, 1.

Kurtenbach, Elaine. 1990. "Japanese Are Facing Up to Land Inflation and Soaring Costs for Real Estate." *Washington Post*, April 21.

Lakonishok, J., A. Shliefer, and R. W. Vishny. 1994. "Contrarian Investment, Extrapolation, and Risk." *Journal of Finance* 49: 1541–1578.

Langer, E. J., and J. Roth. 1975. "Heads I Win, Tails It's Chance: The Illusion of Control as a Function of the Sequence of Outcomes in a Purely Chance Task." *Journal of Personality and Social Psychology* 32 (6): 951–955.

La Porta, R. 1996. "Expectations and the Cross-Section of Stock Returns." *Journal of Finance* 49: 1715–1742.

Laurence, Michael. 1969. "Playboy's Guide to Mutual Funds." *Playboy*, June.

LeBaron, Dean. 1986. Quoted in "LeBaron: Institutions Are Losing Their Grip." *Investment Management World*, March/April, 5.

Lee, Marcus, and Gary Smith. 2002. "Regression to the Mean and Football Wagers." *Journal of Behavioral Decision Making* 15: 329–342.

Levy, Robert A. 1971. "The Predictive Significance of Five Point Chart Patterns." *Journal of Business* 44 (3): 316–323.

Lewis, Michael. 1989. *Liar's Poker*. New York: W. W. Norton.

———. 2000. "The New New Strategy: Do Nothing and Do It Well." *Financial Observer*, February 7.

Lintner, J., and R. Glauber. 1967. "Higgledy, Piggledy Growth in America," presented to the Seminar on the Analysis of Security Prices, University of Chicago, May. Reprinted in Lorie, J., and R. Brealey, eds. 1978. *Modern Developments in Investment Management*, 2nd ed. Hinsdale: Dryden.

Lipper, Michael. 1986. Quoted in Beatrice E. Garcia, "'Nifty 50' Tactic Tied to Growth Is Resurrected." *Wall Street Journal*, March 24.

Little, I. M. D. 1966. *Higgledy Piggledy Growth Again*. Oxford: Basil Blackwell.

Locke, P. R., and S. C. Mann. 2004. "Prior Outcomes and Risky Choices by Professional Traders." Texas Christian University, Dallas. Working paper.

Loeb, G. M. 1965. *The Battle for Investment Survival*. New York: Simon & Schuster, 57.

Loving, Rush, Jr. 1970. "How Cortes Randell Drained the Fountain of Youth." *Fortune*, April, 94–97.

Lowenstein, Roger. 1986. "How a 23-Year-Old Broker Went from Riches to Scandal and Jail." *Wall Street Journal*, February 27.

———. 1990. "Junk Buying Thrifts Made Problems Worse with Purchases Made Before Market Plunge." *Wall Street Journal*, January 15.

————. 1997. "Valuing Gold—or Stocks—From a Desert Isle." *Wall Street Journal*, July 10.

————. 2000. *When Genius Failed: The Rise and Fall of Long-Term Capital Management*. New York: Random House.

Lynch, Peter. 1989. *One Up on Wall Street*. New York: Simon & Schuster.

Lynch, Peter, and John Rothchild. 1994. *Beating the Street*. New York, NY: Fireside.

Malkiel, Burton G. 1977. "The Valuation of Closed-End Investment-Company Shares." *Journal of Finance* (June): 847–859.

————. 1985. *A Random Walk Down Wall Street*, 4th ed. New York: W. W. Norton.

Markowitz, Harry. 1959. *Portfolio Selection: Efficient Diversification of Investments*. New York: John Wiley & Sons.

Maxwell, W. 1998, "The January Effect in the Corporate Bond Market: A Systematic Examination." *Financial Management* 27: 18–30.

McClintick, David. 1974. "How Did Home-Stake Spend All the Money That Investors Put In?" *Wall Street Journal*, August 29.

————. "Rich Investors' Losses in New 'Ponzi Scheme' Could Hit $100 Million." *Wall Street Journal*, June 26, 1974.

McGlone, M. S., and J. Tofighbakhsh. 2000. "Birds of a Feather Flock Conjointly (?): Rhyme as Reason in Aphorisms." *Psychological Science* 11: 424–428.

McGrath, Kathryn. 1986. Quoted in *Money*, September, 13.

McGrave, Reginald C. 1965. *The Panic of 1837*. New York: Russell and Russell, 145.

McKinsey & Company. 1990. "Valuation: Measuring and Managing the Value of Companies."

McQueen, G., K. Shields, and S. R. Thorley. 1997. "Does the 'Dow-10 Investment Strategy' Beat the Dow Statistically and Economically?" *Financial Analysts Journal* 53: 66–72.

McQueen, G., and S. Thorley. 1999. "Mining Fool's Gold." *Financial Analysts Journal* 55 (2): 61–72.

Merrett, A. J., and Gerald D. Newbould. 1982. "CEPS: The Illusion of Corporate Growth." *Journal of Portfolio Management* (Fall): 5–10.

Miller, D. T., and M. Ross. 1975. "Self-Serving Bias in Attribution of Causality: Fact or Fiction?" *Psychological Bulletin* 82 (2): 213–225.

Mintz, Steven. 1986. "Strategies." *Investment Management World* (May/June): 22.

Mitchell, Constance. 1988. "Trapped in a Time Warp, or Simply Looking Ahead?" *Wall Street Journal*, November 4.

Modigliani, Franco, and Richard A. Cohn. 1979. "Inflation, Rational Valuation, and the Market." *Financial Analysts Journal* (March/April): 24–44.

Nelson, D. 2003. "What Poker Can Teach You About Investing." Legg Mason Funds Management Investment Conference, Baltimore, http://www.leggmason.com/billmiller/ conference/illustrations/nelson.asp.

Nicholson, S. Francis. 1960. "Price-Earnings Ratios." *Financial Analysts Journal* 16: 43–45.

———. 1968. "Price Ratios." *Financial Analysts Journal* (January/February): 105–109.

Niederhoffer, Victor. 1997. *The Education of a Speculator*. New York: John Wiley & Sons, 274–277.

Odean, T. 1998. "Volume, Volatility, Price, and Profit When All Traders Are Above Average." *Journal of Finance* 53 (6): 1887–1934.

———.1999. Do Investors Trade Too Much? *American Economic Review* 89: 1279–98.

O'Higgins, M. B., and J. Downes. 1992. *Beating the Dow*. New York: Harper Collins.

Parkman, Allen. 1987. "Using Economic Analysis in Your Practice." *ABA Journal* (February 1): 54–58.

Peavy John, and David A. Goodman. 1983. "The Significance of P/Es for Portfolio Returns." *Journal of Portfolio Management* (Winter): 43–47.

Pennington, N., and R. Hastie. 1988. "Explanation-Based Decision Making: Effects of Memory Structure on Judgment." *Journal of Experimental Psychology: Learning, Memory, and Cognition* 14: 521–533.

Penny Stock Advisor. 1986. Advertisement, Coral Springs, Florida.

Pereira, Joseph, 1988, "Coleco Is Looking for Lettuce as Cabbage Patch Wilts." *Wall Street Journal*, March 18.

Perritt, Gerald W. 1984. "Is the Load Too Much to Bear?" *American Association of Individual Investors Journal* (June): 18–21.

Petruno, Tom. 1996. "The Logic of Rally's Continuing Longevity." *Los Angeles Times*, November 24.

Pierobon, James R. 1981. "Preparing for the 'March Massacre.'" *Houston Chronicle*, March 18.

Poterba, J., and S. Weisbenner. 2001. "Capital Gains Tax Rules, Tax-Loss Trading, and Turn-of-the Year Returns." *Journal of Finance* 56: 353–368.

Pratt, Eugene F. 1966. "Myths Associated with Closed-End Investment Companies." *Financial Analysts Journal* (July/August): 79–82.

Prudential Securities. 1991. "Marketwise," June, 1.

Pulliam, Susan. 2000. "At Bill's Barber Shop, 'In Like Flynn' Is a Cut Above the Rest." *Wall Street Journal*, March 13.

Quint, Michael. 1992. "Crossland Is Seized by the U.S." *New York Times*, January 25.

Raab, Selwyn. 1991. "New York's Largest Savings Bank Investigated for Possible Tax Fraud." *New York Times*, January 20.

Rashes, Michael. 2001. "Massively Confused Investors Making Conspicuously Ignorant Choices." *Journal of Finance* 56: 1911–1927.

Reber, R., and N. Schwartz. 1999. "Effects of Perceptual Fluency on Judgments of Truth." *Consciousness and Cognition* 8: 338–342.

Reber, R., P. Winkielman, and N. Schwarz. 1998. "Effects of Perceptual Fluency on Affective Judgments." *Psychological Science* 9: 45–48.

Regan, Patrick J. 1988. "Japan—Land of the Rising Risk." *Financial Analysts Journal* (July/August): 17, 28.

Reinganum, Marc. 1981. "Misspecification of Capital Asset Pricing: Empirical Anomalies Based on Earnings' Yields and Market Values." *Journal of Financial Economics* 9 (1): 19–46.

———. 1983. "Portfolio Strategies Based on Market Capitalization." *Journal of Portfolio Management* (Winter): 29–36.

———. 1983. "The Anomalous Stock Market Behavior of Small Firms in January." *Journal of Financial Economics* 12: 89–104.

Ritter, Jay R., and Navin Chopra. 1989. "Portfolio Rebalancing and the Turn-of-the-Year Effect." *Journal of Finance* 44 (1): 149–165.

Rohatyn, Felix. 1987. Quoted in James B. Stewart and Daniel Hertzberg, "How the Stock Market Almost Disintegrated a Day After the Crash." *Wall Street Journal*, October 30.

Roll, R. 1983. "Vas Ist Das? The Turn-of-the-Year Effect and the Return Premia of Small Firms." *Journal of Portfolio Management* 9: 18–28.

Rosenberg, B., K. Reid, and R. Lanstein. 1985. "Persuasive Evidence of Market Inefficiency." *Journal of Portfolio Management* 11: 9–17.

Rosenthal, L., and C. Young. 1990. "The Seemingly Anomalous Price Behavior of Royal Dutch/Shell and Unilever NV/PLC." *Journal of Financial Economics* 26: 123–141.

Rotbart, Dean. 1985. "Aggressive Methods of Some Short Sellers Stir Critics to Cry Foul." *Wall Street Journal*, September 5.

Rubenstein, Mark. 2001. "Rational Markets: Yes or No? The Affirmative Case." *Financial Analysts Journal* (May/June): 15–29.

Rukeyser, Louis. 1974. *How to Make Money in Wall Street*. Garden City, NY: Doubleday.

Rumbler, Bill. 2003. "Is It Cheaper to Rent or Buy?" *Chicago Sun-Times*, http://www.suntimes.com/classified/homes/firststeps几.html.

Russell, Fredric E. 1992. Quoted in Steven E. Livingston, "Corporate Treasurers Are Turning Increasingly to Stocks of Firms They Know Best: Their Own." *Wall Street Journal*, October 19.

Salmon, Felix, and Jon Stokes. 2011. "Bull vs. Bear vs. Bot." *Wired*, January, 90–93.

Saunders, E. M. J. 1993. "Stock Prices and Wall Street Weather." *American Economic Review* 83 (5): 1337–1345.

Schacter S., and J. E. Singer. 1962. "Cognitive, Social, and Psychological Determinants of Emotional States." *Psychological Review* 69: 379–399.

Schlesinger, Arthur M., Jr. 1957. *The Crisis of the Old Order*. Boston: Houghton Mifflin, 231.

Schurenberg, Eric. 2012. "How I Did It: John Bogle of the Vanguard Group." *Inc.*, September 25, 21.

Schwed, Fred, Jr. 1940. *Where Are the Customers' Yachts?* New York: Simon & Schuster.

Sease, Donald R. 1989. "Clues Abound for the Small Investor to Divine Market Direction." *Wall Street Journal*, January 3.

Sebastian, Pamela, and Jan Wong. 1986. "Fidelity Is Scrambling to Keep High Flying as Magellan Slows Up." *Wall Street Journal*, August 15.

Secrist, Horace. 1933. *The Triumph of Mediocrity in Business*. Evanston, IL: Northwestern University.

Seyhun, Neijat. 1989. "Fads or Fundamentals: Some Lessons from Insiders' Response to the Crash of 1987." University of Michigan.

Sharpe, William F. 1966. "Mutual Fund Performance." *Journal of Business* (January): 119–138.

———. 1985. *Investments*, 3rd ed. New York: McGraw-Hill, 430.

————. 1997. Interviewed by the Vanguard Group. *In the Vanguard* (Summer): 1.

Sharpe, William F., and Howard B. Sosin. 1975. "Closed-End Investment Companies in the United States: Risk and Return." In *Proceedings of the 1974 Meeting of the European Finance Association*, edited by B. Jacquillat. Amsterdam: North-Holland.

Sherman, Michael H. 1986. "Cash Signals a Lack of Confidence." *Investment Management World* (March/April): 23.

Shiller, Robert J. 1987. "Investor Behavior in the October 1987 Stock Market Crash: Survey Evidence." Yale University, November. Also see *The Wall Street Journal*, "Black Monday: What Really Ignited The Market's Collapse After the Long Climb," December 16, 1987, page 1.

Shulman, Morton. 1985. "The Difference Between Men and Boys Is the Stock Price of Their Toys." *Hume MoneyLetter*, November 26, 1–2.

Siconolfi, Michael. 1989. "Closed-End Funds Open to Gimmicks That Lift Prices." *Wall Street Journal*, April 13.

Simon, Bernard. 2002. "Pledge to Canadian Unit Is Now Haunting AT&T." *New York Times*, February 28.

Sivy, Michael. 1980. "Joe Granville: Messiah or Menace?" *Financial World*, June 15.

Slovic, P., B. Fischhoff, and S. Lichtenstein. 1976. "The Certainty Illusion." *Oregon Research Institute Research Bulletin* 16 (4): 1–38.

Smith, Adam. 1776. *Wealth of Nations*. London, 76.

"Smith, Adam" [pseud.]. 1967. *The Money Game*. New York: Random House, 157–158.

Smith, Gary. 1997. "Do Statistics Test Scores Regress Toward the Mean?" *Chance* (Winter): 42–45.

————. 1982. "A Simple Model for Estimating Intrinsic Value." *Journal of Portfolio Management* (Summer): 46–49.

————. 2003. "Horseshoe Pitchers' Hot Hands." *Psychonomic Bulletin and Review* 10: 753–758.

————. 2014. "Why Are Some Home Values Resistant and Others Resilient?" *International Real Estate Review* 17 (2): 223–240.

————. 2016. "Companies Are Seldom as Good or as Bad as They Seem at the Time." In *Essays in Honor of Joseph Stiglitz*. Place: Publisher, forthcoming.

Smith, Gary, and Jeff Fesenmaier. 2002. "The Nifty-Fifty Re-Revisited." *Journal of Investing* 11: 86–90.

Smith, Gary, Michael Levere, and Robert Kurtzman. 2009. "Poker Player Behavior After Big Wins and Big Losses." *Management Science* 55 (9): 1547–1555.

Smith, Gary, and Teddy Schall. 2000. "Baseball Players Regress Toward the Mean." *American Statistician* 54 (November): 231–235.

Smith, Gary, and Joanna Smith. 2005. "Regression to the Mean in Average Test Scores." *Educational Assessment* 10: 377–399.

Smith, Gary, and Margaret Smith. 2004. "Is a House a Good Investment?" *Journal of Financial Planning* 17: 67–75.

Smith, Gary, and Margaret Smith. 2008. *Houseonomics*. Upper Saddle River, NJ: Financial Times/Prentice Hall Books.

Smith, Gary, and Michael Zurhellen. 2015. "Sunny Upside? The Relationship Between Sunshine and Stock Market Returns." *Review of Economic Analysis* 7: 173–183.

Smith, Greg A. 1987. "Welcome to My Nightmare." Prudential-Bache Securities, August 12, 1.

Smith, Margaret H., Manfred Keil, and Gary Smith. 2004. "Shrunken Earnings Predictions Are Better Predictions." *Applied Financial Economics* 14: 937–943.

Smith, Margaret Hwang, and Gary Smith. 2006. "Bubble, Bubble, Where's the Housing Bubble?" *Brookings Papers on Economic Activity* 37 (1): 1–50.

———. 2008. "Harvesting Capital Gains and Losses." *Financial Services Review* 17 (4): 309–321.

Smith, Randall. 1985. "Some Mutual Funds' Hot Records May Hide Companies' Cool Moves." *Wall Street Journal*, March 14.

Smith, Vernon L., Gerry L. Suchanek, and Arlington W. Williams. 1988. "Bubbles, Crashes, and Endogenous Expectations in Asset Market Experiments." *Econometrica* 56 (5): 1119–1151.

Sobel, Robert. 1996. "The Way It Works: Analysts Began Speculating on What Moves the Market About a Century Ago; They Didn't Agree Then, Either." *Wall Street Journal*, May 28.

Srodes, James. 1987. "We Have All Been Robbed by Deceit of 3 'Geniuses.'" *Los Angeles Times*, March 1.

Stancill, James McNeill. 1982. "Does the Market Know Your Company's Real Worth?" *Harvard Business Review*. September/October, 60 (5): 50.

Starks, L., L. Yong, and L. Zheng. 2006. "Tax-Loss Selling and the January Effect: Evidence from Municipal Bond Closed-End Funds." *Journal of Finance* 61: 3049–3067.

Staw, B. M. 1976. "Knee-Deep in the Big Muddy: A Study of Escalating Commitment to a Chosen Alternative." *Organizational Behavior and Human Performance* 16 (1): 27–44.

Steenbarger, B. 2007. "What We Can Learn from Trading and Poker," April 6, http://traderfeed.blogspot.com/2007/04/what-we-can-learn-from-trading-and.html.

Stewart, James B., and Daniel Hertzberg. 1987. "Speculative Fever Ran High in the 10 Months Prior to Black Monday." *Wall Street Journal*, December 11.

Swensen, David F. 2000. *Pioneering Portfolio Management: An Unconventional Approach to Institutional Investment*. New York: Free Press.

———.2005. *Unconventional Success: A Fundamental Approach to Personal Investment*. New York, Free Press.

Tempest, Rone. 1988. "Swiss Stock Scam Swindled Investors Out of $250 Million." *Los Angeles Times*, September 6.

Thaler, R., and E. J. Johnson. 1990. "Gambling with the House Money and Trying to Break Even: The Effects of Prior Outcomes on Risky Choice." *Management Science* 36 (6): 643–660.

Thomson, James B., 1986. "Errors in Recorded Security Prices and the Turn-of-the-Year Effect." Federal Reserve Bank of Cleveland. Working paper 8611, December.

Thurow, Lester C. 1988. "Brady Group's Answers Miss the Key Questions." *Los Angeles Times*, January 24.

Time. 1929. November 18, 45.

Tobias, Andrew. 1976. "The Broker Made Money, the Firm Made Money (and Two Out of Three Ain't Bad)." *New York Magazine*, June 28, 56–59.

———. 1978. *The Only Investment Guide You'll Ever Need*. New York: Harcourt Brace Jovanovich.

———. 1989. "High Yield Bonds: Aging Analysis of Defaults, Exchanges, and Calls." *Journal of Finance* (September): 923–952.

Tomsho, Robert. 2002. "Stocks Aren't Buzz at Barbershop Anymore." *Wall Street Journal*, July 8.

Train, John. 1987. *The Midas Touch*. New York: Harper & Row.

Treynor, Jack. 1987. "Market Efficiency and the Bean Jar Experiment." *Financial Analysts Journal* 43: 50–53.

Triana, Pablo. 2009. *Lecturing Birds on Flying: Can Mathematical Theories Destroy the Financial Markets?* New York: Wiley & Sons.

Tversky, A., and D. Kahneman. 1973. "Availability: A Heuristic for Judging Frequency and Probability." *Cognitive Psychology* 5: 207–232.

———. 1981. "The Framing of Decisions and the Psychology of Choice." *Science* 211(4481): 453–458.

Value Investors Club. 2001. "AT&T Canada," October 26.

Value Line. 1982. "International Business Machines," August 13, 1101.

———. 1987. "International Business Machines," February 6, 1102.

Wall Street Journal. 1967."Western Oil Shale Corp. Stresses 'Speculative Nature' of Its Shares," May 5.

———.1987. January 19.

———. 1987. "Black Monday: What Really Ignited the Market's Collapse After Its Long Climb," December 16.

———. 1988. "Follies, Foibles, and Fumbles," January 4.

Wasik, John. 2013. *Keynes's Way to Wealth: Timeless Investment Lessons from the Great Economist.* New York: McGraw-Hill.

White, James A. 1989. "How a Money Manager Can Pull a Rabbit Out of a Hat." *Wall Street Journal*, March 16.

Whitefield, Debra. 1987. "Money Talk." *Los Angeles Times*, June 4.

Whitman, Martin J., and Martin Shubik. 1979. *The Aggressive Conservative Investor*. New York: Random House, 184.

Wiesenberger Investment Companies Service. 1987. "Investment Companies."

———.1991. "Investment Companies."

Wiles, Russ. 1991. "Mutual Funds." *Los Angeles Times*, September 22.

Williams, John Burr. 1938. *The Theory of Investment Value*. Cambridge, MA: Harvard University Press.

Williamson, J. Peter. 1974. *Investments: New Analytic Techniques*. New York, Praeger, 152.

Wilson, Jack W., and Charles P. Jones. 1987. "Common Stock Prices and Inflation: 1857–1985." *Financial Analysts Journal* 43 (4): 67–71.

Witter, Dean. 1974. Quoted in "Dean Witter's Market Advice in 1932," *New York Times*, October 13.

Woolley, Suzanne. 1994. "The Dividend Also Rises." *Business Week*, May 2, 28–29.

Wright, W. F., and G. H. Bower. 1992. "Mood Effects on Subjective Probability Assessment." *Organizational Behavior and Human Decision Processes* 52 (2): 276–291.

Wyer, R. S., Jr., and T. K. Srull. 1989. *Memory and Cognition in its Social Context*. Hillsdale, NJ: Lawrence Erlbaum Associates.

Wyndham Robertson. 1973. "Those Daring Young Con Men of Equity Funding." *Fortune*, August, 81–85, 120–132.

Yardeni, Edward. 1985. "Money and Business Alert." Prudential-Bache Securities, November 15.

———. 1985. "Money and Business Alert." Prudential-Bache Securities, November 20.

———. 1986. "Money and Business Alert." Prudential-Bache Securities, October 29, 1.

———. 1987. "Money and Business Alert." Prudential-Bache Securities, February 4, 1.

———. 1987. "Money and Business Alert." Prudential-Bache Securities, September 23.

Zweig, J. 2009. "As Stock Losses Loom, Don't Throw a 'Hail Mary.'" *Wall Street Journal*, February 21, B1.

INDEX